Remembering Air India

The Art of Public Mourning

Remembering Air India

CHANDRIMA CHAKRABORTY,
AMBER DEAN & ANGELA FAILLER, *Editors*

The University of Alberta Press

Published by

The University of Alberta Press
Ring House 2
Edmonton, Alberta, Canada T6G 2E1
www.uap.ualberta.ca

LIBRARY AND ARCHIVES CANADA
CATALOGUING IN PUBLICATION

Remembering Air India : the art of public mourning / Chandrima Chakraborty, Amber Dean & Angela Failler, editors.

Includes bibliographical references and index.
Issued in print and electronic formats.
ISBN 978-1-77212-259-6 (softcover).—
ISBN 978-1-77212-311-1 (PDF)

1. Air-India Flight 182 Bombing Incident, 1985. 2. Collective memory—Canada. 3. Bereavement—Psychological aspects. 4. Creation (Literary, artistic, etc.)—Social aspects—Canada. 5. Terrorism—Social aspects—Canada. 6. Racism—Social aspects—Canada. I. Dean, Amber Richelle, 1975–, author, editor II. Chakraborty, Chandrima, 1973–, author, editor III. Failler, Angela, 1973–, author, editor IV. Title: Art of public mourning.

HV6433.C3R44 2017 363.12'4650916337
C2017-900792-0
C2017-900793-9

First edition, first printing, 2017.
First printed and bound in Canada by Houghton Boston Printers, Saskatoon, Saskatchewan.
Copyediting and proofreading by Kirsten Craven.
Indexing by Judy Dunlop.

The University of Alberta Press is committed to protecting our natural environment. As part of our efforts, this book is printed on Enviro Paper: it contains 100% post-consumer recycled fibres and is acid- and chlorine-free.

The University of Alberta Press gratefully acknowledges the support received for its publishing program from the Government of Canada, the Canada Council for the Arts, and the Government of Alberta through the Alberta Media Fund.

Canadä

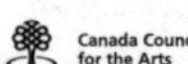

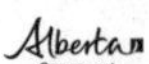

As the families were entering the courtroom to hear the verdict, an old man yelled at all of the family members that were present. He told us to go back home, that we were bringing our problems to Canada. This was very hard to hear on such an emotional and anxiety-filled day. To me this is paradigmatic of the way in which this tragedy has been perceived by many in Canada, including government officials; that this was not a Canadian tragedy, that the issues dealt with people involved in a conflict far away.

—MANDIP SINGH GREWAL, quoted in *The Families Remember: Commission of Inquiry into the Investigation of the Bombing of Air India Flight 182, Phase 1 Report*

Ahakista: one church, two pubs,
inhabitant: Atlantic,
memory orphans June 23, 1985
a widow,
who lists the names of eighty-two children under the age of thirteen
faces in a sundial the hours and a garden, a wall,
three hundred and twenty-nine, thirty, thirty-one
deposited in stone, the flesh of names,
flower and rot   remember-forget
time and its dimensions

—RENÉE SAROJINI SAKḶIKAR, *children of air india, un/authorized exhibits and interjections*

The night before she was to leave for India, Leela dreamed that she was in a plane, cutting through the infinity of space towards an unknown destination. Thousands of feet below, the ocean undulated silently. She could not see it but she knew that it was there. It was dark inside the plane and all around her she could hear the sussuration of her fellow passengers breathing.

—ANITA RAU BADAMI, *Can You Hear the Nightbird Call?*

Contents

Personal Loss, Collective Grief

Acknowledgements

AS THE EDITORS OF THIS BOOK, we would like to acknowledge everyone involved in its publication. A collection such as this is a collaborative effort and relies on the willingness and dedication of contributors to make new meaning of the past, in and for the present. Our sincerest thanks to the artists, writers, and scholars whose work, both original and previously published, appears between its covers, representing various forms of memorial expression, including academic essay, critical commentary, expert witness report, poetry, fiction, film, dance, and painting: Cassel Busse, Rita Kaur Dhamoon, Teresa Hubel, Suvir Kaul, Elan Marchinko, Eisha Marjara, Bharati Mukherjee, Lata Pada, Uma Parameswaran, Sherene H. Razack, Renée Sarojini Saklikar, Maya Seshia, Karen Sharma, Deon Venter, and Padma Viswanathan. We are also grateful to Lata Pada and photographer Cylla von Tiedemann for permission to reproduce the stunning image of Lata's contemporary multimedia dance work, *Revealed by Fire*, on the cover of our book. We would also like to acknowledge the loss, during the production of this book, of the remarkable professor, novelist, and short story writer Bharati Mukherjee. We are deeply grateful to be able to include Dr.

Mukherjee's short story, " The Management of Grief," in this collection. Her work on Air India has touched so many lives profoundly.

We would like to thank the University of Alberta Press and, in particular, senior editor, Peter Midgley, who immediately recognized the importance of this project and helped usher our manuscript into publication. We also benefitted from the process of anonymous review, which served to clarify and highlight the book's intrinsic strengths.

We gratefully acknowledge Cassel Busse and Malissa Phung for their research and administrative assistance during the preparatory stages of the manuscript, and Judy Dunlop for expertly writing the index.

We also acknowledge financial support toward the publication of this book from McMaster University's Arts Research Board, the University of Winnipeg, and the Social Sciences and Humanities Research Council of Canada.

Finally, we wish to acknowledge those who lost their lives to the Air India bombings and the family members, friends, and loved ones who continue to mourn their loss. We hope this book contributes in some small way to sustaining their memory.

—CHANDRIMA CHAKRABORTY, AMBER DEAN & ANGELA FAILLER

The Art of Public Mourning

An Introduction

CHANDRIMA CHAKRABORTY, AMBER DEAN & ANGELA FAILLER

THE AIR INDIA BOMBINGS remain a little-known, little-remembered event in Canadian public memory. Three hundred and twenty-nine passengers were killed by one bomb that detonated on Air India Flight 182 en route to Delhi from Montreal via Toronto on June 23, 1985. Another bomb targeting a second Air India flight the same day caused the deaths of two baggage handlers at the Narita International Airport in Japan. Two years later, writers Clark Blaise and Bharati Mukherjee observed, "the failure to acknowledge the victims of the crash as Canadians remains for most of the families the enduring political grief of Air India 182."[1] Staggeringly, almost twenty-three years later, the Air India Victims' Families Association (AIVFA) was still insisting that Canada "failed to incorporate this tragic event into its collective conscience and history."[2] Feeling ignored, abandoned, and even made suspect by their government and many fellow Canadians, the relatives of the dead have struggled for decades in the face of enormous loss and grief to instill a widespread awareness of the events of June 23, 1985, and to bring about something resembling justice.

But what might it mean to claim the violent loss of so many lives as a loss specifically of and for Canada? Certainly, the lengthy disavowal of the bombings as an event of serious significance to Canada as a nation represents a clear injustice to those who were killed and to the families and friends forced to live on in the aftermath of their loss. And yet, critical questions must also be raised about the timing and strategy behind a renewed state interest in claiming the bombings as "a Canadian tragedy." Following the September 11, 2001, attacks in the United States, the Canadian federal government has expended considerable resources to stake a claim to terror and to trauma by reframing the bombing of Air India Flight 182 as "the single worst act of terrorism in Canadian history."[3] Some notable attempts to do so include pronouncing June 23 as a National Day of Remembrance for Victims of Terrorism in 2005,[4] and titling the Commission of Inquiry into the Investigation of the Bombing of Air India Flight 182 final report, *Air India Flight 182: A Canadian Tragedy*.[5]

Revising its initial representation of the Air India bombings as a foreign event, the government's emphasis is now on reminding the Canadian public that this particular violence was "conceived in Canada, executed in Canada, by Canadian citizens, and its victims were themselves mostly citizens of Canada," even as the suspected perpetrators are described as importing foreign "blood-feuds" from India.[6] Consequently, the collection of scholarly essays commissioned for the commission of inquiry, its findings, and former Prime Minister Stephen Harper's subsequent apology to the relatives of those killed in the bombings all seek to establish for the Canadian public the "facts" of the Air India narrative as a way of offering "closure to those who still grieve for their loved ones."[7] The aim of these efforts would seem to produce, consolidate, and then marshal an official version of the Air India story as a story of Canada's vulnerability to terrorism in order to bolster support for the state's anti-terrorism policy initiatives. This marshalling is not without controversy given how anti-terrorism policies and laws are themselves implicated in perpetuating the very forms of systemic racism that underpin both the bombings and the Canadian government's inadequate treatment of the victims' families in its aftermath. It seems imperative, then, to create openings for conversations on legacies of the Air India bombings that are being glossed over, if not erased, by official forms of remembering.

Strategic reclamations of the bombings are made much more complex by engaging with the varied ways the event and its aftermath are memorialized in creative texts—in fiction, poetry, film, photography, dance, music, and visual art. Artistic and creative renderings of the bombings and their aftermath invite us to remember and grapple with the event quite differently than the strategic memorializing by the state. More specifically, these texts widen the historical record, challenging us to build connections between the events of June 23, 1985, and a host of other historical and ongoing events, policies, beliefs, and practices that demarcate subjects as insiders or outsiders, "us" or "them," in national contexts. They also invite us to encounter the traumatic loss of so many lives and subsequent suffering and grief as forms of "difficult knowledge," not so easily contained or given "closure" as official discourse might promise.[8] While the state *has* begun, belatedly, to memorialize those who were killed on Flight 182, its efforts are strategically nationalist—noting the loss of "future unrecognized Canadian assets," for example—eschewing encounters with the dead that might ask us to consider their complexity, their particularity, even "peculiarity," and thus the incommensurability of their loss.[9] *Remembering Air India: The Art of Public Mourning* generates a different kind of public record. It assembles an archive of creative and scholarly responses to the Air India bombings, as well as legal testimony otherwise not easily accessed, with the intent of troubling the narrow delimiting of the "facts" as sanctioned by official sources.

Seeking to preserve and bring into wider circulation a number of marginalized voices and texts, our collection places emphasis on the traumatic losses experienced by family and friends and their impact on the wider South Asian community in the aftermath of the bombings. Over the past few decades, there have been a significant number of aesthetically based works by artists and writers who have represented these experiences, from Srinivas Krishna's critically acclaimed feature length film, *Masala*,[10] to Renée Sarojini Saklikar's award-winning book of poetry, *children of air india*, and many in between. *Masala* centres on a struggling tough-guy protagonist named Krishna, whose immediate family was killed on a plane that he was also meant to board. Set in Toronto, the film incorporates elements of reality, fiction, and Bollywood camp to tell a tale of survivor guilt, diasporic subjectivity, and intercultural tensions. The filmmaker also uses parody to convey the hypocrisies of liberal multiculturalism and critique state posturings of benevolence, embodied in characters like a blundering Canadian minister of multiculturalism. Breaking from documentary or historiographic mode, this work accomplishes something valuable in reaching beyond "fact" to produce an account that is at once imaginative and resistant. Saklikar's *children of air india*, a series of "exhibits" in poetic form, evokes legal process, evidence, and documentation intercepted by intimate snapshots of lives touched and abbreviated by the Air India bombings. Fragments and traces of these lives are made visible and then redacted through her text, creating a sense of the way in which memories themselves can be felt as tangible and then not. The palimpsestic-style elegy Saklikar builds in *children of air india* takes a slightly different shape in her original contribution to this collection. In "air india, unsent / letters from the archive," the poet addresses her own cousin, whose parents—Saklikar's aunt and uncle—were killed in the bombings. Here the trope of unsent letters brings to mind both the unfulfilled potential of lives cut short and feelings of regret that often accompany loss. However, in their attempt to communicate the incommunicable, the insistence of the letters also speaks to resilience in the face of loss. While our collection does not endeavour to include or exhaustively review every creative account produced on the Air India bombings, it does revisit a number of important earlier works alongside such new ones, resulting in juxtapositions that we hope will enliven scholarly, popular, and official narratives of this history.

By generating conversations between artistic and scholarly works that offer alternative frames for attending to the Air India tragedy, this book refutes the characterization of artistic productions as less reliable than official accounts—a view expressed in the context of the commission of inquiry's hearings. In his summary comments for the first report of the inquiry,[11] Commissioner John C. Major applauds the memorialization of those killed in the bombings through the establishment of public monuments, dedication of scholarships, sporting events, and the publication of memorial books by journalists and family members. He suggests, however, that "these must be distinguished from other books and films based loosely on the events of the tragedy," as "the authors may have used artistic licence to develop stories which are not necessarily based on facts."[12] While he goes on to insist that all of these texts and other memorial gestures "contribute in some way to keeping the memories alive,"[13] we are interested in prying open this perceived need to warn the public not to confuse creative texts with the "facts" of the events. The assumption here, that facts somehow speak for themselves, that they function outside re-presentation, is a limited one. If the purported "facts" are self-evidently "objective" knowledge, then what is the impetus behind Commissioner Major's call for such a distinction between memorialization practices? In contrast with Commissioner Major's apparent unease with "artistic licence," we see in artistic remembrance practices not only the enormous potential to offer new openings and alternatives to the Air India story that necessarily trouble and at times fracture the purported facticity (and thereby objectivity) of official discourse, but also an opportunity to call on the public to reflect on the traces of the past as they impinge on the present, to have a sustained debate about the continuing memorial insistence the Air India bombings and their aftermath make on Canadian public memory.

In this book we encourage an active, ongoing dialogue between official and artistic memorializations and between artists and scholars with the intent of questioning the dominance and recognition accorded to official frames of remembering. As philosopher and queer theorist Judith Butler reminds us, "the frame does not simply exhibit reality, but actively participates in a strategy of containment, selectively producing and enforcing what will count as reality."[14] For the contributors to this book, several of whom are family members of those killed in the Air India bombings and/or vocal participants in the juridical processes, in the media, and active in community organizing, the Air India story begins much earlier than June 23, 1985. The conflicts underpinning the bombings and their aftermath can arguably be traced back to an earlier history of British imperialism, to the Partition of British India, to ongoing attempts at maintaining a white Canada, including anti-Asian riots in Vancouver and the turning back of the *Komagata Maru* from Vancouver's Burrard Inlet, to Operation Blue Star in Amritsar, to anti-Sikh riots in Delhi, and so on. Tracing the history of the Air India bombings to other events, experiences, narratives, and histories in this way reflects how remembrance—both personal and collective—plays an indispensable role in a historical accounting of the past. We also insist that while personal proximity to the losses of the Air India bombings must be privileged in such an accounting, it is important to broaden a sense of inheritance and responsibility to care for the impact of the bombings on our shared present and future.

The government's response to the Air India bombings reflects its assumptions about which injuries do and do not merit public concern. While the bombings are now being harnessed to safeguard the desires of Canadians to have "skies safe for travel,"[15] the racial injuries repeatedly noted by the families in trial testimonies, interviews, and press reports are glossed over and not given recognition. Almost all of the contributors to this book demonstrate the urgency of engaging directly with the issue of racism in relation to the Air India story. Questions raised by sociologist Sherene Razack's expert witness testimony at the Air India inquiry continue to remain unanswered: Why did official agencies and the nation "not care as much as when far fewer Canadians lost their lives in the World Trade Center bombings? What can we say about successive federal governments that made no public space for inquiry into the bombings, could not bring themselves to even express condolences, and were not moved to commemorate the Canadian lives lost that day until more than twenty years after?"[16] The official (re)framing of the Air India bombings as a terrorist attack overshadows these questions and downplays the inadequacy of the Canadian state and public's response to the 1985 bombings and the marginalization of the Air India events in Canadian history. The exclusion of Razack's expert witness testimony from the official report of the commission of inquiry is a clear indication of how the state endeavours to deflect attention away from allegations of racism. We thought it was therefore crucial to reproduce her testimony (in the form of a report she submitted to the inquiry) here in this volume. Although hers is not a creative text, her testimony was treated with contempt and suspicion by lawyers representing the Crown during the inquiry, and then effectively disappeared from accessible public record by a government unwilling to entertain the possibility that racism played a role in its inadequate response to the bombings and to the families whose terrible grief was, from all reports, compounded by the abysmal (lack of) response from the Government of Canada, the nation into which many of the bereft had been born or acquired citizenship.

With contributions by artists, cultural critics, and scholars from a variety of theoretical perspectives and disciplinary approaches that address loss, grief, anger, and trauma, *Remembering Air India: The Art of Public Mourning* offers insights into how systemic racism and contemporary discourses on terrorism shape Canadian national imaginaries, and how our understanding of Canada's past is continually reframed through the present. The contributors interrogate how Air India indexes national and transnational histories of racial injustice that live on in the present and through its post-9/11 reframing by the Canadian state. These scholars and cultural producers challenge straightforward, linear conceptions of past, present, and future, exposing instead the enmeshments of past and present, and how these enmeshments shape the kinds of futures we are encouraged to imagine.

Ashwin Rao, the Canadian-trained Indian psychologist in Padma Viswanathan's novel, *The Ever After of Ashwin Rao*, bemoans the limited scholarship on Air India that contributes to the larger amnesia by serving to confirm that Air India is marginal to the nation's history. Canada, Rao insists, not only "failed to prevent the bombing in the first place" and "failed, for eighteen years, to bring it to trial" but has also "failed to take the bombing up in scholarship."[17] This relative silence, despite (or perhaps, in part, because of?) the striking number of scholars—from undergraduates to the professoriate—among those who were killed on Flight 182, drives Viswanathan's protagonist to initiate his own study of how victim families (including his own) have "coped up" in the aftermath of their losses. By initiating a dialogue between scholars and creative artists working on the remembrance of the bombing of Air India Flight 182, and bringing into circulation the marginalized works of several Canadian cultural producers, this book stems from our understanding of creative works as knowledge—as testimony, remembrance, and witness to Canada's racial past and present. Artistic works, in our view, offer creative modes of engagement that complement but also complicate and extend traditional historiographic accounts. The creative works collected here offer crucial contributions to knowledge about the bombings and their aftermath in and of themselves. By putting these works into conversation with related scholarship, we hope to demonstrate how they are instrumental to generating new and important insights about the events of June 23, 1985. The scholarly essays in this volume are not intended to inform readers about how to interpret the creative works; instead, they see in the creative works forms of knowledge about the Air India tragedy that remain under-acknowledged and under-utilized in official responses and remembrances of this event, and thus they aim to draw out the knowledge contributions of the creative works and further build upon the important insights these texts are making. In addition, through the pairing of scholarly and artistic materials, we hope to make the book more accessible to teachers, students, and to an engaged wider public.

This book also offers an archive of speech acts, such as Razack's testimony, and then Prime Minister Stephen Harper's apology to the Air India families offered at the twenty-fifth commemoration ceremony in Toronto; as well as artistic performances, such as Lata Pada's *bharatanatyam* dance performance, *Revealed by Fire*, that have not otherwise been preserved as a matter of public record or that are ephemeral in nature due to their form, as in the case of Pada's performance.[18] Reproducing Razack's testimony and Prime Minister Harper's speech and generating scholarship on *Revealed by Fire* in the pages of this book help sustain and nurture memories of these events. The contributors to *Remembering Air India* argue for and demonstrate the political potential in remembering and memorializing the past "otherwise." We are indebted here to the work of memory scholar

Roger Simon, who argues that "remembering otherwise" requires an engagement with those traces of the past that "arrive in the public realm making an unanticipated claim that may wound or better, instantiate a loss that haunts those to whom these claims are addressed."[19] In an earlier work, Roger Simon, Sharon Rosenberg, and Claudia Eppert distinguish between remembrance as a strategic practice and remembrance as a difficult return.[20] While strategic approaches to remembrance (such as state reframings of the Air India bombings in a post-9/11 context discussed above) frequently aim to "bolster hegemonic, emergent, and, at times, insurgent nationalisms and ethnocultural identifications," a difficult return of memory requires us to reconsider "how to live with what cannot be redeemed."[21] In its haste to marshal and consolidate a particular version of the past, a strategic remembrance practice eschews complexity in order to be consolatory. Remembering otherwise, as a practice of grappling with memory as a difficult return, requires a different orientation to the past; as Simon suggests, it includes "the production of a historical imaginary within which it is possible to rethink as sensible and justifiable those practices which establish one people's exploitation, dominion, or indifference with regards to others."[22] It is our hope that this volume contributes to the production of one such alternative "historical imaginary" for the Air India bombings, for a reconsideration of how this traumatic history "lives on" in the present seems urgent.

The Air India criminal trials, the commission of inquiry findings, and Prime Minister Harper's apology do not adequately recognize the effects of the Air India bombings and their aftermath on others beyond the immediate families and friends of those killed on Flight 182. This book aims to broaden our understanding of how and why we collectively inherit these effects, along with demonstrating the impact of the Air India events on successor generations who are faced with the legacies of racism, trauma, and loss that the events index.[23] Bringing artistic and scholarly pieces together suggests that the experiences they document are historically significant and shared, and in so doing, they make a plea for public mourning. Our hope is that this book will, therefore, generate debate around what constitutes meaningful forms of remembrance, reconciliation, or redress, as contributors raise questions about the ethics and politics of coming to terms with violent pasts and racial histories of community and national identity.

The book is organized around five thematic clusters. Each cluster consists of creative works and/or testimony or statements not already part of the permanent public record, and a scholarly essay accompanied by a brief commentary. The clusters explore various aspects of the process of remembering, including how state memory projects inhibit other possibilities of memorialization; how questions of facts, truth, and justice are contested and negotiated through artistic and scholarly creations; and how scholars and artists can collaborate to express social realities, build alliances, and trouble/resist state histories and strategic remembrance practices.

The first cluster, "Remembering in Relation," expands the historical timeline leading up to the events of June 23, 1985, by insisting that a more complex understanding of the bombings and their aftermath requires us to remember a largely forgotten (at least until recently) event in Canada's immigration history: the 1914 routing of the *Komagata Maru* from the Vancouver harbour. The 376 passengers aboard the *Komagata Maru*, mostly Sikh men who were subjects of British India, were detained aboard the ship upon their arrival due to an obscure immigration policy, the "continuous journey regulation," which denied entry to Canada for anyone who failed to arrive directly from their point of departure. After two months of being stranded in the harbour, the *Komagata Maru* was driven back out to sea by a Canadian Navy vessel.[24] The recurring presence of the *Komagata Maru* in several creative texts about the bombings, including Anita Rau Badami's novel, *Can You Hear the Nightbird Call?*, Uma Parameswaran's poem "On the Shores of the Irish Sea," and Padma Viswanathan's novel, *The Ever After of Ashwin Rao*, invites us to (re)consider how Canadian immigration practices, both historical and contemporary, that demarcate brown bodies as particularly suspect "outsiders" or "foreigners" to the nation are as much a part of the history of the Air India bombings and their aftermath as the oft-cited partitioning of India or anti-Sikh violence in India in 1984. In this way, these creative texts offer us a richer, deeper, more complex sense of how the history of British imperialism is profoundly implicated in producing the clashes around race, religion, and belonging that underpin the bombing of Flight 182 than what we can discern from the official discourse of either India or Canada. As Rita Kaur Dhamoon suggests in her commentary, the contributors to this cluster "invoke the reader to remember their own connections to Air India and to the *Komagata Maru* by foregrounding the politics of emotions, weaving in and out of love, anger, and grief—for and against the self, Others, and the nation."[25]

The second cluster, "A Nation Outside of History," points to the power of the state to frame documents with an evidential purpose and its constitutive acts of exclusions, which can effectively limit the Canadian public's knowledge of the Air India bombings and privilege the state version of the story.[26] This cluster fills a significant gap in the official archives and brings into public circulation a condemned piece from the Air India inquiry testimony: Dr. Sherene H. Razack's expert witness report commissioned by a lawyer for the families of those killed in the bombings on whether or not systemic racism played a role in the pre-bombing threat assessment, as well as in the post-bombing response. Contributors Maya Seshia, Sherene Razack, and Deon Venter also direct attention to the suffering and grief caused by the government's apathetic response to the families in the aftermath of the tragedy, which the families testify became part of the trauma itself. Redressing this suffering has not been a priority for state officials. For instance, the commission of inquiry's mandated terms of reference made no allowance for recommendations on this front, instead privileging issues of state securitization.[27] By constructing Canada as a (defendable) target of terrorism through post-9/11 reframings of the Air India bombings, the state conveniently sidesteps its own role as perpetrator of past and ongoing violences. Our contributors to this cluster remember and re-centre the ways Canada has been implicated in the Air India bombings saga, challenging a vision of the country as an innocent nation outside of history.

The focus of the third cluster, "The Political Apology," is the apology offered by former Prime Minister Stephen Harper to the relatives of those killed in the Air India bombings, which adds to a litany of declarations of regret for past injustices in the last decade or so offered by the Government of Canada. A number of scholars have suggested that the current moment might be described as an "age of the apology,"[28] in which the "apology has become a form of political speech with increasing significance and power."[29] While Harper's apology to the Air India victim families raises concerns about intent and strategy, concerns that contributors Cassel Busse and Karen Sharma explore in more depth, it is clear that political apologies continue to matter. The symbolism of the gesture often does make a difference to recipients and it also enables the state to demonstrate (however nominally) that it registers the grievances of its minorities. The Air India apology was offered in a commemoration ceremony in Toronto addressed to Air India victim families and friends; it was at one time available on the Government of Canada's website, but today only a small excerpt of the apology is archived there (for this reason, we have reprinted the full text of the apology in this volume).[30] It is notable that the apology was delivered before a gathering of grieving family and friends rather than in Parliament as an address to all Canadians. Evidently, the bombing of Air India Flight 182, although characterized in official discourse as "Canada's 9/11," in other words, a national tragedy, is still not conceptualized as a national loss that could then call for widespread national mourning.[31] Thus, we are pleased to include the then prime minister's speech that, in its acknowledgement of "institutional failings" for the Air India bombings and the treatment of the families thereafter, makes the former prime minister's perspective part of the historical record, and, in this way, a more widely remembered and acknowledged part of the Air India story.

The fourth cluster, "Creative Archive," focuses on Lata Pada's remarkable *bharatanatyam* dance performance *Revealed by Fire*, which provides an alternative affective, political, and aesthetic frame for understanding the trauma of the Air India bombings. Here the body as archive replaces or diverts a notion of archive as strictly document collection or bureaucratic management of "the past." Pada uses corporeal presence and agency (against the spectre of bodies absented by the tragedy) to both remember and express the visceral grief she experienced over the loss of her husband and two daughters who were killed in the bombings. The dance work also meditates on the transnational character and impact of the bombings, which sees grief strewn both "here" and "there" and in the liminal spaces between as Pada addresses the diasporic conditions within which most of those who were killed in the bombings lived, complicating reappropriations of the bombings as a "Canadian tragedy." Elan Marchinko's essay in this cluster attends especially to the potential for this dance work to foster a form of reparation beyond those of judicial-legal framings. She reads the detailed and nuanced choreographies of movement along with the work's layered dramaturgy as contributing to its affective force and thereby its ability to provide an occasion for remembrance and witnessing that commentator Teresa Hubel, in turn, describes as *Revealed by Fire*'s capacity to invite audiences "into a personal relationship with an international tragedy."[32]

While official attempts at redress such as the Air India apology seek to acknowledge the past in order to move on, Bharati Mukherjee's short story, "The Management of Grief," Eisha Marjara's docudrama, *Desperately Seeking Helen*, and Renée Sarojini Saklikar's poem, "air india, unsent / letters from the archive,"[33] which form parts of the fifth cluster, "Personal Loss, Collective Grief," illustrate how grief persists in and shapes the present for those who lost loved ones in the bombing of Air India Flight 182. These deeply personal pieces direct attention to how the impetus that grief be civilly displayed or, better still, sidestepped in multicultural Canada, functions as a mode of managing minorities and their grief, as Chandrima Chakraborty argues in her critical essay in this cluster. Remembering and mourning Air India as a date that is "documented and well known, effaced and forgotten. / One continuing gesture, happened, never happened,"[34] Marjara and Saklikar, in particular, open up their personal history of grief to public gaze. Situating the Air India tragedy within a long history of racial grief suggests it is this everyday grief of racialized subjects that is in need of being recovered, rather than the grief of Air India conceptualized as an odd or aberrant event (or series of events) in Canadian multiculturalism. Critiquing the state's call to be "model mourners," Chakraborty demonstrates how creative remembrances offer compelling understandings of melancholia as an engagement with loss that refuses closure. It is this potential for ongoing grief to foster collective mourning that, according to commentator Suvir Kaul, enables critical remembrance practices and, more importantly, demands action that can reshape the national present and future.[35]

Unlike the Canadian state's myriad attempts to secure the meaning of the past for the present through the lens of a post-9/11 discourse on terror, artistic remembrances of the Air India bombings and their aftermath insist on the dialectical relationship of the past and the present and the ongoingness of grief and mourning, which can potentially encourage the creation of other histories, other memories, and other rememberings. In their attention to grief and loss, the scholarly and creative works collected here encourage us to recognize the trauma that remains, to witness that trauma, and to provide avenues for further public mourning.[36] At the same time, they also demonstrate how lingering grief and trauma trouble notions of abject victimhood—by raising more widespread awareness of the events of June 23, 1985, and by enabling new alliances and community activism, which then puts pressure on the state to accept accountability for the injustices of the past and present. They insist on the necessity of recognizing the role of racism and of racial/imperialist histories in the aftermath and events of June 23, 1985, widening the historical record and the usual "timeline of events" through which the Air India story is too frequently recounted. We hope the conversations produced in this book through our concerted entwining of artistic, scholarly, and official voices will provoke other kinds of exchanges of knowledge and memories that continue the work of remembering Air India *otherwise*.

Notes

1. Clark Blaise and Bharati Mukherjee, *The Sorrow and the Terror: The Haunting Legacy of the Air India Tragedy* (Toronto: Viking, 1987), 203.
2. AIVFA, *Where Is Justice? AIVFA Final Written Submission, Commission of Inquiry into the Investigation of the Bombing of Air India Flight 182* (Ottawa, February 29, 2008), 59.

3. Prime Minister of Canada, Statement Delivered at the Commemoration Ceremony for the 25th Anniversary of the Air India Flight 182 Atrocity, June 23, 2010, accessed August 10, 2012, http://pm.gc.ca/eng/news/2010/06/23/statement-prime-minister-canada-commemoration-ceremony-25th-anniversary-air-india.
4. Prime Minister of Canada, National Day of Remembrance for Victims of Terrorism, June 23, 2011, accessed August 10, 2012, http://pm.gc.ca/eng/news/2011/06/23/national-day-remembrance-victims-terrorism.
5. The public inquiry into the Air India bombing investigation was announced on May 1, 2006, after then Prime Minister Stephen Harper took office, revising Bob Rae's report that called for an administrative inquiry on November 23, 2005. The final report of the commission of inquiry was released in 2010. See Government of Canada, *Air India Flight 182: A Canadian Tragedy, Final Report Volumes 1–5* (Ottawa: Minister of Public Works and Government Services, 2010).
6. Prime Minister of Canada, Commemoration Ceremony. Also, see, for example, the timeline provided in Annex C, Government of Canada, *The Families Remember: Commission of Inquiry into the Investigation of the Bombing of Air India Flight 182, Phase 1 Report* (Ottawa: Minister of Public Works and Government Services, 2007). For an analysis of this shift, see Maya Seshia and Cassel Busse in this volume; Chandrima Chakraborty, "Remembering Air India Flight 182 in an Age of Terror," in *South Asian Racialization and Belonging after 9/11: Masks of Threat*, ed. Aparajita De (Lanham, MD: Lexington Press, 2016), 1–20; Angela Failler, "Remembering the Air India Disaster: Memorial and Counter-Memorial," *Review of Education, Pedagogy, and Cultural Studies* 31 (2009): 150–176.
7. Prime Minister of Canada, Prime Minister Harper Announces Inquiry into Air India Bombing, May 1, 2006, accessed August 10, 2012, http://pm.gc.ca/eng/news/2006/05/01/prime-minister-harper-announces-inquiry-air-indiabombing-0.
8. The concept of "difficult knowledge" is most commonly attributed to the work of educational theorist Deborah Britzman. Building on Britzman, Jessica A. Heybach suggests that difficult knowledge "demands a shattering of self—one's lovely knowledge of the world—to make way for the construction of something not yet defined." Jessica A. Heybach, "Learning to Feel What We See: Critical Aesthetics and 'Difficult Knowledge' in an Age of War," *Critical Questions in Education* 3, no. 1 (2012): 25. See also Alice Pitt and Deborah Britzman, "Speculations on Qualities of Difficult Knowledge in Teaching and Learning: An Experiment in Psychoanalytic Research," *International Journal of Qualitative Studies in Education* 16, no. 6 (2003): 755–776. See also Britzman's *Lost Subjects, Contested Objects: Toward a Psychoanalytic Inquiry of Learning* (Albany, NY: SUNY Press, 1998); Erica Lehrer, Cynthia E. Milton, and Monica Eileen Patterson, eds., *Curating Difficult Knowledge: Violent Pasts in Public Places* (Houndmills, Basingstoke, UK: Palgrave Macmillan, 2011); Roger I. Simon,

"A Shock to Thought: Curatorial Judgment and the Public Exhibition of 'Difficult Knowledge,'" *Memory Studies* 4.4 (2011): 432–449; and Roger I. Simon and Angela Failler, "Curatorial Practice and Learning from Difficult Knowledge," in *The Idea of a Human Rights Museum*, ed. Karen Busby, Adam Muller, and Andrew Woolford (Winnipeg: University of Manitoba Press, 2015), 165–179.

9. Ashwin Rao, the protagonist of Padma Viswanathan's novel, *The Ever After of Ashwin Rao*, raises this concern with state and other official efforts to memorialize the children who died aboard the flight, in particular, as "lost assets" while eschewing their "peculiarity." Padma Viswanathan, *The Ever After of Ashwin Rao* (Toronto: Random House Canada, 2014), 80.
10. *Masala*, directed by Srinivas Krishna (Toronto: Divani Films Productions, 1991), DVD.
11. This report was published in 2007. See Government of Canada, *Families Remember*.
12. Ibid., 139.
13. Ibid.
14. Judith Butler, *Frames of War: When Is Life Grievable?* (London: Verso Books, 2009), xiii.
15. Prime Minister of Canada, Commemoration Ceremony.
16. Sherene Razack, *The Impact of Systemic Racism on Canada's Pre-Bombing Threat Assessment and Post-Bombing Response to the Air India Bombings* (report submitted to the Commission of Inquiry into the Investigation of the Bombing of Air India Flight 182, 2007), 24. Reprinted in this volume.
17. Viswanathan, *Ashwin Rao*, 7–8.
18. Lata Pada, *Revealed by Fire: A Woman's Journey of Transformation*, directed and choreographed by Lata Pada, composition by Timothy Sullivan and R.A. Ramamani, visual design by Cylla von Tiedemann, dramaturgy by Judith Rudakoff (Mississauga, ON: Sampradaya Dance Creations, 2001), DVD.
19. Roger I. Simon, *Touch of the Past* (New York: Palgrave Macmillan, 2005), 4.
20. Roger I. Simon, Sharon Rosenberg, and Claudia Eppert, eds. *Between Hope and Despair: Pedagogy and the Remembrance of Historical Trauma* (Lanham, MD: Rowman and Littlefield, 2000).
21. Ibid., 3, 5.
22. Simon, *Touch of the Past*, 9.
23. For a detailed analysis, see Chandrima Chakraborty, "Official Apology, Creative Remembrances, and Management of the Air India Tragedy," *Studies in Canadian Literature* 40.1 (2015): 111–130.
24. For a more detailed history, see *Continuous Journey*, directed by Ali Kazimi (Toronto: Peripheral Visions Film and Video, Inc., 2005), DVD; Ali Kazimi, *Undesirables: White Canada and the Komagata Maru* (Vancouver: Douglas & McIntyre, 2011).
25. See Rita Kaur Dhamoon in this volume.

26. For scholarly discussions on the archive as an expression of governmental control of its subjects, a hegemonic instrument of the state, see Bernard S. Cohn, *An Anthropologist among the Historians and Other Essays* (Delhi: Oxford University Press, 1987); Nicholas Dirks, *Castes of Mind: Colonialism and the Making of Modern India* (New Delhi: Permanent Black, 2002); Antoinette Burton, *Dwelling in the Archive: Women Writing House, Home and History in Late Colonial India* (New York: Oxford University Press, 2003); Ann L. Stoler, *Along the Archival Grain: Epistemic Anxieties and Colonial Common Sense* (Princeton, NJ: Princeton University Press, 2009).
27. For further discussion, see Angela Failler, "'War-on-Terror' Frames of Remembrance: The 1985 Air India Bombings after 9/11," TOPIA: *Canadian Journal of Cultural Studies* 27 (Spring 2012): 253–269; Angela Failler with artwork by Eisha Marjara, "'Remember Me Nought': The 1985 Air India Bombings and Cultural *Nachträglichkeit,*" *Public: Art/Culture/Ideas* 42 (2010): 113–124; and Failler, "Remembering the Air India Disaster."
28. Roy L. Brooks, " The Age of Apology," in *When Sorry Isn't Enough: The Controversy over Apologies and Reparations for Human Injustice*, ed. Roy L. Brooks (New York: New York University Press, 1999), 3–11; Michael Cunningham, "Saying Sorry: The Politics of Apology," *Political Quarterly* 70, no. 3 (1999): 285–293.
29. Allan Luke, " The Material Effects of the Word: 'Stolen Children' and Public Discourse," *Discourse: Studies in the Cultural Politics of Education* 18, no. 3 (1997): 344.
30. See Prime Minister of Canada, Commemoration Ceremony. The small excerpt of the apology archived on the Government of Canada's website appears at http://news.gc.ca/web/article-en.do?mthd=tp&crtr.page=77&nid=542319&crtr.tp1D=980 (last accessed January 25, 2017).
31. See Chakraborty, "Official Apology."
32. See Teresa Hubel in this volume.
33. Bharati Mukherjee, " The Management of Grief," in *The Middleman and Other Stories* (New York: Grove Press, 1988); Eisha Marjara, *Desperately Seeking Helen* (Montreal: National Film Board of Canada, 1999), DVD; see Renée Sarojini Saklikar in this volume.
34. See Saklikar in this volume.
35. See Suvir Kaul in this volume.
36. In the recent "History, Memory, Grief: A 30th Air India Anniversary Conference," held at McMaster University, Hamilton, Ontario, in May 2016, that brought together for the first time scholars, artists, Air India family members, and the wider public to engage in conversation on the 1985 Air India tragedy and its aftermath, Air India family members who spoke in various panels repeatedly noted that they felt ignored by their government and their fellow citizens. Attendees witnessed the palpable grief

of the families, thirty years after Flight 182 crashed off the coast of Ireland at Cork. The effect of these conversations on the wider public who attended the conference suggests how affect can travel between and among bodies to cultivate a public that feels a shared responsibility for the nation's past and its future. For videos of the conference panels, see https://www.youtube.com/playlist?list=PLzLUWMt2NZLQS PHYi5l7GZwgiyXeKg8Ui.

Works Cited

AIVFA. *Where Is Justice?* AIVFA *Final Written Submission, Commission of Inquiry into the Investigation of the Bombing of Air India Flight 182*. Ottawa, February 29, 2008.

Badami, Anita Rau. *Can You Hear the Nightbird Call?* Toronto: Alfred A. Knopf, 2006.

Blaise, Clark, and Bharati Mukherjee. *The Sorrow and the Terror: The Haunting Legacy of the Air India Tragedy*. Toronto: Viking, 1987.

Britzman, Deborah. *Lost Subjects, Contested Objects: Toward a Psychoanalytic Inquiry of Learning*. Albany, NY: SUNY Press, 1998.

Brooks, Roy L. "The Age of Apology." In *When Sorry Isn't Enough: The Controversy over Apologies and Reparations for Human Injustice*, edited by Roy L. Brooks, 3–11. New York: New York University Press, 1999.

Burton, Antoinette. *Dwelling in the Archive: Women Writing House, Home and History in Late Colonial India*. New York: Oxford University Press, 2003.

Butler, Judith. *Frames of War: When Is Life Grievable?* London: Verso Books, 2009.

Chakraborty, Chandrima. "Official Apology, Creative Remembrances, and Management of the Air India Tragedy." *Studies in Canadian Literature* 40.1 (2015): 111–130.

———. "Remembering Air India Flight 182 in an Age of Terror." In *South Asian Racialization and Belonging after 9/11: Masks of Threat*, edited by Aparajita De, 1–20. Lanham, MD: Lexington Press, 2016.

Cohn, Bernard S. *An Anthropologist among the Historians and Other Essays*. Delhi: Oxford University Press, 1987.

Continuous Journey. Directed by Ali Kazimi. Toronto: Peripheral Visions Film and Video, Inc., 2005. DVD.

Cunningham, Michael. "Saying Sorry: The Politics of Apology." *Political Quarterly* 70, no. 3 (1999): 285–293.

Dirks, Nicholas. *Castes of Mind: Colonialism and the Making of Modern India*. New Delhi: Permanent Black, 2002.

Failler, Angela. "Remembering the Air India Disaster: Memorial and Counter-Memorial." *Review of Education, Pedagogy, and Cultural Studies* 31 (2009): 150–176.

———. "'War-on-Terror' Frames of Remembrance: The 1985 Air India Bombings after 9/11. TOPIA: *Canadian Journal of Cultural Studies* 27 (Spring 2012): 253–269.

Failler, Angela, with artwork by Eisha Marjara. "'Remember Me Nought': The 1985 Air India Bombings and Cultural *Nachträglichkeit.*" *Public: Art/Culture/Ideas* 42 (2010): 113–124.

Government of Canada. *Air India Flight 182: A Canadian Tragedy, Final Report Volumes 1–5.* Ottawa: Minister of Public Works and Government Services, 2010.

———. *The Families Remember: Commission of Inquiry into the Investigation of the Bombing of Air India Flight 182, Phase I Report.* Ottawa: Minister of Public Works and Government Services, 2007.

Heybach, Jessica A. "Learning to Feel What We See: Critical Aesthetics and 'Difficult Knowledge' in an Age of War." *Critical Questions in Education* 3, no. 1 (2012): 23–34.

Kazimi, Ali. *Undesirables: White Canada and the Komagata Maru.* Vancouver: Douglas & McIntyre, 2011.

Lehrer, Erica, Cynthia E. Milton, and Monica Eileen Patterson, eds. *Curating Difficult Knowledge: Violent Pasts in Public Places.* Houndmills, Basingstoke, UK: Palgrave Macmillan, 2011.

Luke, Allan. " The Material Effects of the Word: 'Stolen Children' and Public Discourse." *Discourse: Studies in the Cultural Politics of Education* 18, no. 3 (1997): 343–368.

Marjara, Eisha. *Desperately Seeking Helen.* Montreal: National Film Board of Canada, 1999. DVD.

Masala. Directed by Srinivas Krishna. Toronto: Divani Films Productions, 1991. DVD.

Mukherjee, Bharati. " The Management of Grief." In *The Middleman and Other Stories,* 179–197. New York: Grove Press, 1988.

Pada, Lata. *Revealed by Fire: A Woman's Journey of Transformation.* Directed and choreographed by Lata Pada. Composition by Timothy Sullivan and R.A. Ramamani. Visual design by Cylla von Tiedemann. Dramaturgy by Judith Rudakoff. Mississauga, ON: Sampradaya Dance Creations, 2001. DVD.

Pitt, Alice, and Deborah Britzman. "Speculations on Qualities of Difficult Knowledge in Teaching and Learning: An Experiment in Psychoanalytic Research." *International Journal of Qualitative Studies in Education* 16, no. 6 (2003): 755–776.

Razack, Sherene. *The Impact of Systemic Racism on Canada's Pre-Bombing Threat Assessment and Post-Bombing Response to the Air India Bombings.* Report submitted to the Commission of Inquiry into the Investigation of the Bombing of Air India Flight 182, 2007.

Saklikar, Renée Sarojini. *children of air india, un/authorized exhibits and interjections.* Gibsons, BC: Nightwood Editions, 2013.

Simon, Roger I. "A Shock to Thought: Curatorial Judgment and the Public Exhibition of 'Difficult Knowledge.'" *Memory Studies* 4.4 (2011): 432–449.

———. *Touch of the Past.* New York: Palgrave Macmillan, 2005.

Simon, Roger I., and Angela Failler. "Curatorial Practice and Learning from Difficult Knowledge." In *The Idea of a Human Rights Museum*, edited by Karen Busby, Adam Muller, and Andrew Woolford, 165–179. Winnipeg: University of Manitoba Press, 2015.

Simon, Roger I., Sharon Rosenberg, and Claudia Eppert, eds. *Between Hope and Despair: Pedagogy and the Remembrance of Historical Trauma*. Lanham, MD: Rowman and Littlefield, 2000.

Stoler, Ann L. *Along the Archival Grain: Epistemic Anxieties and Colonial Common Sense*. Princeton, NJ: Princeton University Press, 2009.

Viswanathan, Padma. *The Ever After of Ashwin Rao*. Toronto: Random House Canada, 2014.

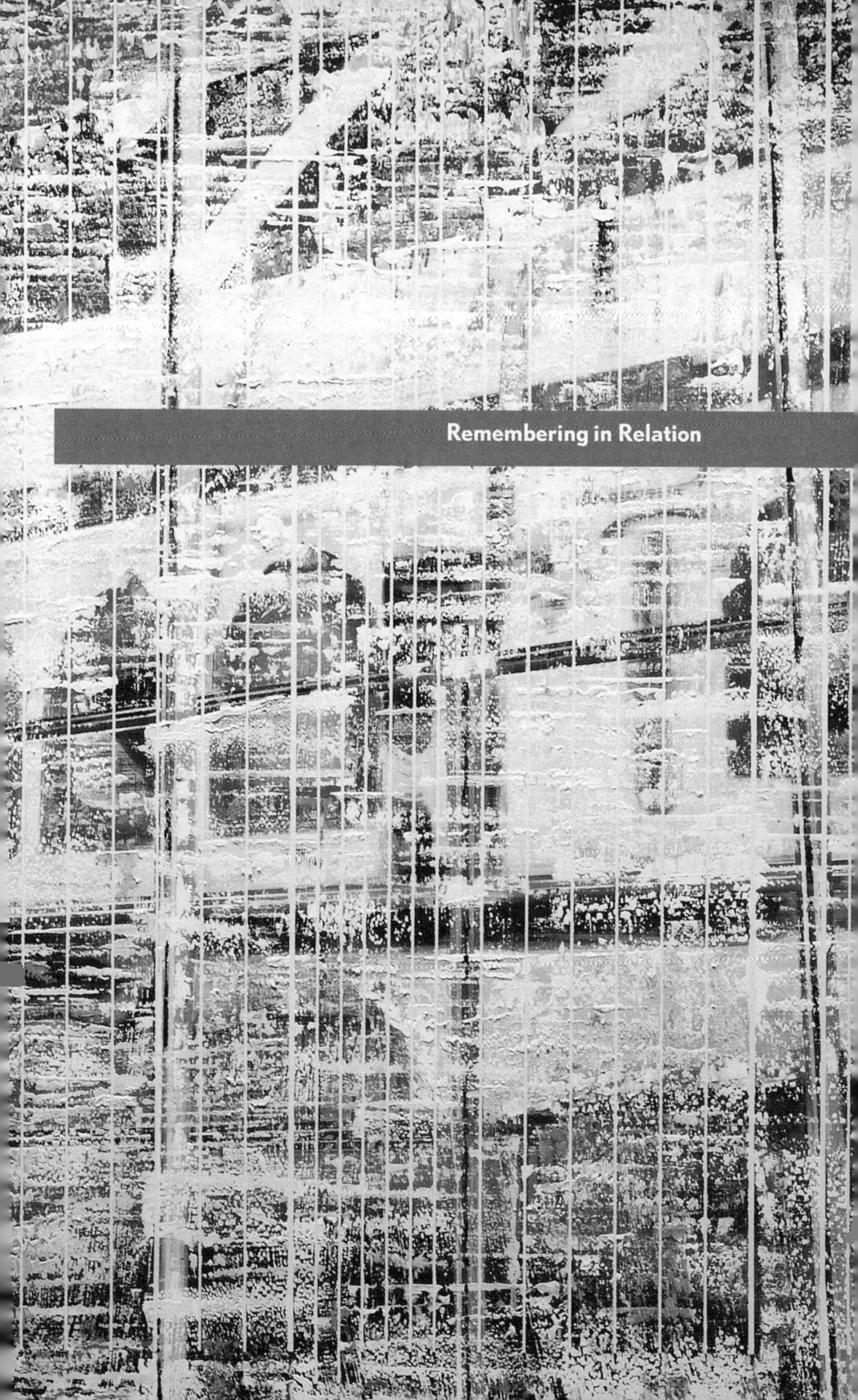

Remembering in Relation

Overleaf: Deon Venter, Flight 182 #2 *(detail) from the* Flight 182 *series, 2007. Oil on linen. 65" x 73". Copyright © Deon Venter, reprinted by permission of the artist. Photo by David Borrowman.*

Remembering in Relation

The Air India and Komagata Maru *Disasters*

AMBER DEAN

Now those Tamils protesting downtown, if they don't like it here and don't want to fit in and just be Canadian, then why don't they just go back where they came from?

—CONVERSATION OVERHEARD between members of the public just before the commencement of the twenty-fifth anniversary commemoration of the Air India disaster, June 23, 2010, in Humber Bay Park, Toronto

If there's one thing Canadians of all political stripes can agree on, it's sending the Tamil wannabe refugees home...In fact, a majority of supporters from all political parties...think the Tamils should be turned away, even escorted back to Sri Lanka by the Canadian Navy.

—BRYN WEESE, "Send 'em Packing: Poll," *Toronto Sun*, August 22, 2010

Jill Weaving, the [Vancouver Parks and Recreation] board's arts and culture co-ordinator, unveiled early plans [for a memorial to the Komagata Maru *incident] at the Coal Harbour Community Centre on Thursday… "There is fear that our memories of times that were unfair will divide people," she said. "But everyone wants not to see this happen again. Canadians and Vancouverites don't want this to happen again." The monument, said Weaving, will allow visitors to reflect on the past and hope for a better future.*

—NATALIE KAUR JOHAL, "Ship Memorial Takes Shape," *Metro News* (Vancouver), January 28, 2011

IN 1914, a ship named the *Komagata Maru* arrived off the coast of British Columbia carrying 376 potential immigrants, mostly Sikh men from India, some of whom desired to settle permanently in the burgeoning colony of Canada.[1] A public sentiment of anxiety about "Hindoo Invaders" and a racist immigration policy caused the ship to be anchored for two months in the Vancouver harbour, during which time the passengers were treated as prisoners and had difficulty gaining access to food and water. The ship was finally forced back to sea under threat from the weaponry of a Canadian Navy vessel. Upon its return to India, the governing British were concerned that the disgruntled passengers of the *Komagata Maru* might be persuaded to join a burgeoning movement for India's independence and decided to try to detain the vessel yet again. The British provoked hostilities and fired on the passengers; several were injured, some were killed, and most were subsequently imprisoned or disappeared.[2] At first glance, this event seems to have little in common with the 1985 bombing of Air India Flight 182, a terrorist act widely believed to have been committed by Sikh separatists fighting for an independent Khalistan, or Sikh homeland, in India. Yet Padma Viswanathan's novel, *The Ever After of Ashwin Rao*, Anita Rau Badami's novel, *Can You Hear the Nightbird Call?*, and Uma Parameswaran's poem, "On the Shores of the Irish Sea" all draw important connections between the *Komagata Maru* incident and the bombing of Flight 182 and its aftermath. In this essay, I argue these creative texts exemplify the crucial importance of remembering these two events *in relation*. How might remembrance of the *Komagata Maru* refract and reframe memories of the bombing of Flight 182 and its aftermath? I turn to recent state-sponsored efforts to memorialize and offer reconciliation for the Air India bombings and *Komagata Maru* incident to demonstrate how failing to remember these events in relation makes it easier to cloak the overt racism underpinning both, maintaining the veneer of "Canada" as a haven for racial diversity and tolerance.[3] By contrast, if public memorials of one event were designed in a way that explicitly make links to the other, a wider public might come to recognize how the unresolved injustice of the *Komagata* incident is deeply implicated in a cascading torrent of violent encounters that affected many in India, Canada, and other parts of the globe, events that are widely believed to have contributed to the bombing of Air India Flight 182 and to the delays in recognizing the bombing as a "Canadian" tragedy.[4] In other words, the state's implication in the (re)production of racial difference and the violence of its racializing practices are not easily surmised from current state-sponsored efforts to memorialize either event, but remembering the two events in relation (as Viswanathan, Badami, and Parameswaran's creative texts insist we must) invites critical reflection on the many ways that historical injustices live on, shaping and delimiting the present.

The approach to remembrance invoked in recent state-sponsored efforts to memorialize and apologize for the state's role in the Air India and *Komagata Maru* disasters is, unsurprisingly, very strategic. Remembrance as a strategic practice, according to Roger Simon, Sharon Rosenberg, and Claudia Eppert, involves "efforts to mobilize attachments and knowledge that serve specific social and political interests within particular spatiotemporal frameworks," while remembrance as a difficult return "unsettle[s] and put[s] into question the very terms of the redemptive promise of a strategic remembrance: that the future will be better if one remembers."[5] Although both of these approaches to remembrance draw attention to something to be done to redress or resolve an injustice, strategic remembrance tends to point toward concrete things a community can do, usually on behalf of less fortunate "others," to redress what is framed as a "historical" (or securely past) injustice in the purportedly more-just present and in the interest of a supposedly brighter future. Strategic remembrance also tends to collapse the distinctions between those who have suffered a loss directly and those who have suffered indirectly as witnesses or bystanders, as then Prime Minister Stephen Harper does in his apology to the family members of those killed in the bombing of Flight 182, when he asserts, "Your pain is our pain. As you grieve, so we grieve."[6] The collapsing of difference here, intended to overcome a perceived *in*difference on the part of the government toward the victims' families in the years following the attack, makes a strategic affective claim for recognition of a shared human suffering that cloaks how vulnerability to such suffering is so unevenly distributed across racial (and other) categorizations of difference.

By contrast, remembrance as a difficult return works quite differently: memorializations with the potential to evoke this kind of remembrance tend to focus much more on the complicated enmeshments of past and present, inviting the public that is called upon to remember or mourn a violent or traumatic event to consider the many ways in which historical injustices "live on" in the present.[7] The focus, then, is not so much on redressing an injustice that is framed as mattering primarily in the past but instead on contemplating how to respond to the many ways the injustice continues to inflect our lives differently in the present. Here are Simon, Rosenberg, and Eppert again, arguing that memory as a difficult return "implicat[es] us in an examination of how it is each of us listens, learns, and responds to those whose identities, bodies, and memories have been fundamentally impacted by such violence—impacts that cannot ever be reduced to versions of our own troubles and traumas."[8] To take seriously the distinction these authors make between remembrance as a strategic practice and remembrance as a difficult return demands a different approach to memorialization, one I believe is much more likely to be accomplished by remembering the *Komagata Maru* incident and Air India bombings in relation.

State-sponsored efforts to memorialize the 1985 bombing of Air India Flight 182 within Canada are quite recent, only undertaken with any seriousness beginning in 2007. An annual memorial service has been held—conspicuously, not in Canada but in Ahakista, Ireland, near where the plane fell into the Atlantic—since the first anniversary of the bombings and a permanent memorial was unveiled there in 1986, built through donations from the Canadian and Indian governments and Cork County's contribution of land and upkeep. The unveiling of this memorial was attended not by the prime minister of Canada, though, but by the minister of external affairs. Not until the twentieth anniversary of the bombings, in 2005, would a Canadian prime minister attend this annual memorial event. Also in 2005, the Government of Canada proclaimed June 23, the date of the bombings, a "National Day of Remembrance for Victims of Terrorism." As Angela Failler argues, this renewed state interest in encouraging and supporting public memorializing of Air India must be read in light of Canada's increasing participation in the "war on terror" and renewed emphasis on securitization sparked by the events of September 11, 2001.[9] In other words, these belated gestures toward public remembrance and reconciliation are highly strategic.

In 2007, twenty-two years after the bombings took place, permanent public memorials for the victims of Air India Flight 182 were installed in Toronto and Vancouver; the following year, a small existing plaque was transformed into a memorial presumed more fitting in Ottawa. In 2011, a fourth, state-sponsored, public monument was unveiled in Montreal. These memorials are remarkably belated, drawing attention to a significant temporal gap between when the bombings occurred and when the losses began to be claimed by the state as losses of and for Canadians. As then Prime Minister Harper acknowledged in his speech at the unveiling of the Toronto monument,

> *Flight 182 may have flown that fateful day under the flag of India, but the murder of its passengers was singularly a Canadian crime and tragedy. And worst of all, many Canadians didn't realize this until much, much later. Like bystanders at a public assault, many initially*

looked the other way and thought it was none of their business. This was a terrible, hurtful mistake—one that Canada will always regret.[10]

However, family and friends of the Air India victims had been advocating for more widespread public memorialization of their loss and acknowledgement of the bombing as a Canadian tragedy for at least two decades. To suggest that the government's belated decision to act on their advocacy serves a strategic purpose is not intended to downplay friends' and families' important work but is instead intended to signal that the state's interest in belatedly memorializing the losses resulting from the bombing of Flight 182 is hardly innocent and not necessarily as benevolent as it may, on the surface, appear.[11] In 2010, on the twenty-fifth anniversary of the Air India disaster, former Prime Minister Harper offered an apology on behalf of the government and the people of Canada to the families of the victims of Flight 182, for the "institutional failings" that contributed to the bombing and the "treatment of the victims' families thereafter."[12]

Efforts by the state to memorialize or apologize for the *Komagata Maru* incident are more recent still, even though the unjust, racist treatment of the ship's passengers took place much longer ago. In May 2008, the Government of British Columbia issued a formal apology in the legislature for its part in the treatment of the passengers aboard the *Komagata*. In August 2008, Prime Minister Harper offered an apology to the Indo-Canadian community on behalf of the Government of Canada, an apology that met with dissent from the largely Sikh crowd attending the Gadri Babian Da Mela celebration at which it was offered. Just after the apology was delivered, angered attendees took control of the stage, arguing (as the PM was whisked away by security) that such an informal apology was unacceptable. " The government has betrayed us," shouted Mela organizer Sahib Singh Thind, "as only yesterday it had promised us that the PM will announce a date here for the apology in Parliament later. Today, they have treated us like they did the *Komagata* passengers in 1914...It was the same racist conservative government then as now. Racism is alive in Canada."[13] Clearly, this is a past that is not so securely historical as the government might like to imagine; some experience the injustice of the state's treatment of the passengers aboard the *Komagata Maru* not as a century-old history but as an event that continues to matter in and for the present. In 2010, thanks to tireless advocacy by many in Sikh communities in Canada, the federal government announced its intention to fund several new projects designed to educate Canadians about the *Komagata*, committing this injustice to more widespread public memory. One of these projects includes a permanent monument built in Vancouver's Harbour Green Park, in partnership with the Vancouver Board of Parks and Recreation and the Khalsa Diwan Society. The monument, designed by Lees and Associates (the same landscape architectural firm that built the permanent Air India memorial in Vancouver's Stanley Park), was unveiled on July 23, 2012.

In each of the state-sponsored efforts to memorialize or apologize for the Air India and *Komagata Maru* disasters outlined in the last two paragraphs, the strategic deployment of memories of these events in the interest of distancing Canada and Canadians from racism is amply evident. For example, despite his expression of regret for how Canadians initially "looked the other way" after the bombing of Flight 182, Prime Minister Harper also asserted at the 2007 unveiling of the Air India memorial in Toronto that the bombing had "nothing to do with Canada."[14] As Failler insists, this statement seems to disregard the fact that those accused of committing the bombings and those aboard the plane were almost all Canadian citizens.[15] It also posits an invitation to forget the racist treatment of passengers aboard ships like the *Komagata Maru*, through which the state and its many apparatuses contributed directly to casting potential immigrants from India as undesirable "outsiders" to an imagined national community. Harper's statement thereby forecloses opportunities for reflecting on the ways that such casting of some potential immigrants has not changed as much in the ensuing years as the prime minister's gestures toward reconciliation and inclusion attest.

Not *all* immigrants to Canada in the early twentieth century received similar treatment, of course. The policy used to deny entry to most of the passengers on the *Komagata*, known as the "continuous journey" policy, was passed specifically to limit or prevent the arrival of non-white, non-European immigrants from other British colonies like India, working in tandem with policies like the Chinese Head Tax, which were designed with the specific goal of keeping those racialized as "other" out of Canada. The contemporary tendency among many Canadians to conflate brown bodies with "immigrant" or "outsider" is a direct legacy of such policies. Such tendencies remain enmeshed with the bombing of Flight 182 more than seventy years later, when many white Canadians still presumed that brown people could not *be* Canadian, making widespread recognition of this event as a specifically Canadian tragedy highly unlikely. It is a past that remains amply evident in the more immediate present as well, for as Ali Kazimi points out in his documentary *Continuous Journey*, the continuous journey policy of the early twentieth century is not so different from the Safe Third Country Agreement that allows Canadian immigration officials to turn away refugee claimants who have not reached Canada by continuous journey from their homeland (when their route took them through another country presumed by the Canadian government to be "safe" for refugees, i.e., the United States). Efforts to overturn this agreement were exhausted on February 5, 2009, when the Supreme Court of Canada decided not to hear an appeal of a prior court decision to uphold this policy.[16] And an even more recent echo of the injustice of the *Komagata Maru* reverberates powerfully in the treatment of Tamil refugee claimants who arrived aboard the MV *Sun Sea* in the summer of 2010.

The hostility with which the migrants aboard the *Sun Sea* were met upon their arrival off the coast of British Columbia stands in stark contrast to the claims of the Vancouver Parks Board spokesperson, who insisted that "Canadians" do not want to witness another *Komagata Maru* incident (cited in my epigraph above).[17] In fact, according to the *Toronto Sun* poll cited as an epigraph above, many Canadians *do* support a strikingly similar repetition of the unjust treatment of those aboard the *Komagata*, right down to the deployment of the Canadian Navy to "escort" the *Sun Sea* from Canadian waters.[18] While I am suspicious about whether the *Sun* poll should be read as representative of the views of a majority of Canadians, what this poll does seem to signal is ongoing support among *Sun* readers for responding to the MV *Sun Sea* in a way that does not just echo but *directly repeats* the 1914 treatment of those aboard the *Komagata Maru*. And although the passengers aboard the *Sun Sea* were permitted to disembark, the government immediately imprisoned them until their refugee claims could be heard, a practice that has been heavily critiqued by human rights activists.[19] Nearly nine months after the ship's arrival, approximately one hundred of the almost five hundred migrants aboard the vessel were still being held in Canadian prisons.[20] Yet, through their efforts to enact remembrance as a strategic practice, state-sponsored efforts to memorialize the *Komagata Maru* insist that such racist practices (and the sentiments of white supremacy that underpin them) are a thing of the past, such that it becomes possible to simultaneously acknowledge and express regret for a racist past while allowing racist immigration policy and practice to continue in the present—unabated and apparently unconnected to this history. This helps to explain how then Prime Minister Harper, in his 2008 apology for the *Komagata Maru* incident, described Canada as "our country that affords opportunity to all, regardless of their background, *our country that offers sanctuary to victims of violence and persecution* [emphasis added]."[21] Yet two years later his government responded as it did to the arrival of the MV *Sun Sea*, apparently without being widely called upon to explain this hypocrisy, because the past and the present are understood and framed through the logic of strategic remembrance as isolatable and largely unrelated.

As Radhika Mongia has argued, policies like the "continuous journey" enact "a racist strategy without naming race."[22] Racism continues to operate in a cloaked fashion in tandem with expressions of regret for past "exclusions" or "mistakes" (which are themselves seldom officially acknowledged as having racist underpinnings). As Hameed and Vukov elaborate,

> *The ways in which the racialized effects of policy exclusions operate virtually, leaving race unnamed and unspecified in the policy text while enacting highly racialized practices and effects, mirrors the Anglo-Canadian tradition of "polite racism": a racism without recourse to explicit naming or to an overtly racist terminology.*[23]

By separating opportunities for remembrance and expressions of regret for the *Komagata Maru* and Air India disasters both temporally and spatially—that is, by never uttering them at the same time and by geographically separating the state-sponsored monuments dedicated to their memories—state actors can more successfully and strategically maintain an image of Canada as "not racist," because linking the two suggests *a pattern* of racist treatment of South Asians in Canada, one that is structural, as well as symbolic. For example, if remembrances of Air India Flight 182 and the *Komagata Maru* are linked, it would be much more difficult for Harper to have claimed, as he did in his speech at the 2007 unveiling of the new Air India memorial in Toronto, that Canada "has long served as a model of a prosperous, peaceful, pluralistic society."[24] "It is little wonder," he continued, "that millions of people from around the world have been attracted to our shores, with each wave helping to further enrich our diverse and unique society."[25] The waves that brought the *Komagata Maru* are conveniently wiped away here, although the reference to "waves" and "shores" causes their haunting resonance to seep through Harper's speech. In 2010, in his speech at the twenty-fifth anniversary commemoration of the Air India disaster, Harper made this point slightly differently: "When we invite from around the world," he said, "those who share our aspirations for a better life, others also come, those who see in our Canada, not new bridges to a hopeful future but only another chance to travel the old roads to the blood-feuds of the past."[26] Here the onus is upon an "us" to "invite" others to make Canada home; Harper here re-enacts the logic of the continuous journey policy, both through his insistence on the right of invitation (and subsequently, although not mentioned, of refusal) and through how his speech invokes the qualities of "good" (i.e., easily assimilated) and "bad" immigrants (i.e., those who refuse to leave the past behind). Such qualities might not map as easily onto skin colour as they did in the popular understandings of race circulating in 1914, but the logic remains much the same.

One of the key ways that overt mention of race or racism is avoided in discussions about contemporary government immigration practice is through the advancement of these sorts of distinctions between good and bad (or, at least, less "desirable") immigrants or refugees. This sort of discursive framing is certainly not restricted to comments like those made by Harper in his apology speech for Air India—indeed, one need only peruse a sampling of comments posted to online articles on the topic of immigration to note how very pervasive such sentiments are. It is the same sort of logic that underpins the comments about the Tamil protestors I overheard just prior to the commencement of the twenty-fifth anniversary Air India commemoration cited in the epigraph to this chapter, a logic that is enabled through the widespread failure to remember the *Komagata Maru* and Air India disasters in relation. To remember these events in relation presents a challenge to such logic, as well as to dominant understandings of Canada as "not racist." Such a practice of remembering in relation can be found, in this instance, not in state-sponsored effort to memorialize or advance reconciliation for these events, but in Canadian literary culture.

In Padma Viswanathan's 2014 novel, *The Ever After of Ashwin Rao*, the bombing of Flight 182 cannot be understood as an isolated event that stands apart from the larger histories of empire and nationalism in India, Canada, or Britain.[27] The novel's protagonist, Ashwin Rao, a psychologist who lost his sister, niece, and nephew on Flight 182, has decided to write a book about how other family members of the victims have "coped up" in the years since the bombing. In a particularly significant scene, Ashwin insists that "the Air India bombing was not simply the result of some limited if collective murderous rage. That rage was fed by a larger sense of outrage, resulting from the under-noticed, under-reported Delhi pogroms."[28] The anti-Sikh pogroms that led to the murder of more than three thousand Sikhs in and around Delhi in 1984 are only the first of many violent events that Ashwin begins to connect to the bombing of Flight 182. Some of these events—the

Delhi pogroms, the Indian government's storming of the Golden Temple, and the subsequent assassination of Indira Gandhi, for example—are quite frequently discussed in connection to Air India, happening as they did in 1984, the year just prior to the bombings. But Ashwin also begins to connect other historical events—the 1975 state of emergency in India, Mahatma Gandhi's assassination, the history of British imperialism in India, and the 1914 routing of the *Komagata Maru* in Canada—events that are seldom, if ever, remembered in relation to the Air India bombings.

Trying to understand the psychic consequences of large-scale events of mass violence and racial injustice, Ashwin points out that the *Komagata Maru* was forced out of the Vancouver harbour in the interests of "exercising Canada's right to Keep Canada White."[29] Reminding readers that Canada's refusal to allow the British Indians aboard the *Komagata* entry to this British colony served as a reminder that "all British subjects were hardly equal within and throughout the Empire," Ashwin contemplates the long-term consequences of these sorts of significant moments of racial injustice. "Each humiliation grew the Sikhs' pride," he writes, "each galvanized a small sub-set into quests for purity and self-rule. Each formed a rough link on history's rattling chains."[30] Although one cannot draw a direct line from the treatment of Sikhs aboard the *Komagata Maru* to the bombing of two Air India flights in support of the Khalistan movement in 1985, Ashwin is nonetheless trying to sift through and connect the "rough links." Certainly, not all—not *nearly* all—people who survive events of mass violence go on to perpetrate such violence against others. But some do, and Ashwin is forced to consider how narrowing the "origins" of such events is one method by which both individuals and states abdicate responsibility for the ways we are all implicated in mass violence, albeit differently. As he concludes,

> *When I think on the Air India disaster, I hear the chain of history rattle. Its links are loops. Loops have holes. Was the bombing a Canadian or an Indian tragedy? Why pose this false division? Canada was colonized when India was, and their fates were ever linked. There is no expiation. The declaration of any single truth is itself an act of violence…Without*

India, could there be Empire? Without Empire, could there be radicalizing? Without Canada, could there have been a bomb?[31]

I read Ashwin's final sentence here as a rebuttal to former Prime Minister Harper's assertion at the unveiling of the Air India memorial in 2007 that the bombings had "nothing to do with Canada"—a contradictory claim, given that part of his aim in this speech is to acknowledge the tragedy as a loss of and for Canadians, but by which I believe he meant to distance the Canadian state and Canadian history from the bombings, drawing a neat line between Canadian and Indian history. Ashwin's version of history as a rattling chain that loops opens possibilities for understanding how and why the violence of British imperialism and the violence of the bombings remain, instead, inseparable. If not for the racist treatment of those aboard the *Komagata Maru*, could there have been a bomb? Ashwin's question is impossible to answer in any definitive way, and yet so important to contemplate.

Anita Rau Badami's novel, *Can You Hear the Nightbird Call?*, a book dedicated in part to the memory of the victims of Air India Flight 182, also demonstrates the potential for remembering differently, and with difficulty, that might arise from mediating remembrance of the Air India disaster by emphasizing its relation to the *Komagata Maru* incident.[32] A work of fiction, it takes as its subject matter the intertwining lives of three women as their personal narratives collide with significant historical events in Canada and India. The novel begins with a story about the *Komagata Maru* and concludes with the murder of one of the novel's three central characters aboard Flight 182. The injustice of the *Komagata Maru* is addressed in Badami's novel as an invitation to the reader to imagine that the characters' lives, and, by extension, history itself, might have turned out differently had the father of central character Sharanjeet (or Bibi-ji) Kaur not had to suffer the injustice of the ship's routing from the Vancouver harbour. By beginning the novel with a recounting of the *Komagata Maru* and the impact of the racist treatment of those on board, the novel also has the compelling effect of putting the histories of Canada and India in relation and positing them, too, as indelible—an understanding of history that Harper's framing of events "here" and "there" works against.

Recounting how the *Komagata Maru* was routed from the Vancouver harbour after its lengthy and difficult time in limbo there, a postman informs Sharanjeet's mother, Gurpreet, that those on the ship "were driven away as if they were criminals!"[33] He also tells her what he has heard about the troubles at Budge-Budge, the port to which the ship returned—that "the British were waiting for [the *Komagata*'s passengers] with guns"—and when Gurpreet wonders why, he asks, "Do the sahibs need an excuse to raise guns to our heads?"[34] Through the postman's question, Badami deftly links the British imperialism so evident in India at the time with its day-to-day workings in that far-away British colony of Canada, challenging assumptions that the routing of the *Komagata* from the Vancouver harbour and the treatment of the ship's passengers upon their return to India can be understood in isolation. The postman then conveys his hope that Gurpreet's husband has survived the encounter and will find his way home. After a month of waiting, Harjot Singh returns to his family, deeply affected by what he has experienced: "here he was, denied entry into Canada, denied a chance to make a better life and finally accused of treason. Since when, he asked Gurpreet bitterly, since when had it been treasonous to wish for a better life?"[35] In Singh's words we hear an echo of the rhetoric underpinning Harper's speeches, of the immigrant's perpetual imagining of "Canada" as synonymous with "a better life," and yet Badami does not allow this assumption to go untroubled. While the characters who do later immigrate to Canada—including Harjot's daughter Bibi-ji—manage to avoid the grinding poverty experienced by the central characters who remain in India, I would argue their lives are not easily interpreted as "better," for they are not protected from the violence and traumatic losses associated with the events that contribute to the bombing of Flight 182, or from the bombing itself. Several years later, never able to "get over" the injustice of being denied entry to Canada, Harjot Singh simply disappears and his wife and family decide to imagine that he has gone to join the struggle for India's independence. After all, Gurpreet tells herself, "Harjot Singh *had* been resentful about his treatment at the hand of the goras who ruled the country, he had never understood why he and the other passengers on the *Komagata Maru*, every one of them British citizens, had been refused entry to Canada."[36] Thus, the racist immigration policy that denied Harjot entry into Canada is cast as indelible from Britain's imperialist policy and practice in India, and the white supremacy of the "goras" *here* and *there* is resituated as another factor underpinning the violent struggles over land and sovereignty yet to come, again challenging common assumptions that the histories of "here" and "there," Canada and India, are actually neatly separable by nation-state borders.

The *Komagata Maru* returns again in Badami's novel when Bibi-ji is trying to understand why her great-nephew and adopted son, Jasbeer, gets into so much trouble at his Canadian school. Bibi-ji wonders if her recounting of the incident and its effects on her father has left the child with "an impossible load, a feeling of grievances unresolved?"[37] Later on, as a teenager, Jasbeer becomes a pupil of Dr. Randhawa, an agitator for an independent Sikh homeland whose calls for militant revolution are implicated, in the novel, in the bombing of Flight 182. Those so-called "old roads to the blood-feuds of the past" that former Prime Minister Harper implied have "nothing to do with Canada" lead squarely back, here in the novel, to Canadian immigration policy, such that it becomes difficult to hold these two events and the histories they mark as separate. Indeed, one might read this passage in Badami's novel as further implying that the unresolved injustice of the *Komagata* incident is itself deeply implicated, along with the violent aftermath of partition, the storming of the Golden Temple in Amritsar, and the anti-Sikh violence following Indira Gandhi's assassination, in the twinning of a vengeful militancy to expressions of Khalistani (Sikh separatist) masculinity. Rather than imagine that such racialized, gendered subjectivities simply "are," remembering the *Komagata* incident in relation to the surge in such militancy as an expression of Khalistani masculinity invites us to contemplate how the derision of mostly Sikh men as "Hindoo invaders" during and after the *Komagata*'s time in the Vancouver harbour can be understood as a racializing practice that helps to *produce* such militancy as an *effect* of the state's racist policy. Such a reading invites us to remember both the *Komagata* incident and the Air India bombing on quite different terms—the *Komagata* seems less likely to be remembered as "ancient history" that "no one" wants repeated and more as an event still bearing heavily on the present, one that could (and does) too easily continue to repeat. And the Air India bombings seem less likely to be remembered as the "mad, militant" actions of "evil" men acting on a "foreign" history, and more likely to be recognized as bound to colonial histories of injustice that cross state lines and remain inseparable from the production of racialized subjects still too frequently marked as "insiders" or "outsiders" to Canada, not just on the basis of skin tone but also on the basis of a willingness to forget the injustices of the so-called past.

Finally, in a poem written for the fifteenth anniversary commemoration of the bombing of Flight 182, Uma Parameswaran draws our attention to the indelible binding of the *Komagata Maru* and Air India disasters:

Dive deeper.
July 23rd, 1914, dark day of ignominy,
when Komagatamaru was driven into the open sea,
while people and newspapers screamed:
Keep Canada White, true north strong and free.
(As though the first nations of this land
never were, had never been.)

Fly higher.
June 23rd, 1985, dark day of ignominy
when Mulroney sent condolences to Rajiv Gandhi
For "your great loss"
after Flight 182 hurtled through the sky
into the Irish sea,
stopping three hundred Canadian hearts
And breaking three thousand more.[38]

The line "Dive deeper" suggests that to fully understand the state's many failures in response to the bombing, one must consider how the injustice of the *Komagata Maru* incident—an event one only discovers by delving more deeply into the histories of British Empire—lives on. Parameswaran also deftly establishes how the very founding of "Canada" is premised on racial injustice when she notes its colonial origins. By drawing attention to the popularity of the " White Canada" rhetoric of 1914 and juxtaposing it with then Prime Minister Brian Mulroney's significant gaffe after the bombing of Flight 182, the poem suggests the lingering effects of such rhetoric on more recent imaginings that continue to conflate whiteness and "Canadian-ness." Thus, the poem invites reflection not just on the racial injustices of the past but on how they continue to inflect and shape the present. The *Komagata Maru* incident, then, is more likely to be understood as enmeshed with racial injustice in the more recent past of the Air India disaster, or even in the immediate present in which the poem was written (for in the next stanza, Parameswaran goes on to decry the many delays in initiating a public inquiry into the state's handling of the Air India case, an inquiry that was not, in fact, established until 2006). The invocation of the *Komagata* in Parameswaran's poem is much more consistent with memory as a form of difficult return than with the more strategic invocations evident in state-sponsored efforts to memorialize or offer reconciliation for the treatment of the vessel and its passengers.

Viswanathan, Badami, and Parameswaran wisely do not imply a direct causal link between the *Komagata* incident and the Air India disaster, but juxtaposing the two events as they do highlights how these events are nonetheless thoroughly enmeshed. That enmeshment challenges conventional ways of understanding these events as entirely separate or separable. The injustice of the *Komagata Maru* incident is commonly imagined as having been "resolved" by the liberalization of Canadian immigration policy, for example, while the Air India bombing is commonly imagined as having arisen solely out of a conflict over land in India. And while both of these assumptions are partly true, remembering the two events in relation, as do Viswanathan, Badami, and Parameswaran, helps to illuminate the ways that colonial histories—the history of British Empire and efforts to uphold the racial hierarchies of that Empire in its colonies, including Canada—were largely about inventing and securing notions of racial superiority and inferiority. So while the immigration policies that prevented the landing of the men aboard the *Komagata* no longer exist (at least, not in the same form), it is impossible to precisely measure the degree to which such policies played a role in effecting the twinning of a violent militancy to Khalistani masculinity, a twinning that is itself key to understanding the Air India bombings. Indeed, I would argue that such a twinning can be read as a subtle-but-tangible gendering and racializing effect of such policies, and that these effects live on long after the policies themselves have been changed. So although it may remain impossible to insist on a direct causal link between the *Komagata* incident and the Air India bombings, such a different understanding allows—indeed, demands—us to connect one to the other, which can be accomplished by remembering these events in relation.

It is not terribly surprising that works of literature seem more likely than memorials, and particularly than state-sponsored remembrance events or monuments, to evoke memory as a difficult return. After all, as James Young insists, " Traditionally, state-sponsored memory of a national past aims to affirm the righteousness of a nation's birth, even its divine election."[39] In fact, as Angela Failler notes, the official public inquiry into the state's handling of the Air India case cast dispersion on creative or fictional interpretations of the event, which works to cement the inquiry's claims of authoritative fact finding but does little to encourage reflection on how public memories of such atrocities could be deployed for other than strategic purposes.[40] As Failler asserts, " This form of exclusion and the suspicions raised around the work of artists speaks precisely to the potential of artworks to disrupt and challenge the symbolic authority that official accounts of the bombings have maintained."[41] Creative texts such as those I analyze above offer us a richer, deeper, more complex sense of how the formation of these two nations, Canada and India, as well as the history of British imperialism that underpins them, are implicated in producing the clashes around race, religion, and belonging that underpin the bombing of Flight 182. But so long as the strategic use of memories of these events remains the paramount form of public memory deployed in Canada, the potential for evoking remembrance as a difficult return evident in these literary works will remain largely unrealized. What are the possibilities for a more widespread evocation of remembrance as a difficult return, made possible by remembering the *Komagata Maru* and Air India Flight 182 in relation? By way of offering a tentative response to this question, I conclude with a reflection on the permanent memorials to the Air India and *Komagata Maru* disasters in Vancouver.

James Young has long advocated the creation of "counter-monuments" as subversive responses to the traditional, state-sponsored use of the memorial form, a counter-monument, he argues, that aims

> *not to console but to provoke; not to remain fixed but to change; not to be everlasting but to disappear; not to be ignored by its passersby but to demand interaction; not to remain pristine but to invite its own violation and desecration; not to accept graciously the burden of memory but to throw it back at the town's feet.*[42]

Unfortunately, the four state-sponsored, permanent memorial structures dedicated to the memory of the victims of the bombing of Flight 182 and the similar monument built in Vancouver in memory of the *Komagata Maru* incident all seem highly unlikely to accomplish any of these counter-monumental aims. Nor do they seem likely to put the events they mark in relation, for although the memorial for the *Komagata Maru* in Vancouver was designed by the same landscape architectural firm that designed and built the nearby Air India memorial, the two monuments make no reference to each other.

In a document outlining the plans for the *Komagata Maru* memorial, the goals of the project are listed as follows:

- *To provide views of the mooring site of the Komagata Maru while respecting existing views;*
- *To retain and benefit the amenity, open space and accessibility of Harbour Green Park; and*
- *To create a meaningful monument that promotes reflection and education.*[43]

When considered alongside Young's explication of the qualities of a counter-monument, it seems likely that the first two goals listed here may significantly impede the realization of the third. For if the monument design must respect existing views and essentially retain the current park setting, it seems unlikely to "provoke" its viewers, as Young insists it must. Rather than exposing the long history of racism in Canada and inviting viewers to reflect on the many ways such racism lives on, it seems likely that the *Komagata Maru* monument, much like the one unveiled for Air India a few years earlier, will blend rather seamlessly into the landscape, primarily inviting forgetting or a casual interest rather than throwing memory "back at the town's feet."

Similarly, the Air India memorial in Stanley Park blends so seamlessly into the park's current landscape that it seems quite possible for passers-by to miss experiencing it entirely, unless one is specifically searching for it.[44] Although the plaque accompanying the monument wall declares Air India to be "a Canadian tragedy," thereby countering those narratives of the event that distance it from Canada, it contains no further text that might provoke reflection on the many ways that racism affected the state's efforts to prevent and respond to the bombings, or the widespread failure among many Canadians to recognize the loss as significant to the national narrative—the sort of reflection that might be more likely to arise from remembering Air India and *Komagata Maru* in relation. The monument wall is built to echo the trajectory of the plane as it fell into the Atlantic, and the names of those who were killed in the bombings are etched into the stone, just as the names of those who were aboard the *Komagata Maru* are etched into the steel ship's hull of the monument in Coal Harbour. Such a list of names is perhaps most meaningful for those who knew those named in life, and thus it remains an important feature of contemporary monuments.[45] But I am inclined to agree with Judith Butler when she writes,

> *Do names really "open" us to an intersubjective ground, or are they simply so many ruins which designate a history irrevocably lost? Do these names really signify for us the fullness of the lives that were lost, or are they so many tokens of what we cannot know, enigmas, inscrutable and silent?*[46]

Both of these physical monuments seem more likely to reproduce the strategic deployment of memory so evident in the state-sponsored memorials and apologies discussed thus far than to be evocative of memory as a difficult return, particularly among visitors who did not personally know those whom the monuments name.

What if, instead, the various points of connection between the *Komagata Maru* incident and the Air India bombings were made explicit in the design of such memorials? Importantly, the connections would need to be drawn not to expose political or religious differences between Canadians of South Asian heritage but to invite reflection on how racist state policies and colonial histories contribute to the (re)production of such differences. In other words, by foregrounding the connections between the communities most directly affected by the *Komagata Maru* and Air India disasters, a unique opportunity exists to expose the many ways that racism and state racializing practices underpin both of these events and continue to inflect state-sponsored efforts to memorialize and redress these histories today. Thus, I remain hopeful that the practice of remembering the *Komagata Maru* and Air India disasters in relation, begun in the literary contributions of Viswanathan, Badami, and Parameswaran, could be powerfully enacted through the design and use of memorials-to-come, if their creators, planners, and organizers are willing to dwell on the complicated enmeshment of these two events.

Notes

1. This is a revised and expanded version of the article, "The Importance of Remembering in Relation: Juxtaposing the Air India and *Komagata Maru* Disasters," originally published in TOPIA: *Canadian Journal of Cultural Studies* 27 (2012): 197–214.
2. For richer and much more in-depth recountings of the story of the *Komagata Maru*, see Ali Kazimi's documentary, *Continuous Journey* (Toronto: Peripheral Visions Productions, 2004, DVD), his more recent book, *Undesirables: White Canada and the Komagata Maru* (Vancouver: Douglas & McIntyre, 2011), and Hugh Johnston's *The Voyage of the Komagata Maru: The Sikh Challenge to Canada's Colour Bar* (Vancouver: UBC Press, 1989).
3. This essay was originally written prior to the election of Justin Trudeau's Liberal government in 2015 and his 2016 apology for the *Komagata Maru* incident, delivered in the House of Commons. As such, close analysis of this most recent apology, along with more recent community, activist, and artistic efforts to commemorate the *Komagata* coinciding with its hundredth anniversary in 2014, is beyond the scope of this essay. The author hopes to develop further analysis of these very recent responses in future work.
4. It is beyond the scope of this essay to repeat the complex histories of the Air India bombings; for a brief overview of the events that are widely believed to have contributed to the bombings, see Chandrima Chakraborty's introduction to the feature section, "Air India Flight 182: A Canadian Tragedy?" in TOPIA: *Canadian Journal of Cultural Studies* 27 (2012): 173–176. Readers desiring more background on the bombings and associated events might also consult any of several journalist's accounts, including Clark Blaise and Bharati Mukherjee, *The Sorrow and the Terror: The Haunting Legacy of the Air India Tragedy* (Markham, ON: Viking, 1987); Kim Bolan, *Loss of Faith: How the Air-India Bombers Got Away with Murder* (Toronto: McClelland & Stewart, 2005); or Salim Jiwa and Donald J. Hauka, *Margin of Terror: A Reporter's Twenty-Year Odyssey Covering the Tragedies of the Air India Bombing* (Toronto: Key Porter Books, 2006).
5. Simon, Roger I., Sharon Rosenberg, and Claudia Eppert, eds., *Between Hope and Despair: Pedagogy and the Remembrance of Historical Trauma* (Lanham, MD: Rowman and Littlefield, 2000), 3–4.
6. Stephen Harper, Statement Delivered at the Commemoration Ceremony for the 25th Anniversary of the Air India Flight 182 Atrocity, June 23, 2010, accessed July 14, 2011, http://pm.gc.ca/eng/news/2010/06/23/statement-prime-minister-canada-commemoration-ceremony-25th-anniversary-air-india. Reprinted in this volume.
7. My interest in how pasts "live on" is inspired, in part, by Wendy Brown, who writes, "[w]e inherit not 'what really happened' to the dead but what lives on from that

happening, what is conjured from it, how past generations and events occupy the force fields of the present, how they claim us, and how they haunt, plague, and inspirit our imaginations and visions for the future"; see Wendy Brown, *Politics Out of History* (Princeton, NJ: Princeton University Press, 2001), 150.

8. Simon, Rosenberg, and Eppert, *Between Hope and Despair*, 6.
9. Angela Failler, "Remembering the Air India Disaster: Memorial and Counter-Memorial," *Review of Education, Pedagogy, and Cultural Studies* 31 (2009): 150–176; Angela Failler with artwork by Eisha Marjara, "'Remember Me Nought': The 1985 Air India Bombings and Cultural *Nachträglichkeit*," *Public: Art/Culture/Ideas* 42 (2010): 113–124; Angela Failler, "'War-on-Terror' Frames of Remembrance: The 1985 Air India Bombings after 9/11," TOPIA: *Canadian Journal of Cultural Studies* 27 (Spring 2012): 253–269.
10. Stephen Harper, Statement Delivered at the Unveiling of the Memorial Dedicated to the Victims of Air India Flight 182, June 23, 2007, accessed July 25, 2011, http://pm.gc.ca/eng/media.asp?id=1719.
11. For specific analyses of how various official or authoritative memorializations of Air India Flight 182 support and advance Canada's role in the post-9/11 "war on terror," see Failler, "Remembering the Air India Disaster"; Failler with Marjara, "'Remember Me Nought'"; and Failler, "'War-on-Terror.'"
12. Harper, Commemoration Ceremony. For an analysis of the prime minister's apology to the families of the victims of Flight 182, see Cassel Busse's essay in this volume.
13. *World Sikh News Bureau*, "Canadian PM Apologizes for *Komagata Maru*, Sikhs Reject Apology: Community Wanted PM to Deliver Apology in House of Commons," August 6, 2008, accessed July 14, 2011, http://worldsikhnews.com/6%20August%20 2008/Canadian%20PM%20apologizes%20for%20Komagata%20Maru.htm.
14. Harper, Unveiling of the Memorial.
15. Failler, "Remembering the Air India Disaster," 164.
16. Edward C. Corrigan, "Courts Allow Safe Third Country Agreement to Operate," *Rabble*, March 17, 2009, accessed February 4, 2012, http://rabble.ca/news/ courts-allow-safe-third-country-agreement-operate.
17. Natalie Kaur Johal, "Ship Memorial Takes Shape," *Metro News* (Vancouver), January 28, 2011, accessed February 6, 2012, http://www.metronews.ca/vancouver/local/ article/756537--ship-memorial-takes-shape.
18. Bryn Weese, "Send 'em Packing: Poll," *Toronto Sun*, August 22, 2010, 4.
19. Amnesty International, "Rights Advocates Decry Detention of Refugee Claimants from MV *Sun Sea*, 10 February," February 10, 2011, accessed July 21, 2011, http://www.amnesty.ca/media2010.php?DocID=247.

20. Canadian Press, "Tamil Migrant No Security Threat, IRB Rules," CBC *News*, March 3, 2011, accessed July 6, 2011, http://www.cbc.ca/news/canada/british-columbia/story/2011/03/07/bc-tamil-migrant-security-threat.html.
21. Alia Somani, "The Apology and Its Aftermath: National Atonement or the Management of Minorities?" *Postcolonial Text* 6, no. 1 (2011): 10–11, accessed July 21, 2011, http://journals.sfu.ca/pocol/index.php/pct/article/viewArticle/1216. For the text of then Prime Minister Harper's apology for the *Komagata Maru* incident, I am indebted to the research conducted by Somani, who went to great lengths to document Harper's speech and make it more widely available. Unlike most of the former prime minister's public speeches, and, in particular, his apologies for past wrongs, the apology he delivered at the Gadri Babian Da Mela celebration on August 3, 2008, was not made available to the public by his office. This inaccessibility of the text of the apology is one of the reasons why members of the Sikh community insisted the prime minister's apology should be formally delivered in Parliament. A transcript of the full speech can be found in Somani's article.
22. Quoted in Ayesha Hameed and Tamara Vukov, "Animating Exclusions: Ali Kazimi's *Continuous Journey* and the Virtualities of Racialized Exclusion," TOPIA: *Canadian Journal of Cultural Studies* 17 (2007): 93.
23. Ibid., 91.
24. Harper, Unveiling of the Memorial.
25. Ibid.
26. Harper, Commemoration Ceremony.
27. Padma Viswanathan, *The Ever After of Ashwin Rao* (Toronto: Random House Canada, 2014).
28. Ibid., 235.
29. Ibid., 240.
30. Ibid., 241.
31. Ibid., 242.
32. Anita Rau Badami, *Can You Hear the Nightbird Call?* (Toronto: Alfred A. Knopf, 2006).
33. Ibid., 17.
34. Ibid.
35. Ibid.
36. Ibid., 13.
37. Ibid., 198.
38. Uma Parameswaran, "On the Shores of the Irish Sea," in *Sisters at the Well* (New Delhi: Indialog Publications, 2002), 12–13.
39. James E. Young, "The Counter-Memorial: Memory against Itself in Germany Today," *Critical Inquiry* 18, no. 2 (1992): 270.

40. Failler with Marjara, "'Remember Me Nought,'" 117.

41. Ibid., 117.

42. Young, "Counter-Memorial," 277.

43. Vancouver Board of Parks and Recreation, Khalsa Diwan Society, and Lees and Associates, Site and Monument Design Proposal, January 2011, accessed July 25, 2011, http://vancouver.ca/parks/info/planning/komagatamaru/pdf/11-01-26_presentationboards.pdf.

44. When I visited the memorial, for example, I found that despite knowing what I was looking for and where to look, I had to search to find the monument and actually walked past it once before realizing that I had missed seeing it.

45. I have elsewhere discussed the complexities of using personal names in memorials in much more detail in "Can Names Implicate Us? The Memorial-Art of Rebecca Belmore and Janis Cole," *Public: Art, Culture, Ideas* 42 (2010): 101–112.

46. Judith Butler, "Spirit in Ashes," review of *Spirit in Ashes: Hegel, Heidegger, and Man-Made Mass Death*, by Edith Wyschogrod, *History & Theory* 27, no. 1 (1988): 69. I first encountered this passage from Butler in Sharon Rosenberg, " Tracing the Textures of an Ethical Relation to the Dead: Trauma, Witnessing, and the 'Montreal Massacre,'" *Canadian Journal of Community Mental Health* 17, no. 2 (1998): 21; see that essay for a more in-depth discussion of Butler's critique of the use of names in memorials.

Works Cited

Badami, Anita Rau. *Can You Hear the Nightbird Call?* Toronto: Alfred A. Knopf, 2006.

Blaise, Clark, and Bharati Mukherjee. *The Sorrow and the Terror: The Haunting Legacy of the Air India Tragedy*. Markham, ON: Viking, 1987.

Bolan, Kim. *Loss of Faith: How the Air India Bombers Got Away with Murder*. Toronto: McClelland & Stewart, 2005.

Brown, Wendy. *Politics Out of History*. Princeton, NJ: Princeton University Press, 2001.

Butler, Judith. "Spirit in Ashes." Review of *Spirit in Ashes: Hegel, Heidegger, and Man-Made Mass Death*, by Edith Wyschogrod. *History & Theory* 27, no. 1 (1988): 60–70.

Chakraborty, Chandrima. Introduction to "Air India Flight 182: A Canadian Tragedy?" TOPIA: *Canadian Journal of Cultural Studies* 27 (2012): 173–176.

Continuous Journey. Directed by Ali Kazimi. Toronto: Peripheral Visions Productions, 2004. DVD.

Dean, Amber. "Can Names Implicate Us? The Memorial-Art of Rebecca Belmore and Janis Cole." *Public: Art, Culture, Ideas* 42 (2010): 101–112.

Failler, Angela. "Remembering the Air India Disaster: Memorial and Counter-Memorial." *Review of Education, Pedagogy, and Cultural Studies* 31 (2009): 150–176.

———. "'War-on-Terror' Frames of Remembrance: The 1985 Air India Bombings after 9/11." TOPIA: *Canadian Journal of Cultural Studies* 27 (Spring 2012): 253–269.

Failler, Angela, with artwork by Eisha Marjara. "'Remember Me Nought': The 1985 Air India Bombings and Cultural *Nachträglichkeit*." *Public: Art/Culture/Ideas* 42 (2010): 113–124.

Hameed, Ayesha, and Tamara Vukov. "Animating Exclusions: Ali Kazimi's *Continuous Journey* and the Virtualities of Racialized Exclusion." TOPIA: *Canadian Journal of Cultural Studies* 17 (2007): 87–109.

Jiwa, Salim, and Donald J. Hauka. *Margin of Terror: A Reporter's Twenty-Year Odyssey Covering the Tragedies of the Air India Bombing*. Toronto: Key Porter Books, 2006.

Johnston, Hugh. *The Voyage of the Komagata Maru: The Sikh Challenge to Canada's Colour Bar*. Vancouver: UBC Press, 1989.

Kazimi, Ali. *Undesirables: White Canada and the Komagata Maru*. Vancouver: Douglas & McIntyre, 2011.

Parameswaran, Uma. "On the Shores of the Irish Sea." In *Sisters at the Well*, 11–13. New Delhi: Indialog Publications, 2002.

Rosenberg, Sharon. "Tracing the Textures of an Ethical Relation to the Dead: Trauma, Witnessing, and the 'Montreal Massacre.'" *Canadian Journal of Community Mental Health* 17, no. 2 (1998): 15–26.

Simon, Roger I., Sharon Rosenberg, and Claudia Eppert, eds. *Between Hope and Despair: Pedagogy and the Remembrance of Historical Trauma*. Lanham, MD: Rowman and Littlefield, 2000.

Somani, Alia. "The Apology and Its Aftermath: National Atonement or the Management of Minorities?" *Postcolonial Text* 6, no. 1 (2011): 1–18.

Viswanathan, Padma. *The Ever After of Ashwin Rao*. Toronto: Random House Canada, 2014.

Young, James E. "The Counter-Memorial: Memory against Itself in Germany Today." *Critical Inquiry* 18, no. 2 (1992): 267–296.

On the Shores of the Irish Sea

UMA PARAMESWARAN

for June 23, 2000:
15th anniversary of the crash of *Emperor Kanishka*, Air India Flight 182

i.
On the Shores of the Irish Sea

Fifteen years have passed.
Fifteen summers,
with the length of fifteen long winters.
I reach out to feel her little fingers
that so trustingly encircle mine
as we wade along the beach,
only to see her floating on spindrift foam
far on the open sea.
On winter nights, snow on my window,
I curve my legs to entwine his warmth
and feel the empty chill of cold sheets.

Fifteen summers we have met
On the shores of this Irish sea;
victims twice over, mourning
our ever-young dead
with our slowly-aging eyes
and ever-aching hearts.

ii.

Long a celebrant
of this lovely land of endless skies,
whose earth I've walked into horizons,
whose skies I've flown from sea to sea,
in whose rivers I've seen my own –
    the singing waters of my native Narmada,
    Kaveri whose rapids feed ancestral fields –
I come, bearing votive incense and a pledge.

I, who have brought Ganga to our land, our Assiniboine,
and built my temples where it flows into the Red, and where
the fluteplayer dances on the waters of La Salle,
now stand on the ocean's shore
and know
I must walk farther,
fly higher, dive deeper
to find the fire
that is now but ember
in empty pyres
that smoulder ever
waiting for the hopes,
the bodies, that lie strewn
on ocean floor.

Earth, air, fire, water,
Progenitors of all life,
Inspire, exhort, goad, needle,
nag us night and day
I pray
That all who live
in this lonely land of endless skies
Remember now and forever
the dates etched in caves of memory
where there and here come together
to make us who we be.

Dive deeper.
July 23rd, 1914, dark day of ignominy,
when Komagatamaru was driven back into the open sea,
while people and newspapers screamed:
Keep Canada White, true north strong and free.
(as though the first nations of this land
never were, had never been.)

Fly higher.
June 23rd, 1985, dark day of ignominy
when Mulroney sent condolences to Rajiv Gandhi
for "your great loss"
after Flight 182 hurtled through the sky
into the Irish sea,
stopping three hundred Canadian hearts
and breaking three thousand more.

Cry rivers.
June 23rd, 2000, dark day of ignominy,
when the criminals who sent limbs and hearts
hurtling through the sky into the Irish sea,
have still not been brought to book
because of a government that drags its feet.

She said, Dark, dark your memories.
Surely there are sunnier ones that shine
thru the spruce green of your prairie mind:
November 2nd, 1949, when Jawaharlal in person
Stood on the Pacific shore and thanked
the Ghadars for their part in freedom's cause.
February 21st, 2000, when Ujjal took oath of office
to the sound of India's drums and dance.

Yes, yes, and I have sung psalms to those.
But I come today to light camphor markers,
stupa, gnomon, pyramid, obelisk,
and to sing dirges to the dead, who,
denied funeral pyres,
shall glow forever
in history books and hearts
of all who live from sea to sea.

Source

The Ever After of Ashwin Rao (excerpt)

PADMA VISWANATHAN

9 June 2004

At three in the morning, New Delhi's air is mostly remnants. This is its quietest hour, though the city is not still. The sounds of night business concluding, morning business being prepared, all sorts of shrouded transactions: these carry. But the air itself is nostalgic with acrid exhaust, cookstove smoke, the dying breaths of jasmine and bougainvillea breaking down into each other, night exhaling the prior day.

Please excuse: poetic lapse. I orient by smell. The night-scent excited me as I locked my door and ascended, then stopped, descended and re-entered the flat to check again: taps off, windows locked, no food anywhere. I don't normally second-guess this way—I have many neuroses, just not this one—but I would be away in Canada for a year. I would leave my key with a fellow resident but didn't want to leave her a reason to use it.

I locked the door again, and went upstairs to lay the key in its envelope on Vijaya's threshold. She was a widow I barely considered a friend, particularly since she wanted to be more than that. Fetching my bag from the landing, I trotted briskly down the stairs, across the courtyard and into the carport, clicking my tongue for the cat. Dirty-orange fur, three rickety legs, strangely swollen jowls; it slunk around as though hoping to be hit.

I put out last night's take-away, lamb biryani, at the usual spot. I had never wanted to keep a pet, but was overcome by the urge to feed the patchy creature. A memory knocked. My nephew, Anand, at six months maybe. When do they start with the pabulum? My sister, Kritika, was feeding him. She called me over—" Watch, Ashwin!"—as she lifted the little spoon toward his face and he opened his mouth, SO wide, his head bobbing a little, the eyes so serious, as though this were a contract he had agreed to fulfill: survival. My sister and I laughed until our sides hurt.

And two years after Anand came my niece, Asha.

Asha, my Asha. The child of my life. Sometimes I thought I recalled a whisper of her smell—green grapes and the pages of books; perhaps a hint of nutmeg?—but even the motion of my mind turning toward it fanned it away.

The cat still hadn't appeared and my auto-rickshaw was waiting. "Airport," I told the driver, no *good morning* necessary. He had been, for fifteen years, my favourite among those at the corner rank—almost surly, always prompt. He tossed his beedi and unthrottled his engine.

Two weeks from today, June 23, would be the nineteenth anniversary of a jet bombing that killed 326 people I didn't know, and three I did: Kritika, Anand, Asha. It had taken nearly eighteen years to drag two perpetrators into court. Last spring, April 2003, I had gone to Vancouver to witness the trial's start. My first time back in Canada since 1985. A Screaming Reluctance to See It had battled in me with a Driving Compulsion to See It. Guess which won?

Victims' families, along with various other concerned parties and/or gawkers, came from all over. They milled in the grand atrium at the provincial courthouse in Vancouver, their hot, thick optimism mingling with a slight steam from the bloodthirsty and giving me…what is it? When one's skin crawls. The *heebie-jeebies*.

The atrium's high, glass walls gave the all-too-obvious image of transparency. Kafka's trial could never happen here. Glass houses: Canadians don't throw stones. On the government side, the excitement was both more stately and more tawdry: press releases, security expenditures, and a bullet- and bomb-proof courtroom custom-built several circles of hell underground, down where the sun don't shine.

Only two of the many hot-air buffoons allegedly involved in the bombing were standing trial. I would name them, but what's in a name? I try to block their faces, but they rise in my mind's eye. Specimens. Bad examples of their community, their race, their species. Bad men.

I felt the trial to be a sham and yet I had gone to see it. Why? And furthermore, Why?

Why a sham? Because it came so very late—and after so much had changed, from the political situations that fed the bomb plot to the security situations that permitted it—that it would do nothing to prevent future terrorist acts. The accused did not regret what they had done, but neither would they plant any other bombs.

But what of punishment? you might ask. I *hated* those men. I might gladly have punished them with my own hands, not that I have ever done such a thing. But for the government to mete out, what—justice? Hardly. No government in the world possessed a moral scepter weighty enough to flog these puny fellows.

So. Why had I gone? At the time, I didn't know why. In the courtroom, it wasn't the accused who interested me but the bereaved, the others like myself, those who had lost the people most important to them. Apart from my now-late parents, I had only ever spoken to one other living victim: my brother-in-law, Suresh, Kritika's husband. A good fellow, but we had not been in contact since a year or two after the disaster. I looked for him in the courthouse crowds, fruitlessly.

How is he? I thought, for the first time in years. Perhaps it was the first time I had ever thought that. When the bomb struck, my first thoughts were not for the suffering of others. Except my parents. Well, except my father.

How was Suresh? How were these people around me? These people *like me?*

In the therapeutic context, such a question would be no problem. I am a psychologist. Put me across from a client and I will ask, intuit, tease or ferret out everything either of us needs to know. Surrounded by the crowds at the trial, though, I didn't know where to start. Every two hours, after each break in the trial (lawyers need their Starbucks), I would have someone new next to me, such as the heavy woman in a *salwar kameez* whose homey aroma of frying dough couldn't quite cover an inky, pooling despair. She leaned on a young man with a serious brow and neatly trimmed beard, who supported her on one arm while taking notes with his other. Two hours later, it was a tiny, twiggy-smelling couple in outdated business suits who sat without touching until, hearing some detail I didn't catch, they took each other's hands without meeting each other's eyes. Across the room, I saw a famous dancer whose husband and daughters had been killed. She had become active in the victims' advocacy group, and I had seen her name and photo in news reports. She had remarried, a gentleman whose wife and children had been on that same plane.

This was why I had come, I realized, to find out how these people had coped up. Not only *how* as in *how well*, but rather *by what means* did they go on?

There were so many of them there, but not a single one I could sit down with and ask. I should have contacted Suresh, I thought, then. Was he still in Montreal? Was he still alive? Who had he become in the years since losing his family—since losing my family?

Last spring, I had booked a month in Vancouver, but after only a few days attending the trial, I could take no more. What to do with the three-plus weeks left to me? Try to answer my questions, perhaps. So instead of returning to India early, I retreated to my comfort zones: the university, the library.

Surely others had written about this, I was thinking. Over the years, in psychology journals, I had come across so many studies on victims of mass trauma. Longitudinal, informational, survey- or interview- or standardized-test-based. Beirut, Belfast, Kigali. I had never seen one on the Air India disaster, but then, I'd never properly searched.

After the World Trade Tower attacks, nearly half of all Americans showed PTSD symptoms. How did the researchers think to test for that? They must have observed the symptoms in others; they might have felt them themselves. Had Canadians suffered similarly, following the bombing? The US has about ten times Canada's population. Three thousand plus people were killed in the September 11 attacks, three hundred plus in the Air India disaster. Do the math. It should add up, but it doesn't.

Canadians at large did not feel themselves to have been attacked, although nearly every passenger aboard that flight was a born or naturalized Canadian. Canada's prime minister infamously sent a telegram of condolences to the Indian government, who had lost what? A jet. Oh, and a couple of pilots. No wonder Canada failed to prevent the bombing in the first place. No wonder they had failed, for eighteen years, to bring it to trial.

And, I learned now, failed to take the bombing up in scholarship. I found no articles that addressed my questions. I looked, though it seemed even more improbable, for books. I found the same three I had read over fifteen years ago, one sensational, one implausible, and one by Bharati Mukherjee and Clark Blaise.

Mukherjee: tough broad. I've never met her but I'd like her, even if we would almost certainly fight. I loved her novels back when I lived in Canada: she was one of the very first to write about the no-man's land—or, more often, no-woman's land—of the transplant. I might have felt nothing in common with her protagonists had I met them in life, but I identified with them as I never had with fictional characters before.

Her book on the bombing was called *The Sorrow and the Terror*. (That title, in huge block letters and lurid flame-tones: really?) I sat with it in the reading room of the Vancouver public library. Much of it was good, far better than I had given it credit for the first time around, back when my pain was most acute.

Like all of us, Mukherjee and Blaise were appalled by the Canadian government's refusal for six months to acknowledge that the jet had been destroyed by a bomb, even given that another Air India jet, also originally departing from Vancouver, had blown up an hour earlier in Tokyo. Officials didn't want to admit their negligence. An FBI plant had met radical Sikhs who wanted to blow shit up in India, poison the water supply, disrupt the economy, kill thousands. The newly formed Canadian Security and Intelligence Service had tailed a motley crew of brown radicals who kept muttering to one another in secret code in Punjabi, a language none of CSIS's west coast agents spoke, despite five generations of Sikh settlement here. Phones were bugged, conversations were taped and sent back to Ottawa for transcription, all routine, no sense of urgency. After transcription, translation. After translation, decoding. ("Ready to write the book?" asked a pay phone caller. " Yes, let's write the book," responded the man who had picked up in some suburban home.) After decoding, perhaps alarm. (Wait a sec, is this—? *What* are they—?) But then, of course, it was too late.

And right after the tapes were transcribed, they were erased, per routine, leaving no original evidence to present at a future trial.

All that is laid out in the first part of Mukherjee–Blaise's book, a very serviceable catalogue of failures. Part two "honours" the victims, telling their stories in their voices, but framing and bending them so that this stream converges with the first to become a single roaring river of accusation: that the Canadian government failed to see this as a Canadian problem and a Canadian tragedy, even though it was a plot hatched by Canadians in Canada that resulted in hundreds of Canadian deaths.

"But it is never so simple!" I said, slapping the book's face, even though they were right. It was their methods and their tone that I disagreed with—but more on that in time.

Whatever I thought of the analysis, the interviews were a generation old. Had no one tried to learn what had happened to these people since? I hunted again for articles. I enlisted librarians to double-check my search terms. They were as puzzled as I—*What a good question*, they said. *I can't believe no one has asked it before.* "Sorry, sir. Looks like you're going to have to do a study," one gentleman in wire-rimmed glasses told me, glancing away from his screen to flash me a grin, then freezing when he saw my frozen face.

I had been in a thick, paralyzing fog, less and less able to work—I still believed in my work, but had lost faith in my ability to do it. I overcame this tower of self-doubt, this mountain of lassitude, to come to Canada, to witness the start of the trial. This decision, this trip, was the single meaningful thing I'd done in a year, which is not to say I had known what it meant. I had been suspicious, because it couldn't be the trial I was coming for. Rather, the trial led me to this: the subject of my next book. I should have known, as they say.

Fifteen months later, the trial was still dragging on, and I was returning to Canada to begin work on that book. I had avoided Air India on my last trip, but this time, I made myself fly Delhi–Heathrow–Montreal, reversing the route of all those dear departed and retracing my own of so many years ago.

At Indira Gandhi International's security gate, I slipped my bare feet back into my sandals and tried to see the X-ray of my single carry-on through a security guard's eyes.

[The following section refers to the anti-Sikh violence that erupted in Delhi following Indira Gandhi's assassination. Ashwin recalls here the ways that seeing those riots first-hand changed his father.]

I thought of my father, of how he was galvanized by the Delhi pogroms. He had been in his late sixties at the time, retired, contented. A good career, a life well lived, service to his country, his country as a cause. He had always voted for Congress. These were his beliefs.

The Delhi pogroms of 1984 gave this life the lie. So he changed his life. He joined peace organizations; he helped Sikh widows fill out forms as they sought reparations; he volunteered in slum schools. If he had not seen what he had, on our street, and others, perhaps he would have blamed the murders of our loved ones on "the Sikhs." Losing Kritika and the children slowed him down, it's true. But then he plunged in once more.

I have mentioned in this account only two books about the pogroms and their aftermath, including my own. *Who Are the Guilty?* And *Who Are the Victims?* There are practically no others—why?

Some ten years after the violence, Amitav Ghosh, a novelist of extraordinary scope, wrote a piece for an American magazine, asking the same question. He had been living in Delhi at the time. His neighbourhood was attacked, though he didn't witness the burnings. He, too, was reluctant to march, though he did, in the same protests as I. "Writers don't join crowds," he writes. "But what do you do when the constitutional authority fails to act? You join and in joining bear all the responsibilities and obligations and guilt that joining represents." And yet, he says, "Until now I have never really written about what I saw in November of 1984. Nobody, so far as I know, has written about it except in passing." Why silent for so long? "As a writer," he says, "I had only one obvious subject, the violence. From the news report, or the latest film or novel, we have come to expect the bloody detail or the elegantly staged conflagration that closes a chapter or effects a climax." He is a writer mostly of fiction; I suppose those temptations are particularly present for them.

Ghosh's article has three climaxes: a busload of people protecting a Sikh fellow commuter; a Hindu serving her Sikh neighbour tea in the muffled hush of her parlour while the mob sieges their street; and a moment I must have seen but which is effaced from my own memory: a group of thugs approached us, "brandishing knives and steel rods…A kind of rapture descended on us, exhilaration in anticipation of a climax…all the women in our group stepped out and surrounded the men; their saris and *kameezes* became a thin, fluttering barrier, a wall around us. They turned to face the approaching men, challenging them, daring them to attack. The thugs took a few more steps toward us and then faltered, confused. A moment later, they were gone."

Part of the reason he didn't write about the bloodshed is that he was spared the trauma of witnessing it. "What I saw at first hand," he said, "was not the horror of violence but the affirmation of humanity…the risks that perfectly ordinary people are willing to take for one another."

His representation is honest and necessary. Still, it doesn't fully unlock my understanding of that time. The key, for me, was more ephemeral, less dramatic than either the violence or the resistance. Something in the middle, something about surviving and shifting. About seeing. The critical moment, the thing I remember and want to record, was my father's transformation: one citizen awakened to his own blindness, his own complicity; my father's hands held to his eyes in pain as the scales fell.

Those who alter the course of history by being party either to violence or resistance are, in my experience, a minority. History happens *to* most people, not because of them. As for me, Ashwin Thrice-Struck. Or perhaps, more accurately, Thrice-Missed.

[Ashwin has now been in Canada, conducting his study, for more than six months. He has become embroiled in the lives of one family, the Sethurathnams, who are connected to the bombing via a family friend, Venkat, whose wife and son were on the plane. Just before the next section, Ashwin learns that Venkat's response to his bereavement has been to become a supporter of Hindu chauvinists in India. Ashwin reveals to the reader why he calls himself Ashwin Thrice-Struck: he not only was witness to the 1984 anti-Sikh violence, not only lost loved ones in the 1985 Air India bombing, but also was in Ahmedabad in 2002 for grisly anti-Muslim riots rumoured to have been sponsored by groups of the sort Venkat is supporting.]

At the time, I was ashamed of not participating in any of the public acts of resistance, yet I continued to refuse. This was the third strike, and I had been spared. What for?

Mostly, in those days, I was musing on how limited the catalogue is of horrors people have perpetrated on one another through history. Unless they were Nazis. They, it has to be admitted, took the possibilities of ethnic warfare to a new level—managing nearly to eliminate the role of emotion from their methods. Most organizers of similar projects have not had the Nazis' resources and imagination. Fear and greed flow close to the surface and are easily tapped, but an oily slick of ignorance has greased the machines from Turkey to Nazi Germany to Bosnia to Rwanda to here.

The BJP: the Hindu nationalists' political party. The VHP: their cultural wing. The RSS: their paramilitary volunteers. Whoever you consider to be behind the Godhra attacks, did not have the Nazis' ingenuity, and they had the task of convincing an astonishingly diverse people of their essential homogeneity. But they did take the Nazis' lessons to heart. Sparky youth camps full of chanting and games; a plan of national assimilation and standards by which to judge it. They controlled education, so that school history books told a story of a past India remarkably similar to the India they wanted to create: valorous, prosperous, unitary, Hindu.

This was their plan: a consummately modern ideal of a nation-state unified by an apocryphal identity resurrected for people who didn't know the difference. A key tenet: elimination of the Muslims. The Hindu nationalists were more generous in this than others have been. The Muslims didn't have to be killed. They could convert. They could leave. But those willing to do neither had to be exterminated, which task now devolved to the mob. *Pakistan or Kabristan!*

I needed badly to get back to my apartment. I turned the key, again, started the car, drove.

I had laid in whisky the night before, knowing I was going to Venkat's house today. I congratulated myself on my foresight, but now hesitated at the bottom of the fire escape, knowing the fire water waited above. It was barely noon, and I thought at first that was why I stopped, feeling the gods of decorum tugging at my sleeve.

No, it wasn't that. I stopped because I didn't want to deaden my self-analysis, the way I had for nearly twenty years.

Why dredge all this up?

I needed to understand it. Understand what?

This: what happened to me?

This: could it have been stopped?

I didn't mount my iron stairs. I turned away, up my alley, and began to walk.

Alone. Always alone. I needed a guide, a hand-holder, a Krishna to my Arjuna. Who?

I wanted my Appa.

Think on what you know, Ashwin, I heard as I walked, his voice booming as though from behind the distant mountains, a voice Marlon Brando might have used to play a Bollywood don.

The breezes across Lohikarma's slopes were bracing. My cheeks chapped in the dry winter air.

Think back, my son. Appa's voice gained strength and intimacy in my mind. *Not about yourself.*

Ah.

I began, tentatively:

The Air India bombing was not simply the result of some limited if collective murderous rage. That rage was fed by a larger sense of outrage, resulting from the under-noticed, under-reported Delhi pogroms.

The pogroms? The doing of overzealous party functionaries, using the Dragon Lady's assassination as an excuse to wage an intimidation campaign against Sikhs.

The assassination? A reprisal for her having ordered the invasion of the Golden Temple in Amritsar.

Keep going. Amritsar?

I had circled my neighbourhood to land at the Chinese restaurant downtown. Thirty tables at least, no more than six occupied at any given time. Red carpet, stained near the door. A tank of carp I stood and watched until a bobbing-frowning waiter reminded me that I should seat myself.

Sikhdom's holiest shrine rises as a lily from a pool; the city is named for that water—*amrit*, the Sikhs' holy nectar, drunk by the devoted when they are baptized. The generals had been told not to destroy the temple. "We entered with humility in our hearts and prayers on our lips," said one, in the true spirit of Indian secularism, which means not that the state governs without God, but rather that every god governs at once.

The Dragon Lady upturned that bowl of amrit, drowned fleeing fighters and praying pilgrims, blew fiery breath ahead of the spreading nectar, drenched Sikhs around the world. They tasted ash in it; they tasted blood. They burned the Dragon Lady in effigy, and hung her, and stomped upon her. Prominent Sikhs in India returned their government awards, resigned their parliamentary seats, and so found themselves allied with a movement whose aims and leadership they had never admired.

The government's response was to pull out the Terrorism and Disruptive Activities Act—TADA! No need to steal your neighbour's apples; if you wanted his tree, all you needed to do was accuse him of being a Khalistani sympathizer. "Suddenly there was no crime in Punjab," said a former police officer, "only terror." Thus began the long summer that led up to the Dragon's slaying.

But again, said my father, as I twirled a noodle that seemed to have no beginning and no end, *think. There comes a time to act, but...*

Not for me?

Do not put words in my mouth. You eventually must act, but for now you must think.

To act is to do violence.

Bullshit, my son.

That was me putting words in his mouth—Appa never would have said that. The expression suited him, though, and it made me smile to hear him use it.

My father was growing impatient. *Think! What came before?*

The Emergency.

In 1975, a resolution was introduced by the government of Punjab—a state poor in cash but rich in resources—suggesting a devolution of power into the hands of the states. The young PM, Indira Gandhi, did not take kindly to it. And she was having other problems: on trial for election hanky-panky. She took care of all of it by declaring a national State of Emergency.

I was in Canada, then. My father wrote me letters throughout, so that the Emergency happened, for me, in the measured, regretful voice of his reportage. At that time, he thought the prime minister did what had to be done, no more, no less.

I don't think that anymore, he interjected gruffly.

I always thought you were fooling yourself.

So you say.

Mass demonstrations followed. The first? In Amritsar. Yes, the Sikhs of Punjab were the first to raise the cry, and after twenty-one months, as protests were squashed and silence spread, the Sikhs were the last men standing, even if behind bars: 33 per cent of the Emergency's nearly 150,000 detainees were said to have been Sikhs, who make up 2 per cent of the Indian population.

Given this, how could some of them not start to imagine a Sikh nation?

They had taken on several strange bedfellows (are bedfellows always strange?): Hindu nationalists, who, since they oppose Congress, are natural allies for any other opposition. Thus they opposed the storming of the Golden Temple. Thus they in fact helped Sikhs during the post-assassination riots of 1984.

But they also, later, encouraged destruction of mosques and churches, professed expulsion or forced conversion. And, earlier, they encouraged the killing of that much more famous Gandhi—no dragon, no lady—in the service of this abhorrent idea: India for Hindus.

I left the restaurant, slipping and sliding over icy patches in my inappropriate shoes until finally I scrambled up my fire escape.

I put the kettle on for tea, looking guiltily at my bottle of whisky, as we do in the presence of our parents.

Ah, what the hell, he said, *I'll join you.*

I smiled and poured two shots. We toasted. I drank.

So, carry on.

The Mahatma's assassination. I was eight. The man who had killed him thought that Gandhiji and Nehru were Muslim-lovers, that this (and not the longstanding British policy of divide and rule...) had led to the creation of Pakistan, a Muslim state lopped off India's northwest and northeast corners, like ears on that sacred cow's face. West Pakistan was cut from the Sikhs' holy land, Punjab, with a double-edged sword. The Sikhs were balanced on the blade. Forced, they jumped toward India, a self-proclaimed secular democracy, where their rights would exist on paper, at least.

Sikhs had served in the British army through multiple generations, multiple wars, but this had become tougher as they came to realize that was all the white man wanted them for. Second-generation Sikh Canadians, receiving Second World War conscription notices from Ottawa, asked why they got soldiers' uniforms but not the vote. First-class fighters; second-class citizens. Sure, we'll battle the Krauts and Japs; let's see you open the doors to your white-collar world.

In 1919, they had endured another Amritsar massacre, when General Dyer's troops opened fire on peaceable, picnicking Punjabis, part and parcel of the period's paranoia. After the First World War, Canada, Australia and New Zealand gained greater sovereignty, the Empire's thanks for so many donated lives. India? Not. There, His Majesty's forces put themselves to much trouble quelling a nascent independence movement. They were just wiping their brows, having publicly executed nearly a hundred such violent dreamers, supporters of the Ghadars. This was a party started by North American Sikhs, which envisioned a United States of India for all Indians, a free, secular, democratic nation—plainly a ridiculous notion, of which the inferior races needed to be disabused.

We, Indians, have never given them sufficient credit for that.

As one Canadian parliamentarian put it, with quaintly rough-hewn grammar: " The Hindoos never did one solitary thing for humanity in the past two thousand years and will probably not in the next two thousand."

Canada had always courted European immigrants while barring the Brown Peril, exercising Canada's right to Keep Canada White. In 1914, under newly written (and, because of successful legal challenges, repeatedly rewritten) immigration laws, Canada famously turned a shipload of Indians back at Vancouver harbour. "Hindoo Invasion Repelled!" the headlines hollered, floating on strains of " White Canada Forever!" an anthem sung by mobs ten thousand strong.

When the emigrés returned to India, they were fired on by the Brits, who feared that this rejection—demonstrating that all British subjects were hardly equal within and throughout the Empire—might have converted some of them to the Ghadars' cause.

Which it did.

Each humiliation grew the Sikhs' pride. Each galvanized a small subset into quests for purity and self-rule. Each formed a rough link on history's rattling chains.

Once upon a time—

No, be specific.

Punjab, the Land of Five Rivers, at the dawn of the sixteenth century.

Better.

There was a Hindu who was bothered by empty ritual and hierarchy. His name was Nanak. He founded a cult devoted to humility, service, and meditation on the word of God. Its adherents were called Sikhs, which means, I think, only "disciple." His fame spread; his following grew.

On his deathbed, Guru Nanak appointed a successor from among his disciples, who begat another guru in the same manner, until this lineage culminated in the *Guru Granth*: a book composed of centuries of wisdom from the Sikh Gurus and from others: devotees, mystics and saints professing Hinduism, Islam, and shades of belief in between. The final guru: a perfect admixture, a true immortal, a book.

Was there persecution, over these years? There was. Martyrs were made. Sikhs believe in valour. But I recall a young Sikh telling me the story of the ninth guru, who was killed while defending Hindus. "Sikhs are in the world not for Sikhs alone, but for anybody who needs a Sikh," he said, eyes shining.

And yet.

By the time I came back to India, Sikhs were no longer seen as defenders of any interests but their own. "It used to be that if we were riding on a train and saw a Sikh in our carriage, we would feel safer," my mother told me, in the midst of the riots. "Nowadays if we see one, we feel scared."

When I repeated to a Sikh colleague what my mother had said, he grew heartsick. " They are tarring us all with the same brush," he said. "Khalistan, land of the pure!" Disgusted, he had become tempted to shave his beard and yank off his turban. Others had been convinced, by repeated acts of oppression and discrimination in India, England, Canada, the USA, that self-determination was the only way, but most of them still would not follow the self-appointed guardians of orthodoxy, so the purists were attacking them. The terrorist's dilemma: acting on behalf of constituencies who cannot be convinced except by their own deaths. Purity: the old lie.

When I think on the Air India disaster, I hear the chain of history rattle. Its links are loops. Loops have holes. Was the bombing a Canadian or an Indian tragedy? Why pose this false division? Canada was colonized when India was, and their fates were ever linked. There is no expiation. The declaration of any single truth is itself an act of violence.

Once upon a time—here, I cannot be specific—Hinduism arose, perhaps on the soil south of the Indus; perhaps brought by Northern invaders. Without Hinduism, there would not have been Sikhism. Without India, could there be Empire? Without Empire, could there be radicalizing? Without Canada, could there have been a bomb?

Once upon a time: poetry, syncretism, mysticism, death.

Once upon a time: evolution, matter, being.

Once upon a time: time.

Source

Remembering across Place and Time

The Komagata Maru *and Air India*

RITA KAUR DHAMOON

IN THIS VOLUME, Amber Dean, Uma Parameswaran, and Padma Viswanathan poignantly and provocatively raise some key themes about how Air India is remembered. First, they weave together memory and place. Parameswaran's poem stands at the shores of Ireland, the Ganges, the Assiniboine in Canada, and Vancouver to remember the deaths in the oceans and "all who live from sea to sea."[1] For Parameswaran, the connections between these places lie in the experiences of South Asians affected by the Air India bombings, the funeral pyres of the murdered, and the *Komagata Maru* passengers who were detained and refused entry into Canada over a hundred years ago. For Viswanathan, the injustices of the Air India bombings, the failed investigation, the sham trial, and the delayed memorials connect Vancouver, where the bombers lived and one of the memorials is erected, Ireland, as the site of the explosion, Tokyo, where another bomb went off an hour earlier, and colonial India and Canada. Dean draws on the writings of Parameswaran and Viswanathan and weaves these into thinking about Air India and the *Komagata Maru* "in relation," as sites of injustice that necessarily link together Vancouver, memorial sites across Canada, and Punjab.

Second, collectively the three authors journey through time, locating contemporary Sikh nationalism and anger to the shifts and disjunctures of history. They explicitly do not justify the actions of the Air India bombers but instead try to make sense of the bombing by considering flashpoints in history. In doing so, they illuminate, for example, connections between British colonialism of the past (including the Partition of India, which created deep divisions among Sikhs, Muslims, and Hindus), the 1984 state-sanctioned attacks on Sikhs in Amritsar and Delhi in India, and the contemporary ways in which Canadian governments have forgotten the Air India bombings or have tokenistically remembered them after being pushed by family and community members. Methodologically, then, this section of the book points toward the necessity of genealogy as a way to historicize and contextualize what is remembered across history.

Third, in making these connections across place and time, Amber Dean, Uma Parameswaran, and Padma Viswanathan punctuate a third theme of remembering Air India: how competing nationalisms demarcate memory and nationalizing practices of memorialization. Rather than framing memory in terms of a nationalist or conversely anti-nationalist stance, they provoke a series of questions about the relationship between nation and memory: Did abuses of power by British colonial and then Hindu nationalist governments in India prompt versions of Sikh minority nationalism that led to the Air India bombings? Does this matter to how the bombers are remembered, and why? After the bombings, why did the Canadian prime minister send his condolences to the Indian nation even though most of the passengers were Canadian? How does the Canadian nation make and remake myths of multiculturalism and tolerance by remembering racism against the passengers of the *Komagata Maru* as past events, even as Sri Lankan Tamil migrants are detained and denied rights in contemporary Canada? How do memorials for the Air India and *Komagata Maru* events become used by the Canadian nation as tools to mask over ongoing settler colonialism that dispossesses Indigenous peoples? As Dean shows, there is a difference between remembering in strategic ways that reinforce myths of Canadian multiculturalism and remembering as a "difficult return," in which past and present racisms and colonialisms are linked.

A fourth theme runs through these works: the role of art, writing, poetry, novels, and academic theorizing as sites of resistance and collective voice against injustice. The emptiness that exists in the "caves of memory" (a phrase used by Parameswaran) can be named, spoken, and navigated through art, in this case the art of writing. This is the powerful message of these three pieces—the capacity to speak up, speak against, and speak for those who are remembered after murder and injustice, and those who are living and carrying those memories.

Finally, these pieces invoke the reader to remember their own connections to Air India and to the *Komagata Maru* by foregrounding the politics of emotions, weaving in and out of love, anger, and grief—for and against the self, Others, and the nation. These can be distant memories, with people we never meet but who nonetheless shape our diaspora journeys. As I read these ways of remembering Air India, I, too, remembered, for the pieces pulled me in and suspended the pain of violent memories. I remember the assassination of an uncle in England in the 1980s, a practicing Sikh and critic of Indira Gandhi's Hindu nationalist government; memories of my first years in Canada, with signs that said "No dogs, No Indians allowed" and learning that these Indians were Indigenous peoples, people who are regularly forgotten and denied on these stolen lands of Canada; memories of the Twin Towers falling on September 11, 2001, and the making of Muslims and Arabs as terrorists, brown bodies like those on the *Komagata Maru* and Air India Flight 182, who are spectres of colonialism in the past and the present. Some of these memories are of people we never know but who nonetheless flow through our skin, our anger, and our hearts.

Memory and remembering are rooted in networks of places, time, nations, genres, and emotions, and, in the case of these three contributions, care for the Other. It is with this care for the Other that Amber Dean, Uma Parameswaran, and Padma Viswanathan remember Air India.

Note

1. See Parameswaran's "On the Shores of the Irish Sea," reprinted in this volume.

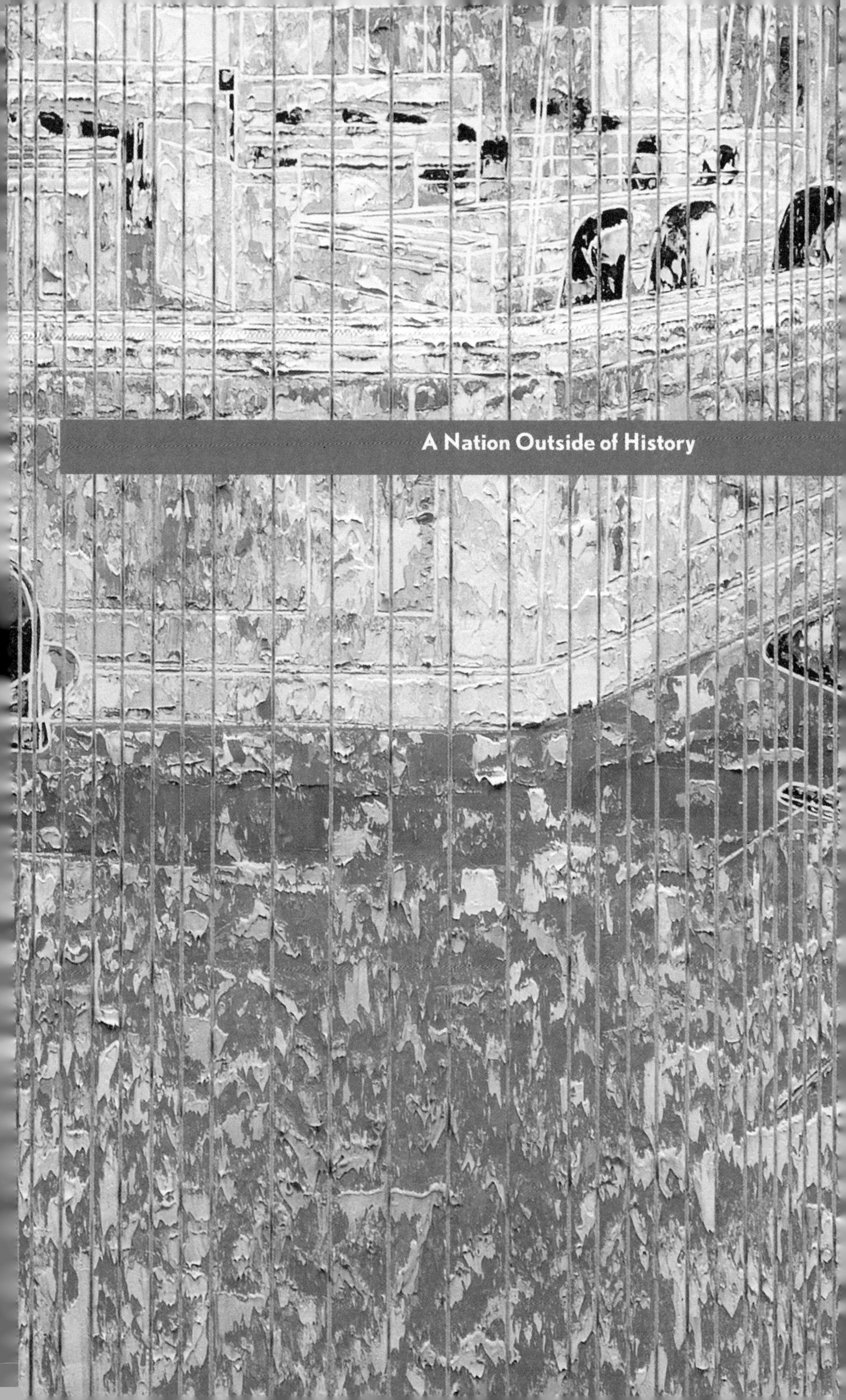

A Nation Outside of History

Overleaf: Deon Venter, Courtroom #3 *(detail) from the* Flight 182 *series, 2008. Oil on linen. 39" x 73". Copyright © Deon Venter, reprinted by permission of the artist. Photo by David Borrowman.*

From Foreign to Canadian

Air India and the Ongoing Denial of Racism

MAYA SESHIA

There were no Canadian people to wipe my tears.

—DONNA RAMAH PAUL, quoted in Government of Canada, *The Families Remember*, 2007, p. 115; Paul's brother Vinubhai Bhatt, her sister-in-law Chandrabala Paul, and her two nieces Bina and Tina Bhatt perished on Air India Flight 182

Let it be said clearly: the bombing of the Air India flight was the result of a conspiracy conceived, planned, and executed in Canada. Most of its victims were Canadian. This is a Canadian catastrophe, whose dimensions and meaning must be understood by all Canadians.

—BOB RAE, *Lessons to Be Learned*, 2005, p. 2

I would ask the Honourable Member to be very careful not to imply, even by innuendo, or leave open the interpretation that there is some sort of racist connotation in the entire issue.

—HOUSE OF COMMONS SPEAKER, quoted in Parliament of Canada, House of Commons, *Official Report—Second Session—Thirty-Third Parliament*, Volume X, 1987–1988, p. 11807

AIR INDIA FLIGHT 182 exploded over the North Atlantic on June 23, 1985, killing all 329 passengers and crew aboard the flight.[1] An hour before this incident, a bomb went off at Tokyo's Narita International Airport, killing two baggage handlers—Hideo Asano and Hideharu Koda—and injuring four others.[2] These bombings were a catastrophe connected to Canada: 280 of the 329 passengers and crew aboard Air India Flight 182 were Canadian citizens; the two bombs originated from the Vancouver International Airport; and a number of the suspects were Canadian citizens.[3] The catastrophe occurred at the height of national discourses about increased inclusivity and anti-discriminatory measures in Canada. The adoption of multiculturalism as an official state policy in 1971, and the enactment of the Immigration Act, 1976–1977, whose alleged purpose was to remove racial, ethnic, national, religious, and gender discrimination, were celebrated as making Canadian policies, institutions, and practices more accepting and fair toward non-white immigrants and non-white Canadian citizens.[4] Yet reactions to Air India tell another story about the state of national inclusivity and the existence of racism within Canadian government institutions and culture. In the immediate aftermath of the 1985 bombings, Canada's then prime minister, Brian Mulroney, responded by sending condolences to the Government of India.[5] A common theme found in *The Families Remember: Commission of Inquiry into the Investigation of the Bombing of Air India Flight 182, Phase I Report* (hereinafter referred to as the *Phase 1 Report*) was that families of the victims reported "that they felt that they were not viewed as 'real Canadians' and that this was somehow not considered to be a Canadian tragedy" involving Canadian citizens.[6]

Falling outside the whiteness that continued to shape dominant conceptions of Canadian-ness, Air India was not grieved as a national tragedy involving Canadian citizens. Victims, victims' families, and suspects did not fit popular ideas about what a Canadian looked like and who belonged to Canada's national community. The violence believed to motivate the attacks clashed with white settler colonial mythologies of the Canadian nation, mythologies that erase colonial racial violence out of national narratives and, instead, exalt Canada as a peaceful, innocent nation.[7] The incongruence between Air India—a catastrophe that was connected to Canada but occurred outside Canadian borders and involved primarily non-white citizens and an Indian airline—and white imaginings of Canadian citizenship and nation resulted in the distancing and abandonment of victims, victims' families, and the bombings themselves. Despite being the worst act of contemporary terrorism against the travelling public in Canada's history and, until 9/11, the worst act of terrorism against the travelling public globally,[8] it took more than twenty-one years of government debate and organizing by victims' families to establish the Commission of Inquiry into the Investigation of the Bombing of Air India Flight 182 (hereinafter referred to as the Air India inquiry).

In light of the above observation, this essay examines the Canadian government's perception and treatment of Air India over time. Specifically, I am concerned with tracking shifts and continuities in articulations of racism, Canadian citizenship, and conceptions of the Canadian nation within government discourse and action. I offer an in-depth analysis of House of Commons debates and attend to victims' families' testimonies about their interactions with, and overall treatment by, the Canadian government. In order to track change—and continuity—the following two time periods are examined: 1985 through to 1990; and 1999 through to 2009. By temporarily tracking parliamentary discourses and the government's treatment of the Air India tragedy, we can examine whether narratives of Air India and, more specifically, articulations of racism, citizenship, and nation have shifted or stayed the same over time. Through this analysis, we can gain a better understanding about what factors contribute to this change and continuity.

Drawing on the 2007 *Phase 1 Report*, the 2005 *Lessons to Be Learned* report by the Honourable Bob Rae (hereinafter referred to as the *Rae Report*), and House of Commons debates, I argue that government discourses initially constructed the 1985 bombings as a non-Canadian tragedy involving non-Canadian citizens; hence victims, victims' families, suspects, and the bombings themselves were discursively distanced from the Canadian nation. During this period, victims' families were situated in a state of "national non-existence" within the Canadian context. Citing their Indian ancestry, and alluding to racist conceptions of who is a Canadian, they described being abandoned by the Canadian government, and feeling invisible to government officials. In consequence, victims' families were treated as non-Canadians by the government. They were offered little support in the years following the bombings, and their suffering, plight, and very humanity were largely ignored. However, the events of 9/11 and persistent counternarratives have helped create a climate in which particular concerns expressed by victims' families have been heard by the Canadian government. Calls for enhanced security measures have resonated with government policy, but victims' families' allegations that racism played a role in the government's pre- and post-bombing actions have consistently been denied. In recent years, the Air India case has been reframed as an act of terror that directly affected Canada, and the victims and surviving families have been embraced as "Canadians." This redefinition is partially related to attempts to bolster support for anti-terrorism initiatives.[9] While unquestionably significant, this shift not only enhances security measures that predominantly—and often unjustly—target racialized subjects but also is premised on a colour-blind approach that ultimately obscures the central role systemic racism has played throughout the history of the Air India case.

It is intriguing to consider Canada's reaction to 9/11 to the nation's response to June 23, 1985. Many Canadians identified strongly with the events of 9/11, reacting with deep sorrow and anger to the bombings of the World Trade Center and the Pentagon. In the days after September 11, 2001, then Prime Minister Jean Chrétien declared a national day of mourning. Most Canadians expressed solidarity with the American nation, and engaged in acts of American patriotism to express their grief and demonstrate their support. The attacks were interpreted as an assault not only on the United States but also on Canada and, more specifically, on Western values of freedom, equality, and democracy.[10] In the aftermath, Canada's national and foreign policies were altered. National security increased and a number of anti-terrorism laws were enacted with little debate.[11] More recent terrorist attacks in Paris and Brussels have been met with similar acts of solidarity and identification. While Air India occurred in a different time period and international context, the lack of support and solidarity toward Air India victims is startling. Canadians were doubtlessly horrified by the Air India bombing but did not embrace the bombings as a national catastrophe involving Canadian citizens. Audrey Macklin points out that Canadian media, government officials, and the public did not initially denounce the 1985 attacks "as a fundamental assault on our nation, our values, our people" and, furthermore, "no foreign leader declared 'we are all Canadians.'"[12] Juxtaposing September 11 to Air India, journalists John Geddes and Ken MacQueen observe that while the Air India bombings are now described as Canada's 9/11, that description misrepresents the response in 1985.[13] Despite the magnitude of the event, its consequences for the victims and their families, and its connection to the Canadian nation, Air India was rendered an invisible "tragedy" in the popular imagination, rather than a national catastrophe and an act of terrorism.[14] The connection between racism and lack of national mourning over Air India victims raises critical questions about the extent of racism within the Canadian state, culture, and institutions. Although Canada is often perceived as an inclusive multicultural mosaic, the story of Air India suggests a different reality.

The theoretical premise of this essay is that the Canadian state is a racial state whose very foundations and prevailing composition are premised on colonial racial violence. Within this context, the politics of life and death—whose lives and deaths matter—is often shaped by race and racism.[15] As the history of slavery, genocidal violence against Indigenous peoples, and racist nation-building projects (such as the building of the Canadian Pacific Railway) demonstrate, racialized conceptions of life, death, and who ultimately was considered human were crucial to the development of modern nation-states such as Canada. The racialized valuing of life and death is also present today. Racism very often governs the politics of life and death in the modern world. It commonly influences whose lives are capriciously sacrificed, whose lives are or are not protected, and whose deaths are or are not considered worthy of national and international mourning.[16] As a result, racialized citizens have been marked as outsiders, non-Canadians, foreigners, and/or "quintessential latecomers,"[17] whose natural geographic home territories are assumed to align with their perceived race.[18] The designation of racialized Canadians as foreigners has consequences. Such positioning obscures "knowledge about the older histories of their communities in the country,"[19] and it naturalizes citizen subjects marked as white as "indigenous" to Canada, thereby erasing Canada's past and present colonial reality, as well as heterogeneous settler experiences.[20] Within this context—a context whereby Canadian citizenship, national belonging, and national value are equated to whiteness—the legal citizenship status of Air India victims, victims' families, and suspects was initially rendered obsolete. The racism involved in conceptions of Canadian citizenship and belonging to the nation is apparent when we examine the Canadian government's treatment of Air India victims' families and parliamentary discourses in the years immediately following the bombings.

From the period of June 24, 1985, through to June 24, 1990, the bombings were widely perceived as a foreign "tragedy," involving "foreign" victims and "foreign" suspects. Hence, the bombing of Flight 182 was distanced from Canada and the Canadian public, and victims and their families were discursively positioned as "internal foreigners"—subjects who, despite possessing formal citizenship status and residing within Canadian borders, are marked as non-Canadian outsiders.[21] Despite changes to Canada's immigration system and the introduction of official multiculturalism, reactions to Air India demonstrate that the equation of Canadian citizenship and imaginings of who substantially belonged to Canada remain firmly rooted in whiteness. Victims did not fit popular imaginings of who is a Canadian citizen. The coming together of race and nation, and specifically the equation of whiteness to Canada and Canadians, continued to impact ideas about who was a Canadian and what events were considered nationally significant. Race overwhelmed victims' Canadian citizenship status, and the equation of Air India to Indian politics and territory overshadowed Canada's connection to the bombings. In consequence, the Canadian government abandoned victims' families. Irish and Indian government officials offered support, and residents of Cork, Ireland, welcomed victims' families into their homes and shared their grief and mourning. In contrast, the Canadian government disassociated itself from the catastrophe and failed to reach out or demonstrate meaningful responsibility to victims' families during the immediate days, weeks, and years following the bombings. An analysis of Canadian government action and discourses during the 1985–1990 period demonstrates that Air India was predominantly perceived as a foreign issue involving foreign victims and suspects by the Canadian government.

This perception is vividly illustrated by Brian Mulroney's reaction to the bombing. In the immediate aftermath, Mulroney "called Mr. Gandhi [then the prime minister of India] to extend condolences and offer help."[22] The results of this gesture were to distance Air India from Canada and to alienate Canadians affected by the bombings from their national government.[23] Krishna Bhat's remarks illustrate both the alienation and the frustration articulated by a number of other victims' families: "Perhaps he [Mulroney] never thought that it happened in our own backyard. Alas, what a twist of irony. Are we not Canadians?"[24] Yet Mulroney's phone call was not simply the result of an individual misunderstanding of the event. An analysis of parliamentary discussions from 1985 to 1990 suggests he "was simply acting in accordance with the government's perception that Indians and not Canadians had been the major victims of flight 182."[25] In other words, his gesture reflected widespread perceptions about who belonged and who did not belong to Canada, and what events were "Canadian." Racialized Canadians, particularly non-white subjects, are often conflated with their perceived immigrant, ethnic, and cultural statuses. "Difference" from the Canadian white norm results in the racist assumption that non-white Canadians are foreigners rather than Canadian citizens.[26] While seemingly innocent, such utterances differentiate between those who belong to the Canadian nation and those who do not.[27] In other words, the boundaries of the Canadian nation, and lines between insiders/outsiders, are drawn on the basis of race, as well as additional intersecting systems of oppression such as gender, sexuality, and class. These dynamic, yet always racialized, boundaries of who belongs and who does not belong to the Canadian nation work to "congeal the insider status of [white] members of the nation" and contribute to white imaginings of Canada, whereby whiteness is predominantly associated with the nation and its citizens.[28] From 1985 to 1990, government utterances about Air India underscored the victims' Indian origins and recent immigrant status (despite the fact that many were born and raised in Canada or had lived in Canada for decades, and some were not of Indian ancestry), and emphasized their Indian ethnic community ties rather than Canadian national belonging.[29] For instance, in 1985, Honourable Edward Broadbent (Oshawa) mistakenly implied that many of the victims were newly arrived immigrants: "Many of the victims are members of the Indo-Canadian community. Disaster has shattered their peaceful lives in *their new land* [emphasis added]."[30] Yet, beyond obscuring the racist colonial systems of power and oppression underpinning the Canadian state, the configuration of Air India victims as foreigners, as non-Canadian citizens, fundamentally impacts victims' families in a number of ways.

One of these consequences was the Government of Canada's abandonment of victims' families. Perceived as non-Canadians, the Government of Canada treated victims' families as such. A theme found through victims' families' narratives is the lack of support they received from the Canadian government. In the weeks following the bombings, victims' families testified that Canadian government officials did not offer condolences or support in the immediate aftermath. In fact, victims' families described receiving little to no guidance from the Canadian government as they struggled to navigate through the difficult process of flying to Ireland to identify their relatives. When relatives arrived in Cork to identify victims, it was overwhelmingly reported that Canadian government officials were "nowhere to be seen."[31] Kalwant Mamak, who lost his wife, asserts that when he arrived in Cork, "there were no Canadian officials," and he "was totally lost."[32] In the absence of guidance from Canadian government officials, victims' families relied on one another's support and direction. Murthy Subramanian, who lost his wife and daughter, noted that "there was no assistance provided to us at Heathrow by the Canadian government, no psychologists, no counsellors. We comforted each other."[33] Dr. Bal Gupta, whose wife died aboard Air India Flight 182, reported that "there was no emotional, psychological, physical or administrative help or grief counselling or guidance from any government agency."[34] Viewed as "non-Canadian" citizens, the Canadian government felt little responsibility to assist victims' families. Eric Beauchesne, who lost his father in the bombing, reports, "I don't think the Canadian government felt any responsibility for helping us in any way, shape or form."[35] Haranhalli Radhakrishna—who lost his wife, son, and daughter—observes that "in spite of the fact that this was the largest mass murder in the recent times of Canadian history, there was no victim services offered to us. We did not receive any type of counseling to cope with this immense tragedy in our lives."[36] Clearly, victims' families were highly critical of the Canadian government's treatment, and their vocal criticism in the weeks following the catastrophe marked the start of ongoing activism around the Canadian government's treatment of Air India. Such inaction, according to Rama Bhardwaj, who lost a relative in the attack, "was unthinkable cold treatment."[37] Summarizing testimonies from victims' families, Commissioner John Major writes, "If one theme dominated the family hearings, it was the expression of frustration and disappointment at what the families saw, and continue to see, as the absence of information, moral support, counselling, guidance and general concern from agencies of the Government of Canada."[38]

In their testimonies and submissions to the Air India inquiry, numerous family members linked their abandoned state and treatment by the Canadian government to their contradictory place within the Canadian nation, whereby they possessed legal citizenship but were not treated as substantial members by the Canadian government and public. Citing the discrepancy between their legal Canadian citizenship status and the Canadian government's abandonment of them, victims' families described being in a state of national invisibility and national "non-existence." According to victims' families, in the eyes of the Canadian government, their loss, suffering, and very humanity did not exist. When asked if the Canadian government ever contacted him to offer support or extend its condolences, Satrajpal (Fred) Rai, whose cousin perished aboard Air India Flight 182, responded, "No, never. Actually, I'm very, very upset and disgusted, to be honest with you. I thought at the least somebody would call, send a letter. It's almost like we never existed. I'm a Canadian citizen."[39] Victims' families recognized that the association of Air India to India, and the common equation of Canadian citizenship and belonging with whiteness, contributed to their abandonment and national nonexistence. Dr. Ramji Khandelwal lost his two daughters in the Air India bombing. He states, " We also started to think that nobody wants to do anything because we are Canadians of Indian origin. We thought at that time, and I think it may be true today too, that it is not taken as a Canadian problem and nobody cares about the lives of Canadians of Indian origin."[40] Renée Sarojini Saklikar, who lost her aunt and uncle, asserts, "My family has put its heart and soul into raising us to view the world as Canadians and yet when we look at the series of failures in relation to this tragedy I think we might ask, well, have we truly been accepted as Canadians?"[41] Vijay Kachru, who lost her mother in the Air India bombing, testified that "her younger brother renounced Canada, his Canadian citizenship and his Canadian passport."[42] Kachru went on to state, " The community as a whole has been broad-brushed with you're not worth it, move on, this happens, there are wars, just move on."[43]

In addition to casting victims and their families outside of the nation, governmental discourses during the 1985–1990 period depicted the suspects as non-Canadians and suggested that the bombings were primarily tied to conflicts within India. Thus, as Failler found in her 2012 analysis of the documentary *Air India 182*, suspects were discursively positioned as "dangerous internal foreigners"—citizens who, despite possessing legal citizenship status and residing within the nation, are nevertheless marked as threatening outsiders.[44] Despite immediate knowledge that the bomb that went off at Tokyo's Narita airport originated from Canada, for example, the possibility that the attack was planned and conceived in Canada by Canadian citizens was not, initially, considered. The Canadian nation was not only equated with whiteness but was also imagined as peaceful, nonviolent, and innocent. This colonial mythologizing, coupled with the racialized assumption that the Flight 182 victims were Indian, contributed to the misperception that Canada could not be implicated or connected to the catastrophe. Rather than considering Canada's connection to the bombings, governmental speculation attributed the violence to "international terrorism"; this event and the individuals directly affected by it were thus distanced from Canada.[45] In early November 1985, it was revealed that the suspects were, in fact, Canadian citizens; nevertheless, the bombings continued to be blamed on foreigners who had brought their "foreign" conflict to Canada, thereby upsetting the peaceful fabric of the nation. In 1988, Liberal Member of Parliament Sergio Marchi (York West) asserted, "this issue of an independent homeland is clearly a foreign issue which is sovereign only to the citizens of India who in the end, in their own time, in their own way, must come to grips with that."[46] As Amber Dean notes in her essay in this volume, such utterances conceal the long history of imperial racial politics underpinning Canada's connection to Air India, and this concealment is necessary for framing the bombings as having little, if anything, to do with Canada.

Victims' families and a handful of journalists and politicians have criticized the dominant construction of Air India as foreign. Commenting on the discursive construction of the bombings as a "foreign" problem involving "foreign" people, Clark Blaise and Bharati Mukherjee write,

> *The initial reaction of too many Canadians, especially of government officials, was that the Air India disaster was an Indian post-colonial tragedy in which newly independent peoples try to redraw provincial boundaries. It was a tragedy affecting only Hindus and Sikhs...A foreign carrier had crashed off foreign seas. Canada, as a nation, though hugely sympathetic to human distress, seemed to distance itself from the guilt by viewing this incident as "their" rather than "our" tragedy.*[47]

Similarly, remarking on the dominant national imagining of Air India, the former British Columbia premier and Liberal Member of Parliament Ujjal Dosanjh states, "Canadians, and particularly Canadian politicians and public leaders, felt these were brown guys fighting over something happening 15,000 miles away."[48] Beauchesne also cogently notes that June 23, 1985, is Canada's "invisible tragedy" because the Canadian government treated the bombings "as something remote, something that happened far away on a non-Canadian airline, unrelated to Canada."[49] Commissioner Major writes, "The Government's position was that no finding could be made that Canadian security measures were inadequate. Underlying the position was an apprehension that a finding that Canada was blameworthy would bring about unavoidable political and financial costs, including the obligation to compensate the families, something the Government was fiercely determined to avoid."[50] In short, between 1985 and 1990, the framing of Air India as an act of international terrorism helped to dissociate this event and those involved in it from Canada. The idea that this act was conceived on Canadian soil and committed by Canadian citizens against Canadian citizens was difficult for the Government of Canada and the majority of the Canadian public to fathom. The racialized marking of Air India coupled with perceptions—rooted in white innocence—that Canada is a peaceful, nonviolent, and innocent nation made it difficult for many to fathom Air India's connection to Canada. As a result, a particular reconstruction of Air India emerged. This dominant narrative of the catastrophe disassociated Air India from Canada and ignored the role racism played in pre- and post-bombing responses. In the minds of most Canadians, not only was Canada a peaceful nation free from violent acts and atrocities but Canadian citizenship was predominantly equated with whiteness. As such, the idea that Air India might be significantly tied to Canada was antithetical to popular imaginings of Canada—imaginings that obscure Canada's racist colonial foundations and contemporary structures—and the disaster was, therefore, largely dismissed as a foreign event.[51]

Beyond distancing the bombings and those directly affected by them from the Canadian nation, the discursive construction of this event as a foreign issue gave rise to anti-immigrant sentiments. In 1987, Member of Parliament Ian Waddell (Vancouver–Kingsway) stated,

> *There is also concern, and one which I have to deal with in the Vancouver context, and I will deal with it honestly, about violence in the Indo-Canadian community. They see Sikhs coming into Canada, and in some instances, the presence of representatives of revolutionary organizations in the Sikh community...The majority of people in the country do not want the Khalistan issue fought in Canada, or fought from Canada...I will remind Canadians that we are a charitable, thoughtful, and civilized people. We are people from all parts of the world. We have tried to adopt the best of the other countries in the world. We have always had a fair process for refugee claims. At the same time we are listening to what our [constituents] are saying on the telephone and in letters. They want a fair process. They want to kick out unscrupulous people and keep genuine refugees. They do not want battles of other countries fought in Canada.*[52]

Such anti-immigrant sentiments had real implications for the relatives of the victims. Testimony from Mandip Singh Grewal, whose relatives died in the Air India bombing, aptly illustrates this.

> *As the families were entering the courtroom to hear the verdict, an old man yelled at all of the family members that were present. He told us to go back home, that we were bringing our problems to Canada. This was*

very hard to hear on such an emotional and anxiety-filled day. To me, this is paradigmatic of the way in which this tragedy has been perceived by many in Canada, including government officials; that this was not a Canadian tragedy; that the issues dealt with people involved in a conflict far away.[53]

In addition, surviving relatives of victims experienced difficulties when applying for Canadian visas that would enable them to travel to Canada to assist and support family members, and some reported that "Canadian visa officers had acted suspicious, as though this were not family rallying in time of monumental tragedy, but just one more immigrant scam to sneak into Canada."[54] Clearly, the effects of constructing Air India as a foreign event involving foreign victims and suspects were many. Not only did the Canadian government ignore the victims' families' plight during the immediate aftermath but the pain experienced by those who lost loved ones was exacerbated by continued neglect and poor treatment by the Canadian state in the months, years, and decades following the bombings.

As the analysis above demonstrates, in the initial period immediately following the Air India bombing, the event was understood as the product of a foreign conflict, affecting a foreign nation. Canada's involvement was primarily limited to the origin of the flights, and, grudgingly, to the reluctant acknowledgement that many of the victims and their families were Canadian—but only nominally so, it seemed. This caveat regarding the Canadian-ness of the families was deeply hurtful to those directly affected by the bombing.[55] Their success in forcing the Canadian government and the media to confront the contradictions in Canada's espoused multicultural inclusiveness exposed by the disavowal of Air India's Canadian-ness and, of course, the effects of 9/11, contributed to a substantial shift in the interpretation of the Air India bombings in the 2000s.

The events of September 11, 2001, have altered security discourses and the techniques used to carry out national security strategies.[56] Within this climate, the articulation of Muslims as the nation's Other has been magnified. Muslim and Arab individuals (and those perceived to be Muslim and/or

Arab) in Western nations are increasingly monitored, interrogated, imprisoned, and deported, and their citizenship is being reconfigured.[57] Jasbir Puar points to another, perhaps less obvious, shift: to bolster support for the War on Terror, certain bodies that were previously cast outside of the nation have been tentatively incorporated back into the nation.[58] In light of contemporary reconfigurations of security and terrorism, it is important to ask: How has the construction of the 1985 bombings and its victims, their surviving families, and the suspects shifted in recent years? In the post-September 11 period, governmental discourses have reframed Air India as an act of terror that directly affected Canada, and the victims and surviving families have been discursively embraced as "Canadians."

An analysis of House of Commons utterances expressed in the two years prior to 9/11 and two years after point to a noteworthy shift in initial representations of Air India. From 1999 to September 2001, the few references made to Air India depicted this event as a "crash,"[59] or a "tragedy."[60] The sole reference to this event as a terrorist attack came from Member of Parliament John Nunziata (York South–Weston, Independent):

> *The biggest mass murder in Canadian history took place 14 years ago when 300 Canadians were blown out of the sky on an Air India flight off the coast of Ireland. To date no one has been charged with respect to that* terrorist act *[emphasis added] and there has been no royal commission of inquiry in Canada, notwithstanding that the Government of Ireland has had a royal commission as well as the Government of India.*[61]

Beyond Nunziata's statement, prior to 9/11, parliamentary discourses often depicted Air India as stemming from a foreign conflict rather than a terrorist attack intimately affecting Canada and Canadians.

In the two-year period following 9/11, a significant discursive shift occurs: conservative government officials represent Air India as an act of terror that directly affected Canada rather than an act of international terrorism dislocated from the nation. On September 24, 2001, Member of

Parliament Darrel Stinson (Okanagan–Shuswap, Canadian Alliance) argued that "Canada shared vulnerability to terrorist infiltration...until this week the largest *terrorist strike* [emphasis added] was the downing of the Air India jet in 1985 where more than 330 people were killed."[62] In 2002, Member of Parliament Val Meredith (South Surrey–White Rock–Langley, Progressive Conservative/Democratic Representative Caucus) noted that Canada "was home to a *terrorist attack* [emphasis added] in 1985."[63] And nearly two years after 9/11, Member of Parliament James Moore (Port Moody–Coquitlam–Port Coquitlam, Canadian Alliance) declared,

> *Mr. Speaker, on June 23, 1985, a* terrorist bomb *[emphasis added] killed 329 innocent people on Air India 182. Like other major terrorist attacks on civil aviation, the process of identifying, locating, and bringing those involved is lengthy and complex...As this trial unfolds, the Canadian Alliance extends our best wishes to the families of the victims of Air India Flight 182.*[64]

Following 9/11, dominant discourses effectively renationalized Air India as Canadian and cited the catastrophe as an example of Canada's vulnerability to terrorism. This re-remembering not only failed to acknowledge the initial foreign construction of this event but, importantly, it ignored the power dynamics and systemic racism that led to the initial distancing of Air India from Canada.

When in power, the Conservative government cited the Air India event and embraced it as an act of terror that impelled Canada and Canadians to bolster support for anti-terrorism initiatives. In 2007, in order to further their push to extend two emergency provisions of the Anti-Terrorism Act, several members of the Conservative Party of Canada (CPC) emphasized the terrorist aspect of Air India Flight 182 and its intimate links to Canada. For instance, Member of Parliament Gord Brown (Leeds–Grenville, CPC) declared, "Families of the 9/11 and Air India terrorist attacks want us to place the safety and security of Canadians ahead of partisan politics and support these provisions. Will the opposition leader stop playing partisan politics and join Canada in its fight against terrorism?"[65] Indeed, some CPC members, including then Prime Minister Stephen Harper, argued that not extending these provisions would hinder the RCMP's investigation into the 1985 bombings.[66] In 2009, in order to garner support for including the term "suicide bombing" under the definition of "terrorist activity," Member of Parliament Ed Fast (Abbotsford, CPC) argued,

> *The third and final reason for my interest in this bill is the impact that terrorism has had on Canada. Sadly, Canada is not immune to the ideology, extremism, and hatred that motivate terrorists. We kid ourselves if we believe terrorists are not interested in Canada. It would be a mistake to forget that 24 innocent lives were lost during the tragic events of 9/11. Canadians also remember and continue to mourn the tragic loss of hundreds of lives in the Air India bombings, a terrorist act spawned right here in our own country.*[67]

In October 2009, the Honourable Peter Kent (for the minister of public safety) underscored the terrorist element involved in the 1985 attacks in order to argue in favour of Bill C-35, an act aimed at addressing terrorism: "Canada is not immune to this threat. Hundreds of Canadians were killed in the bombing of Air India Flight 182, the worst act of terrorism in Canadian history, and the biggest in North America before the September 11 tragedy."[68] A significant redefinition and reframing of the Air India bombings is evident in the remarks of these Canadian politicians, a reframing that has also shaped the government's responses to Air India victims' families in recent years.

In addition to redefining Air India as an act of terror that directly affected Canada, public discourse has reconstituted victims and their surviving families as Canadians. The events of 9/11 partially explain this shift, but the twenty-plus years of tireless activism undertaken by victims' families also play a crucial role in this reconfiguration. The ongoing activism of victims' families, as well as the persistence of a small number of governmental officials (such as John Nunziata and Ujjal Dosanjh), show that dominant discursive constructions of the Air India story have been subjected to ongoing resistance and counternarratives. The convergence of the events of 9/11 and persistent counternarratives created a climate in which *selections* of victims' families' concerns—concerns that resonated with post-9/11 securitization policies but simultaneously did not challenge Canada's race-neutral, inclusive, multicultural mythology—were heard by the Canadian government. The shift in the construction of both the event and the victims and their surviving families is most apparent in the 2005 *Rae Report*, as well as the 2007 *Phase 1 Report*. In both reports, a great deal of effort is placed on emphasizing that the 1985 attacks were a Canadian terrorist attack involving Canadian citizens (see, for example, the epigraph from the *Rae Report* at the start of this essay). The *Phase 1 Report* by the Air India inquiry emphasizes that the attack "remains the greatest loss of Canadians at the hands of terrorists."[69] While the reframing of this event is highly significant and the completion of the Air India inquiry is crucial, so, too, would be the recognition and acknowledgement—persistently and emphatically expressed by victims' families—that processes of racism contributed to the Canadian government's inadequate pre- and post-bombing responses, and ultimately distanced victims, victims' families, and suspects from the Canadian nation.[70] But in addition to potentially enhancing discrimination and criminalization experienced by racialized peoples through the enactment of anti-terrorism laws—laws that often unjustly profile Muslims and Arabs (or those perceived to be Muslim or Arab)—the reconstitution of June 23, 1985, as a "Canadian terrorist attack" involving "Canadians citizens" ultimately erases the central role racism has played throughout the Air India case.

The Canadian state's aggressive and determined denial that racism played a role in the government's pre- and post-bombing response has been constant throughout the history of the Air India case. During one 1987 parliamentary debate, in response to Member of Parliament John Nunziata's comments that "if it was a British Airways flight or an American Airlines flight, the Government would be a little more sensitive to what happened," several honourable members labelled Nunziata a "racist," and, significantly, the Speaker himself stated, "I would ask the Honourable Member to be very careful not to imply, even by innuendo, or leave open the interpretation that there is some sort of racist connotation in the entire issue."[71] Sherene Razack experienced similar hostility when she presented her submission to the Air India inquiry hearing. As noted in her commentary in this volume, Razack's suggestion that systemic racism played a role in the Air India case was depicted as extreme, and she was condemned by Barney Brucker, the counsel for the Attorney General of Canada, for her lack of knowledge about the case and for premising her arguments on selective information.[72] Likely alluding to Razack's testimony and submission to the inquiry for which she was chastised, Commission Chair John Major writes,

> *The Commission finds that the term "racism" is not helpful for the purposes of understanding the Government response. "Racism" carries with it so many connotations of bigotry and intolerance that even the most careful definition that purports to focus on effects rather than on intent ends up generating a great deal more heat than light.*[73]

The denial of racism is also present in the *Phase 1 Report* and the *Rae Report*, which both adopt a colour-blind approach to understanding this event.[74] As a consequence, the central role racism played in state and social perceptions and responses to the case of Air India is concealed, and the victims' families' conviction that racism has been present throughout the case is dismissed as unfounded. The *Phase 1 Report* briefly considers whether racism was a factor by posing the question: "If Air India Flight 182 had been an Air Canada flight with all-fair skinned Canadians, would the government response have been different?"[75] In response to this question, the commission quickly concludes, "there is no way to answer that," and, furthermore, "as a country we would hope not."[76] Likewise, the *Rae Report* questions whether individual racism (versus systemic racism) may have played a role in governmental response. The report, however, concludes that "no evidence of racism on the part of anyone in a position of authority" was found, and "mistakes in the investigation cannot be traced to such bias."[77]

Acknowledging that racism played a role in the Air India case would challenge Canada's exalted multicultural, race-neutral, inclusive image;[78] the eliding of race via the liberal colour-blind reframing of Air India, as well as the embracing of victims and their families as Canadian, strengthens this imagining. For the Government of Canada to accept the role racism played in Air India, a radical rethinking of Canada's liberal multicultural imagining is required, in which relations of power are acknowledged and accounted for, and issues of racism and colonialism can be discussed and debated openly and free from hostile defensiveness. Such an undertaking is, however, unlikely, as it would disrupt Canada's celebrated race-neutral multicultural image and, more importantly, expose the white supremacist ideology that infiltrates Canada's structures and compromises the very foundations of the Canadian state.

Parliamentary discourses are revealing and powerful sources of information. These speech acts are significant because they influence public policy and public opinion. Moreover, these iterations congeal national imaginings about Canada's past and present, and they help construct dominant ideas about Canada, and who is and is not a Canadian.[79] Examining parliamentary discourses about Air India enables us to track shifts and continuities in power relations, as well as conceptualizations of race, racism, citizenship, and nation, over time. Such an undertaking also allows us to compare and contrast divergences and convergences between dominant narratives, articulated by state officials, and counternarratives, predominantly voiced by victims' families. Like the Air India inquiry and public memorials, parliamentary discourses act as "sites of remembrance," for they contribute to a selective dominant national remembering of Air India.[80] As Failler notes, "these sites invoke memory in limited, strategic ways to construct a particular version of the past, of the reconstruction of the present and the past, and of who or what matters in this relationship."[81] Sites of remembrance, such as parliamentary debates, help determine how, and even if, a nation recognizes, remembers, and understands a catastrophe.

This analysis demonstrates that the dominant national story woven through the nearly three-decade history of the Air India case is a racial one: it erases racism out of its narrative and ultimately imagines Canada and the country's citizens as predominantly white. Parliamentary discourses initially constructed the 1985 bombings as a non-Canadian tragedy involving non-Canadian citizens; hence, this event, victims, victims' families, and suspects were discursively distanced from the Canadian nation and thus memorialized as foreign. In contrast to initial framings of Air India, state discourses have recently insisted that we recognize and embrace the Canadian-ness of this catastrophe. This shift is significant, particularly in light of the tireless activism undertaken by Air India victims' families to have Canada's link to this catastrophe recognized and remembered by the Canadian state and public. While unquestionably significant, only *selections* of victims' families' articulations—articulations that resonated with post-9/11 securitization policies but simultaneously do not challenge Canada's race-neutral, inclusive, multicultural mythology—have been heard and accepted by the Canadian government, and concerns that discrimination and racism played a role in the Canadian state's pre- and post-bombing actions have been dismissed. As such, a dominant national remembering of Air India, one that erases race and racism out of its narrative, has emerged, and the state and much of the Canadian public have ignored more critical perspectives that shed light on the relationship between systemic discrimination and pre- and post-bombing responses.

To address systemic inequalities, first they must be named and then widely recognized and acknowledged.[82] The continued denial of the role racism has played throughout the Air India case, and the colour-blind lens adopted by the Government of Canada and Air India inquiry commissioner, John Major, raise the question: Has the story of Air India shifted over time or is the dominant narrative very much the same as the one told in the years immediately following the 1985 bombings? This analysis suggests that while there has been a significant shift in the framing of the bombing, in terms of how readily its victims and the tragedy itself are discussed and represented as Canadian, the initial power structures—power structures that ultimately determine whose voices are heard and whose lives are worthy of recognition and mourning—are still very much in place. While dominant discourses have selectively reframed, re-remembered, and renationalized Air India as a Canadian terrorist attack involving Canadian citizens, those in power have failed to listen—and have often rebuffed—counternarratives that insist racism influenced national responses toward the bombings. As Failler notes, this strategic framing "[shields] the state and its agencies from the full implications of what it might mean to critically reflect upon its powers and operations in light of the disaster."[83] In sum, with the completion of the Air India inquiry and subsequent policy recommendations resulting from John Major's reports, a close eye must be kept on the relations of power that originally resulted in the definition of June 23, 1985, as a non-Canadian tragedy involving non-Canadian victims and suspects.

Notes

1. This is a revised and expanded version of the article, "From Foreign to Canadian: The Case of Air India and the Denial of Racism," which was originally published in TOPIA: *Canadian Journal of Cultural Studies* 27 (2012): 215–231.
2. Due to delays to Canadian Pacific Air Lines Flight 003 (Vancouver to Tokyo), the bomb intended for Air India Flight 301 exploded at Tokyo's Narita airport.
3. Bob Rae, *Lessons to Be Learned: The Report of the Honourable Bob Rae, Independent Advisor to the Minister of Public Safety and Emergency Preparedness on Outstanding Questions with Respect to the Bombing of Air India Flight 182* (Ottawa: Air India Review Secretariat, 2005), 1. While suspected motivations behind the attacks are connected to Indian politics, Angela Failler points out that these "conflicts… were connected to Canada and did involve Canadians by virtue of their relation to/ impact on Canada's Sikh and Indian communities, and by virtue of RCMP and CSIS investigations into specific tensions arising from conflicts prior to the attacks." See Angela Failler, "Remembering the Air India Disaster: Memorial and Counter-Memorial," *Review of Education, Pedagogy, and Cultural Studies* 31 (2009): 164.
4. Sunera Thobani, *Exalted Subjects: Studies in the Making of Race and Nation in Canada* (Toronto: University of Toronto Press, 2007); Sherene H. Razack, *Casting Out: The Eviction of Muslims from Western Law and Politics* (Toronto: University of Toronto Press, 2008); Yasmeen Abu-Laban, " The New North America and the Segmentation of Canadian Citizenship," *International Journal of Canadian Studies* 29, no. 1 (2004): 17–40; Himani Bannerji, *The Dark Side of the Nation: Essays on Multiculturalism, Nationalism and Gender* (Toronto: Canadian Scholars' Press, 2000).
5. "PM Rejects Criticism on Terrorism," *Globe and Mail*, July 9, 1985, 5; see also "Aide of PM Will Meet Crash Families," *Globe and Mail*, July 22, 1985, 15.

6. Government of Canada, *The Families Remember: Commission of Inquiry into the Investigation of the Bombing of Air India Flight 182, Phase 1 Report* (Ottawa: Minister of Public Works and Government Services, 2007), 99.
7. Thobani, *Exalted Subjects*.
8. Rae, *Lessons to Be Learned*, 1–2; Government of Canada, *Commission of Inquiry into the Investigation of the Bombing of Air India Flight 182*, last modified June 17, 2010, accessed July 28, 2014, http://epe.lac-.gc.ca/100/206/301/pco-bcp/commissions/air_india/2010-07-23/www.majorcomm.ca/en/reports/finalreport/default.htm.
9. Failler, "Remembering the Air India Disaster," 159; see also Angela Failler with artwork by Eisha Marjara, "'Remember Me Nought': The 1985 Air India Bombings and Cultural *Nachträglichkeit*," *Public: Art/Culture/Ideas* 42 (2010): 113–124.
10. Audrey Macklin, "Borderline Security," in *The Security of Freedom: Essays on Canada's Anti-Terrorism Bill*, ed. Ronald J. Daniels, Patrick Macklem, and Kent Roach (Toronto: University of Toronto Press, 2001), 383–404.
11. Paul H. Chapin, "Into Afghanistan: The Transformation of Canada's International Security Policy since 9/11," *American Review of Canadian Studies* 40, no. 2 (2010): 189–199.
12. Macklin, "Borderline Security," 399.
13. John Geddes and Ken MacQueen, "Air India: After 22 Years, Now's the Time for Truth," *Maclean's*, May 28, 2007, 16; see also Patrick Brethour, "Mass Murder: Why Canada Chose to Unremember Air India and Disown Its Victims," *Globe and Mail*, June 25, 2010, A23.
14. Geddes and MacQueen, "Air India," 16.
15. See Sherene H. Razack, " When Place Becomes Race," in *Race, Space, and the Law: Unmapping a White Settler Society*, ed. Sherene Razack (Toronto: Between the Lines, 2002); Michel Foucault, *Society Must Be Defended: Lectures at the Collège de France, 1975–1976*, trans. David Macey (New York: Picador, 2003); Achille Mbembe, "Necropolitics," trans. Libby Meintjes, *Public Culture* 15, no. 1 (2003): 11–40.
16. Mbembe, "Necropolitics"; Foucault, *Society Must Be Defended*.
17. Thobani, *Exalted Subjects*, 91.
18. Lois Harder and Lybov Zhyznomirska, "Claims of Belonging: Recent Tales of Trouble in Canadian Citizenship," *Ethnicities* 12, no. 3 (2012): 293–316; David Theo Goldberg, *The Threat of Race: Reflections on Racial Neoliberalism* (Malden, MA: Blackwell Publishing, 2009), 7; A. Falguni Sheth, *Toward a Political Philosophy of Race* (Albany, NY: SUNY Press, 2009); Razack, *Casting Out*, 122; Jacqueline Stevens, *Reproducing the State* (Princeton, NJ: Princeton University Press, 1999).
19. Thobani, *Exalted Subjects*, 158.
20. Yasmeen Abu-Laban and Rita Dhamoon, "Dangerous (Internal) Foreigners and Nation-Building: The Case of Canada," *International Political Science Review* 30,

no. 2 (2009): 166; Bannerji, *The Dark Side of the Nation*; Harder and Zhyznomirska, "Claims of Belonging"; David Pearson, " Theorizing Citizenship in British Settler Societies," *Ethnic and Racial Studies* 25, no. 6 (2002): 989–1012; Debra Thompson, "Is Race Political?" *Canadian Journal of Political Science* 41, no. 3 (2008): 525–547.

21. Abu-Laban and Dhamoon, "Dangerous (Internal)," 169.
22. "PM Rejects," 5.
23. Clark Blaise and Bharati Mukherjee, *The Sorrow and the Terror: The Haunting Legacy of the Air India Tragedy* (Toronto: Viking, 1987), 67; Kim Bolan, *Loss of Faith: How the Air-India Bombers Got Away with Murder* (Toronto: McClelland & Stewart, 2005), 69; Government of Canada, *Families Remember*, 111.
24. Bhat quoted in Government of Canada, *Families Remember*, 26. Bhat's wife and son perished on Air India Flight 182.
25. Sherene H. Razack, *The Impact of Systemic Racism on Canada's Pre-Bombing Threat Assessment and Post-Bombing Response to the Air India Bombings* (report submitted to the Commission of Inquiry into the Investigation of the Bombing of Air India Flight 182, 2007), 20.
26. Yasmin Jiwani, *Discourses of Denial: Mediations of Race, Gender, and Violence* (Vancouver: UBC Press, 2006), 1.
27. Nandita Sharma, *Home Economic: Nationalism and the Making of "Migrant Workers" in Canada* (Toronto: University of Toronto Press, 2006), 21–22.
28. Thobani, *Exalted Subjects*, 168; Razack, *Casting Out*, 122.
29. Parliament of Canada, House of Commons, *Official Report—First Session—Thirty-Third Parliament*, Volume IV, 13 May 1985 to 28 June 1985 (Ottawa: Queen's Printer for Canada, 1985), 6132–6133, 6134. Gar Pardy, the former director of the South Asian and Southeast Asia Relations Division of External Affairs, observes that the persistent referral to "victims as 'Canadians with Indian origin'" reflects the difficulty Canadians had in conceiving "the victims as Canadians and not Indians." Pardy quoted in Blaise and Mukherjee, *Sorrow and the Terror*, 70.
30. House of Commons, *Official Report—First Session*, Volume IV, 6137.
31. Lorna Kelly quoted in Government of Canada, *Families Remember*, 100.
32. Mamak quoted in ibid.
33. Subramanian quoted in ibid., 101.
34. Gupta quoted in ibid.
35. Beauchesne quoted in ibid., 103.
36. Radhakrishna quoted in ibid.
37. Bhardwaj quoted in ibid., 105.
38. Major quoted in ibid., 99.
39. Rai quoted in ibid., 105.
40. Khandelwal quoted in ibid., 102.

41. Saklikar quoted in ibid., 104.
42. Kachru quoted in ibid., 64.
43. Ibid., 65. The sole positive remark relating to Canadian government action reported in the *Phase 1 Report* is from Thomas Hayes, a superintendent in the national police force in Ireland, who was involved in confirming identities of victims in Cork and releasing identified bodies to relatives. He testifies that "he recalled someone from the Canadian High Commission in London being on the scene from the first day" and he "acknowledged excellent cooperation from the RCMP, particularly in obtaining fingerprint records in Canada and in following up inquiries that came from the investigative team in Cork." Quoted in ibid., 90.
44. Abu-Laban and Dhamoon, "Dangerous (Internal)," 68, 71; see also Bonnie Honig, *Democracy and the Foreigner* (Princeton, NJ: Princeton University Press, 2001).
45. Parliament of Canada, House of Commons, *Official Report—First Session—Thirty-Third Parliament*, Volume X, 2 June 1986 to 24 July 1986 (Ottawa: Queen's Printer for Canada, 1986), 14057; House of Commons, *Official Report—First Session*, Volume IV, 6136, 6137.
46. Parliament of Canada, House of Commons, *Official Report—Second Session—Thirty-Third Parliament*, Volume XI, 24 February to 12 April 1988 (Ottawa: Queen's Printer for Canada, 1988), 13583.
47. Blaise and Mukherjee, *Sorrow and the Terror*, 174.
48. Dosanjh quoted in Brethour, "Mass Murder," A23.
49. Beauchesne quoted in Government of Canada, *Families Remember*, 40.
50. Government of Canada, *Commission of Inquiry*, 140.
51. Failler, "Remembering the Air India Disaster"; Razack, *Impact of Systemic Racism*; Razack, " When Place Becomes Race," 2.
52. Parliament of Canada, House of Commons, *Official Report—Second Session—Thirty-Third Parliament*, Volume VII, 11 August 1987 to 21 September 1987 (Ottawa: Queen's Printer for Canada, 1987), 7955–7957. This discourse reverberates beyond the first five years after the bombings. Referring to the 1985 attacks in 1993, Derek Blackburn (Brant) said, "Canada is also used as a haven, a safe haven, for international terrorists. They can come here and sleep it off for a few days, a few weeks, a few months in relative peace and tranquility. To say this is irritating is to put it mildly. I recall that a number of years ago previous governments were warned that certain elements were coming from Asia, that the Asian gangs were arriving in this country. I know it was extremely difficult to try to survey them, to try to investigate them and determine who were legitimate refugees and who were gangsters, political thugs and so on." Blackburn quoted in Parliament of Canada, House of Commons, *Official Report—Third Session—Thirty-Fourth Parliament*, Volume XIV, 24 March 1993 to 3 May 1993 (Ottawa: Queen's Printer for Canada, 1993), 17901.

53. Grewal quoted in Government of Canada, *Families Remember*, 106.

54. Blaise and Mukherjee, *Sorrow and the Terror*, 75.

55. Brethour, "Mass Murder," A23.

56. Janine Brodie, "From Social Security to Public Safety: Security Discourses and Canadian Citizenship," *University of Toronto Quarterly* 78, no. 3 (2009): 687–708; Rita Dhamoon, *Identity/Difference Politics: How Difference Is Produced and Why It Matters* (Vancouver: UBC Press, 2009); Razack, *Casting Out*.

57. Razack, *Casting Out*; A. Falguni Sheth, "Unruly Muslim Women and Threats to Liberal Culture," *Peace Review: A Journal of Social Justice* 18 (2006): 455–463.

58. Jasbir K. Puar, "Mapping US Homonormativities," *Gender, Place and Culture* 13, no. 1 (2006): 70; Sheth, *Toward a Political Philosophy of Race*, 129–145.

59. Parliament of Canada, House of Commons, *Official Report—First Session—Thirty-Sixth Parliament*, Volume 135, Number 225, 10 May 1999 (Ottawa: Queen's Printer for Canada, 1999), 14936.

60. Parliament of Canada, House of Commons, *Official Report—Second Session—Thirty-Sixth Parliament*, Volume 136, Number 039, 14 December 1999 (Ottawa: Queen's Printer for Canada, 1999), 2959.

61. Nunziata quoted in House of Commons, *Official Report—First Session*, Volume 135, Number 225, 14936.

62. Stinson quoted in Parliament of Canada, House of Commons, *Official Report—First Session—Thirty-Seventh Parliament*, Volume 137, Number 84, 24 September 2001 (Ottawa: Queen's Printer for Canada, 2001), 5502.

63. Meredith quoted in Parliament of Canada, House of Commons, *Official Report—First Session—Thirty-Seventh Parliament*, Volume 137, Number 153, 11 March 2002 (Ottawa: Queen's Printer for Canada, 2002), 9480.

64. Moore quoted in Parliament of Canada, House of Commons, *Official Report—Second Session—Thirty-Seventh Parliament*, Volume 138, Number 91, 29 April 2003 (Ottawa: Queen's Printer for Canada, 2003), 5548.

65. Brown quoted in Parliament of Canada, House of Commons, *Official Report—First Session—Thirty-Ninth Parliament*, Volume 141, Number 119, 27 February 2007 (Ottawa: Queen's Printer for Canada, 2007), 7377.

66. Parliament of Canada, House of Commons, *Official Report—First Session—Thirty-Ninth Parliament*, Volume 141, Number 116, 22 February 2007 (Ottawa: Queen's Printer for Canada, 2007), 7203–7206, 7210.

67. Fast quoted in Parliament of Canada, House of Commons, *Official Report—Second Session—Fortieth Parliament*, Volume 144, Number 111, 17 November 2009 (Ottawa: Queen's Printer for Canada, 2009), 6885.

68. Kent quoted in Parliament of Canada, House of Commons, *Official Report—Second Session—Fortieth Parliament*, Volume 144, Number 104, 30 October 2009 (Ottawa:

Queen's Printer for Canada, 2009), 6385. A full discussion of Canadian policies aimed at addressing terrorism is beyond the scope of this essay. For an elaboration of policies enacted in the post-September 11 period, see Yasmeen Abu-Laban, "Liberalism, Multiculturalism and the Problem of Essentialism," *Citizenship Studies* 6, no. 4 (2002): 459–482.

69. Government of Canada, *Families Remember*, 1.
70. Razack, *Impact of Systemic Racism*.
71. Parliament of Canada, House of Commons, *Official Report—Second Session—Thirty-Third Parliament*, Volume X, 14 December 1987 to 23 February 1988 (Ottawa: Queen's Printer for Canada, 1987–1988), 11807.
72. Failler, "Remembering the Air India Disaster," 159–160.
73. Government of Canada, *Commission of Inquiry*, 38.
74. For discussions on colour-blindness and its consequences, see Ashley Doane, "What Is Racism? Racial Discourse and Racial Politics," *Critical Sociology* 32, no. 2–3 (2006): 255–274; Philomena Essed, *Understanding Everyday Racism: An Interdisciplinary Theory* (Newbury Park, CA: Sage Publications, 1991); David Theo Goldberg, *The Racial State* (Malden, MA: Blackwell Publishing, 2002), 200–238; Amit Sen, "Policing the Border: Regulating Race, Gender, and Sexuality," *The Georgetown Journal of Gender and the Law* 67 (2007): 67–91.
75. Government of Canada, *Families Remember*, 3–4.
76. Ibid.
77. Rae, *Lessons to Be Learned*, 4.
78. Thobani, *Exalted Subjects*.
79. Brodie, "From Social Security to Public Safety," 693.
80. Failler, "Remembering the Air India Disaster," 151.
81. Ibid.
82. Jiwani, *Discourses of Denial*.
83. Failler, "Remembering the Air India Disaster," 172.

Works Cited

Abu-Laban, Yasmeen. "Liberalism, Multiculturalism and the Problem of Essentialism." *Citizenship Studies* 6, no. 4 (2002): 459–482.

Abu-Laban, Yasmeen. "The New North America and the Segmentation of Canadian Citizenship." *International Journal of Canadian Studies* 29, no. 1 (2004): 17–40.

Abu-Laban, Yasmeen, and Rita Dhamoon. "Dangerous (Internal) Foreigners and Nation-Building: The Case of Canada." *International Political Science Review* 30, no. 2 (2009): 163–183.

Bannerji, Himani. *The Dark Side of the Nation: Essays on Multiculturalism, Nationalism and Gender*. Toronto: Canadian Scholars' Press, 2000.

Blaise, Clark, and Bharati Mukherjee. *The Sorrow and the Terror: The Haunting Legacy of the Air India Tragedy*. Toronto: Viking, 1987.

Bolan, Kim. *Loss of Faith: How the Air-India Bombers Got Away with Murder*. Toronto: McClelland & Stewart, 2005.

Brodie, Janine. "From Social Security to Public Safety: Security Discourses and Canadian Citizenship." *University of Toronto Quarterly* 78, no. 3 (2009): 687–708.

Chapin, Paul H. "Into Afghanistan: The Transformation of Canada's International Security Policy since 9/11." *American Review of Canadian Studies* 40, no. 2 (2010): 189–199.

Dhamoon, Rita. *Identity/Difference Politics: How Difference Is Produced and Why It Matters*. Vancouver: UBC Press, 2009.

Doane, Ashley. " What Is Racism? Racial Discourse and Racial Politics." *Critical Sociology* 32, no. 2–3 (2006): 255–274.

Essed, Philomena. *Understanding Everyday Racism: An Interdisciplinary Theory*. Newbury Park, CA: Sage Publications, 1991.

Failler, Angela. "Remembering the Air India Disaster: Memorial and Counter-Memorial." *Review of Education, Pedagogy, and Cultural Studies* 31 (2009): 150–176.

———. "'War-on-Terror' Frames of Remembrance: The 1985 Air India Bombings after 9/11." TOPIA*: Canadian Journal of Cultural Studies* 27 (Spring 2012): 253–269.

Failler, Angela, with artwork by Eisha Marjara. "'Remember Me Nought': The 1985 Air India Bombings and Cultural *Nachträglichkeit*." *Public: Art/Culture/Ideas* 42 (2010): 113–124.

Foucault, Michel. *Society Must Be Defended: Lectures at the Collège de France, 1975–1976*. Translated by David Macey. New York: Picador, 2003.

Geddes, John, and Ken MacQueen. "Air India: After 22 Years, Now's the Time for Truth." *Maclean's*. May 28, 2007, 16–20.

Goldberg, David Theo. *The Racial State*. Malden, MA: Blackwell Publishing, 2002.

———. *The Threat of Race: Reflections on Racial Neoliberalism*. Malden, MA: Blackwell Publishing, 2009.

Government of Canada. *The Families Remember: Commission of Inquiry into the Investigation of the Bombing of Air India Flight 182, Phase I Report*. Ottawa: Minister of Public Works and Government Services, 2007.

Harder, Lois, and Lybov Zhyznomirska. "Claims of Belonging: Recent Tales of Trouble in Canadian Citizenship." *Ethnicities* 12, no. 3 (2012): 293–316.

Honig, Bonnie. *Democracy and the Foreigner*. Princeton, NJ: Princeton University Press, 2001.

Jiwani, Yasmin. *Discourses of Denial: Mediations of Race, Gender, and Violence*. Vancouver: UBC Press, 2006.

Macklin, Audrey. "Borderline Security." In *The Security of Freedom: Essays on Canada's Anti-Terrorism Bill*, edited by Ronald J. Daniels, Patrick Macklem, and Kent Roach, 383–404. Toronto: University of Toronto Press, 2001.

Mbembe, Achille. "Necropolitics." Translated by Libby Meintjes. *Public Culture* 15, no. 1 (2003): 11–40.

Parliament of Canada. House of Commons. *Official Report—First Session—Thirty-Ninth Parliament.* Volume 141, Number 116, 22 February 2007. Ottawa: Queen's Printer for Canada, 2007.

———. *Official Report—First Session—Thirty-Ninth Parliament.* Volume 141, Number 119, 27 February 2007. Ottawa: Queen's Printer for Canada, 2007.

———. *Official Report—First Session—Thirty-Seventh Parliament.* Volume 137, Number 84, 24 September 2001. Ottawa: Queen's Printer for Canada, 2001.

———. *Official Report—First Session—Thirty-Seventh Parliament.* Volume 137, Number 153, 11 March 2002. Ottawa: Queen's Printer for Canada, 2002.

———. *Official Report—First Session—Thirty-Sixth Parliament.* Volume 135, Number 225, 10 May 1999. Ottawa: Queen's Printer for Canada, 1999.

———. *Official Report—First Session—Thirty-Third Parliament.* Volume IV, 13 May 1985 to 28 June 1985. Ottawa: Queen's Printer for Canada, 1985.

———. *Official Report—First Session—Thirty-Third Parliament.* Volume X, 2 June 1986 to 24 July 1986. Ottawa: Queen's Printer for Canada, 1986.

———. *Official Report—Second Session—Fortieth Parliament.* Volume 144, Number 104, 30 October 2009. Ottawa: Queen's Printer for Canada, 2009.

———. *Official Report—Second Session—Fortieth Parliament.* Volume 144, Number 111, 17 November 2009. Ottawa: Queen's Printer for Canada, 2009.

———. *Official Report—Second Session—Thirty-Seventh Parliament.* Volume 138, Number 91, 29 April 2003. Ottawa: Queen's Printer for Canada, 2003.

———. *Official Report—Second Session—Thirty-Sixth Parliament.* Volume 136, Number 039, 14 December 1999. Ottawa: Queen's Printer for Canada, 1999.

———. *Official Report—Second Session—Thirty-Third Parliament.* Volume VII, 11 August 1987 to 21 September 1987. Ottawa: Queen's Printer for Canada, 1987.

———. *Official Report—Second Session—Thirty-Third Parliament.* Volume X, 14 December 1987 to 23 February 1988. Ottawa: Queen's Printer for Canada, 1987–1988.

———. *Official Report—Second Session—Thirty-Third Parliament.* Volume XI, 24 February 1988 to 12 April 1988. Ottawa: Queen's Printer for Canada, 1988.

———. *Official Report—Third Session—Thirty-Fourth Parliament.* Volume XIV, 24 March 1993 to 3 May 1993. Ottawa: Queen's Printer for Canada, 1993.

Pearson, David. " Theorizing Citizenship in British Settler Societies." *Ethnic and Racial Studies* 25, no. 6 (2002): 989–1012.

Puar, Jasbir K. "Mapping US Homonormativities." *Gender, Place and Culture* 13, no. 1 (2006): 67–88.

Rae, Bob. *Lessons to Be Learned: The Report of the Honourable Bob Rae, Independent Advisor to the Minister of Public Safety and Emergency Preparedness on Outstanding Questions with Respect to the Bombing of Air India Flight 182*. Ottawa: Air India Review Secretariat, 2005.

Razack, Sherene H. *Casting Out: The Eviction of Muslims from Western Law and Politics*. Toronto: University of Toronto Press, 2008.

———. *The Impact of Systemic Racism on Canada's Pre-Bombing Threat Assessment and Post-Bombing Response to the Air India Bombings*. Report submitted to the Commission of Inquiry into the Investigation of the Bombing of Air India Flight 182, 2007.

———. "When Place Becomes Race." In *Race, Space, and the Law: Unmapping a White Settler Society*, edited by Sherene Razack, 1–20. Toronto: Between the Lines, 2002.

Sen, Amit. "Policing the Border: Regulating Race, Gender, and Sexuality." *The Georgetown Journal of Gender and the Law* 67 (2007): 67–91.

Sharma, Nandita. *Home Economic: Nationalism and the Making of "Migrant Workers" in Canada*. Toronto: University of Toronto Press, 2006.

Sheth, A. Falguni. *Toward a Political Philosophy of Race*. Albany, NY: SUNY Press, 2009.

———. "Unruly Muslim Women and Threats to Liberal Culture." *Peace Review: A Journal of Social Justice* 18 (2006): 455–463.

Stevens, Jacqueline. *Reproducing the State*. Princeton, NJ: Princeton University Press, 1999.

Thobani, Sunera. *Exalted Subjects: Studies in the Making of Race and Nation in Canada*. Toronto: University of Toronto Press, 2007.

Thompson, Debra. "Is Race Political?" *Canadian Journal of Political Science* 41, no. 3 (2008): 525–547.

■

The Impact of Systemic Racism on Canada's Pre-Bombing Threat Assessment and Post-Bombing Response to the Air India Bombings

SHERENE H. RAZACK

The Air India bombings, which claimed 331 lives, most of them Canadian, almost 22 years ago, has belatedly been called Canada's 9/11. In truth, it was never close to that. The date, June 23, 1985, is not seared into the nation's soul. The events of that day snuffed out hundreds of innocent lives and altered the destinies of thousands more, but it neither shook the foundations of government, nor transformed its policies. It was not, in the main, even officially acknowledged as an act of TERRORISM. *The political word "tragedy" seemed safer somehow.*

—KEN MACQUEEN AND JOHN GEDDES, "Air India Inquiry Reveals Intelligence Faults," *Maclean's*, May 28, 2007

Introduction

The assessment that the date of the Air India bombings, June 23, 1985, is "not seared into the nation's soul" is virtually undisputed.[1] It would be hard to find anyone who believes that as a nation, our national response to this terrorist act bore even a passing resemblance to our response to the World Trade Center and Pentagon bombings on September 11, 2001. Given the tremendous loss of life on that June day in 1985, and the fact that the majority of persons who died were Canadian, an obvious question arises as to why this act of terrorism had so little impact. An obvious answer is not forthcoming, although Canadians of Indian origin have offered their own view that racism is at least a part of the reason for national indifference. As many have speculated, the disappearance of the Air India bombings from public memory has something to do with the fact that the bombings were an act of violence largely against a Brown people, and an act intended to intimate or coerce a Brown state, in this case, India. In what follows, I examine the role systemic racism played in the pre-bombing threat assessment and the post-bombing response. It goes without saying that no single factor can account for the institutional response to the bombings. I focus here on systemic racism, offering an assessment of the information available from the Commission of Inquiry into the Investigation of the Bombing of Air India Flight 182 (hereafter referred to as the inquiry).

Part One: Canadian Social Context

What Is Systemic Racism?

Although the term "systemic racism" has now entered the lexicon of everyday speech, there is confusion about its meaning. For most people, systemic racism stands in comparison to individual racism. While individual racism is understood to be a practice arising from the belief that one racial group is superior to another, systemic racism is meant to capture the idea that policies and practices that appear neutral on the surface can have the effect of disadvantaging certain racial or ethnic groups. Systemic racism commonly refers to collective, unintentional practices whereas individual racism is linked to the behaviour of individuals and is often considered intentional. In practice, however, the distinctions between systemic and individual, covert and overt, and intentional and unintentional are messy. In the first instance, systems involve people. Secondly, motivation is notoriously hard to discern, either in individual behaviour or when it shapes systems that disadvantage some groups.

The difficulties of capturing what systemic racism is are readily apparent in the Air India bombings. 331 people lost their lives in the crash, the vast majority of whom were of Indian ancestry. There were also white victims. The bomb, or more accurately, the bomb makers did not discriminate. One is tempted to conclude, then, that no matter what policies and practices, intentional or unintentional, collective or individual, might have contributed to the terrible final outcome, no victim was especially advantaged or disadvantaged by them. All lost their lives. However, if the series of actions that ended with the bombings can be shown to have unfolded because it was assumed that the victims would, in fact, be mostly of Indian ancestry, that is to say, if government, transport, and security personnel were able to throw caution to the winds because they were not sufficiently worried about the possible outcome of doing so, then we can say that systemic racism was a factor.

In a nutshell, systemic racism operates when all lives do not count the same and when those charged with protection are not inspired to do their best to ensure that no life was lost. In this context, we would have to ask what would have been the response in 1985 if there had been a series of terrorist threats against the United States. Would outbound American aircraft have been subjected to a higher security scrutiny? This is indeed the case at the present time when passengers bound for Washington's Dulles airport are required to undergo extra scrutiny of their person and their luggage. Although it is hard to pinpoint what moves institutions to take extra caution, or to feel a greater sense of urgency, that we do so in some instances and not others is something that we must examine.

Throughout its deliberations, the Commission on Systemic Racism in the Ontario Criminal Justice System found itself having to grapple with where systems ended and people began. As one of the commissioners, Toni Williams, points out, coming to terms with systemic racism meant having to determine the relationship between apparently neutral laws, policies, standards and procedures, *and* the individual exercise of discretion.[2] If one focuses on how individuals misuse power, it is easy to miss how the systems themselves foster this outcome; conversely, if one focuses on systemic rules that disadvantage, it is easy to miss that subconscious attitudes remain a significant factor in the production of differential treatment.[3] It is therefore necessary to examine both systems and individuals and their interplay when considering systemic racism. In the case of the pre-bombing threat assessment and the post-bombing response, it is important to consider the routine practices of CSIS, the RCMP, the Ministry of Transport, and the federal government examining the role that race played in terms of assumptions about the nature of the terrorist threat and who would most likely be affected by it.

Unconscious Racism

Although intent is very often the focus when we seek to explain racist outcomes, it is clear that both conscious and unconscious racist attitudes produce differential treatment. In the case of unconscious racist attitudes, several scholars, myself included, show how individuals are socialized through a variety of social institutions to understand themselves within a racial hierarchy. Individuals learn who counts socially and who does not, and in cases where they have restricted opportunities to learn something other than the dominant social messages, they will generally act on the basis of these hegemonic assumptions. If individuals act within systems that operate to the benefit of dominant groups, their own attitudes compound the exclusionary effects of these systems, even as these attitudes themselves shape how systems develop.

Canada is a white settler society, a society established by Europeans on non-European soil. Its origins lie in the dispossession of Indigenous populations, a dispossession accompanied by the mythology that the land was largely empty and populated by pre-modern peoples unable to develop it.

White settler mythologies cast Europeans as the bearers of civilization. If in these mythologies Indigenous peoples are confined to pre-history, people of colour are seen as late arrivals who come to the shores of North America after development has occurred. The Chinese who built the railway and the Sikhs who worked in the lumber industry are handily forgotten in this story of who the nation's original citizens are and who developed the land. Forever consigned to the role of guests and late arrivals in the national imagination, people of colour are then experienced as crowding the ordered spaces of the settler and disturbing that order through the introduction of alien cultures and values.[4] Canadians of colour, Himani Bannerji has famously argued, are seen as stains on a snowy landscape.[5] As I and others have shown, the white settler story of origins, a manifestly racial story, has material impact. It underpins, for example, a number of legislative initiatives in the area of immigration concerning who is entitled to full citizenship and who is not. Racialized immigrants, and refugees in particular, on the whole are consistently seen in the law as outsiders to the nation who simply want what original Canadians have.[6] White Canadians come to know themselves in this settler story as rights-bearing citizens against Indigenous and racial others, and social institutions such as the justice system, the media, and education are profoundly shaped by their knowledge, even as these institutions shape how citizens come to know who they are.

Canadians imagine themselves as a peacekeeping nation that is largely uninvolved in the world's crises. As I showed in my study of Canadian peacekeepers in Somalia, both the Canadian public and Canadian soldiers imagined that they were superior people from the land of "clean snow" who must go to help clean up the messes that chaotic, tribal, and underdeveloped Third World peoples make for themselves.[7] Canadians do not imagine that we are implicated in global crises, and that, for example, our activities in mining seriously destabilize communities in several countries in Africa and contribute to internal strife. If immigrants come to our shores, we consider that they are merely seeking a place to live in one of the nicest countries on earth. We do not pause to reflect upon the economic, social, and political processes that drive people out of their home countries, crises in which we are implicated. It is common to find the view in Canadian newspapers, as one columnist wrote in 1985 in response to the Air India bombings, that "Canada, as a nation, has been studiously uninvolved and disengaged from the blood feuds of these several murderous factions, as becomes a lesser power with a prudent policy of protecting its own interests and its nationals by avoiding even the appearance of intervention."[8]

Our sense of ourselves as an innocent nation outside of history means that we often account for the violence in the world as something that has nothing to do with us. From this premise, one can come to believe that violence is a property of Third World cultures and peoples and not a product of various social, political, and historical factors. It was easy in 1985, and as it is today, to believe the simple explanation that terrorist acts are borne of inherently violent cultures and religions, a violence that has nothing to do with Canadians who are not of those cultures and religions. This simple "clash of civilizations" reassures some Canadians of their racial superiority and their innocence. In the everyday phrase, "they are not like us," we convey notions of biological and cultural superiority.

Indo-Canadians

According to Statistics Canada, more than one-third of racial minorities in Canada, a category that includes Blacks, South Asians, Chinese, and other visible minorities, report experiences of racism in the last five years. More than 41 per cent of visible minorities who had been in Canada for at least a generation still reported discrimination at least rarely.[9]

Like other racialized groups, Indo-Canadians (or more broadly South Asians) are often seen as foreigners, guests who are here largely due to the generosity of Canadians. That they, in fact, *make up* Canada and are central to its prosperity is not something that is uppermost in the minds of many white Canadians. The dominant story of an Anglo-Saxon and French majority who are the original citizens pervades everyday life. In the media, for example, itself a social institution that remains largely white, racial minorities are represented as culturally *different* from the normative citizen. The difference is represented as inferiority. Images and stories about oppressed Indian women are a staple in the media, with headlines frequently proclaiming that men from South Asian and Middle Eastern cultures treat women more badly than do white Canadian men.[10]

In a study of Vancouver newspapers for the last one hundred years, Doreen Indra showed that South Asians were near the bottom of the list of desirable members of the national community.[11] Others have traced the ways in which some minorities, such as the Black and Indo-Canadian communities, are associated with violent behaviour.[12] When crime is discussed in reference to a racial group, it is presumed that every member of the group shares a proclivity to crime.[13] Gladys Symons,[14] for example, found that the police consider the violence of ethnic groups as linked to their culture whereas the violence of white gangs remains a violence that is never linked to race.[15] Any quick perusal of Vancouver's newspapers over the past few decades reveals not only ongoing reports of racism against Indo-Canadians (white violence against Indo-Canadian families; professional associations excluding Indo-Canadians; soccer teams excluding Indo-Canadian kids; violence against South Asian elders and farmworkers; and so on) but also columnists who believe that historical acts of discrimination such as the *Komagata Maru* incident amount simply to a justified response to illegal migrants. The media shares its frames about racialized peoples as foreigners with other social elites, notably the justice system and education system.

When we consider systemic racism, it is important to keep in mind both the social context in which racial minorities are perceived as coming from underdeveloped cultures and the material arrangements of inequality (for example, a race-stratified labour force, where visible minorities hold less than 7 per cent of jobs in the federal public service, constitutes the vast majority of migrant workers, and are paid less than other workers). The symbolic and the material constitute each other. As Yasmin Jiwani explains, drawing on Stuart Hall, if we consider systemic racism in the media, for example, the problem is not that active racists run the media. Instead, the media draw on particular kinds of representations to communicate "a common sense stock of knowledge" about racial minorities. This common sense stock of knowledge sustains the material interests of dominant groups. Added to this, few racial minorities work in the mainstream media, and minorities are almost entirely absent at the top ranks. Such structures privilege particular accounts of social reality and the everyday systemic practices of the media—the interpretive frames of stories, decisions made on what is news, and so on, operate to privilege certain narratives about who counts and who does not.[16] It is important to note that elites pre-figure racism, as Teun van Dijk has shown.[17] Racism is in this sense a top-down phenomenon.

In the same way as the media, police officers also work in an institution that is majority white. The police form a social elite that has a key role to play in the symbolic and material arrangements of a racially ordered society. As a commissioner for the Commission on Systemic Racism in the Ontario Justice System suggests of social institutions such as the justice system:

> *These social institutions may subtly inculcate ideas about the legitimacy of a social order in which material success and positions of power are enjoyed overwhelmingly by males of Northern European ancestry. Decision-makers responsible for maintaining that social order typically form a homogeneous group of common ethnicity that shares similar values and understandings of the world. Interactions among peers implicitly confirm the rightness of their world view and the legitimacy of their position in the social order. Their more limited contact with people from racialized communities—typically in situations where the decision-maker is exercising power—is unlikely to challenge the assumptions about "who belongs where" that stem from historical constructions of race.*[18]

With little to disturb the dominant frames (for example, training in the economic, political, and historical contexts of racial minority Canadians, the context of immigration, and so on), those professionals involved in the pre-bombing threat assessment and post-bombing response would have relied on their own knowledge of the world, a world in which Indo-Canadians are little known and where they are often seen as foreigners whose culture is an inferior one. Crucially, in 1984, there were only fourteen Indo-Canadian members of the RCMP, of whom only two were stationed in Vancouver.[19]

The effects of a racist world view on how professionals associated with threat assessment and with post-bombing responses conducted their everyday lives, and particularly how their superiors made decisions about resources and protocols, should not be underestimated. Equally, how deeply they were moved to respond to the bombing would surely have been conditioned by their own understandings of Indo-Canadians in general. It is entirely possible that a plane full of people of Indian ancestry, an aircraft belonging to Air India that crashed far from Canadian shores, and a violent act committed in the name of a Sikh independent state in India would have struck many Canadians as a tragedy, but not one close to home. If they came to any conclusion at all about the Air India bombings, Canadians were most likely to see the "tragedy" as "just another ethnic thing," as William Warden, Canadian ambassador to India in 1985 has suggested of Canadians.[20] When police, political, and media elites all consistently treated the Air India bombings as a foreign event, it is not surprising that Canadians do not recall June 23, 1985. As a nation, we were not shaken, transformed, and moved to change our own institutional practices for a tragedy we considered had little to do with us.

Part Two: The Air India Bombings

Pre-Bombing Threat Assessment and Post-Bombing Response

To what extent does the social context of a white settler society cast a shadow on the events leading up and subsequent to the bombings? The residue of race is in evidence wherever it becomes apparent that systems are in place that have the impact of providing less protection to Indo-Canadians (and arguably all Canadians) at risk of terrorist attacks. Since systems are also people, we can see the shadow of race whenever individuals appear to make decisions based on their own ethnocentric and racist assumptions.

Pre-Bombing Threat Assessment Warnings

In June 1984, the Indian government took control of the holiest Sikh shrine, the Golden Temple in Amritsar. One thousand people died in the assault on the temple. In October 1984, Sikh bodyguards assassinated Indian Prime Minister Indira Gandhi. Thousands of Sikhs were subsequently murdered in retaliation and a great deal of Sikh property was destroyed. These events greatly heightened Sikh separatism and extremism in India and abroad. Violent incidents and acts of terrorism directed at the Indian government and Indian institutions and at representatives abroad began to occur more frequently. In Canada, prior to the bombings, there had been incidents of violence, including an attack on the acting Indian high commissioner.[21]

In the five years leading up to the bombing of Air India Flight 182, there was considerable discussion of the imminent threat of extremist Sikh terrorism in Canada. In 1984 and 1985, warnings of increasing Sikh extremist violence came regularly from the government of India and from the Canadian high commissioner to India, William Warden. Some of these warnings included information that Indian intelligence felt that an Air India plane would be targeted. As the Rae report noted, between July 1984 and June 1, 1985, the government of India conveyed that there were seventy-three threats of which thirteen were devoted to Air India. For CSIS, the number of warnings merely indicated that the government of India was exaggerating the threat.[22]

The RCMP received information in September of 1984 that there was an alleged plot to bomb an Air India aircraft leaving from Mirabel Airport in Montreal. On June 12, 1985, surveillance audiotapes of a meeting of suspected Sikh extremists in Vancouver revealed information that something was being planned for two weeks. A Vancouver police department official has candidly admitted that when he listened to the Khuruna surveillance tapes and heard that something was being planned for the middle of June, he believed that it was "just another hothead beating his chest."[23] On June 19, 1985, an RCMP informant advised the force that certain individuals were planning a possible hijacking of an aircraft. James Bartleman, a security analyst who later became Ontario's lieutenant-governor, has now revealed that he received and passed on information about a possible aircraft bombing on the weekend of the 23rd.[24] The RCMP was advised by one of its sources on June 9 that Hamilton Sikhs had been told not to fly Air India because it was unsafe to do so.[25]

Finally, in the months immediately prior to the bombings, Air India began issuing repeated warnings to CSIS, the RCMP, and transport officials. On January 9, 1985, Air India held a meeting at Pearson International Airport in Toronto with officials of Transport Canada, the RCMP, and Air Canada to communicate its new security arrangements. The airline asked for the X-ray of all bags and/or the use of the PD-4 explosives detection device and RCMP supervision of the baggage area. Sniffing dogs were also requested, but this request was denied.[26] More ominously, Air India warned the RCMP on June 1, 1985, that it was especially at risk for time-delayed bombs on board its aircraft. Special precautions were delineated (but not, however, for connecting flights). The airline noted the possibility of a terrorist attack from Sikh extremists.[27] Air India updated the RCMP on the threat of sabotage of its aircraft on June 6, 1985.[28] What, then, were the institutional responses to the information received about the possibility of a terrorist act, and specifically to the bombing of an aircraft?

Canadian security and airline officials were remarkably inattentive to Air India's warnings, given the intensity of the warnings. Canadian Pacific Air Lines, for instance, which transported the suitcase with the bomb to Toronto, maintained throughout that it had no knowledge that Air India was specifically threatened.[29] In the year leading up to the bombings, when the warnings were coming in thick and fast from Air India and from the government of India, the main official at the Department of Transport headquarters was never briefed or trained in any way on the issue of Sikh extremism in the context of terrorism.[30] Dr. Peter St. John concluded of the situation in 1985, "I don't think that Canadian airport security or Transport Canada or any of our security people were ready for Air India. And in fact, when it happened they didn't even think it was Canadian. They thought it was Indians from India."[31]

Both the report prepared by the Canadian Air Transport Authority Advisory Panel and the Rae report concluded that human error was a part of the security failures. Notably, there was poor threat communication among all the players.[32] It is important, however, to contextualize human error. At least one reason for the inattention of Canadian officials to the threat environment in June 1985 lies in the general response to Air India itself. As letters and minutes indicate, CSIS believed that Air India was exaggerating the threat.[33] For its part, many members at the January 9 meeting, which included the RCMP and others, felt that Air India was simply trying to have increased security at no extra cost. They note that Air India preceded every flight with a letter outlining a threat to the airline.[34] While the prospect of spending extra money on overtime payments and resources can often produce this response, the idea that racial others are crying wolf and are likely wanting something for nothing is a solidly entrenched one. In immigration debates in the House of Commons, politicians often express the idea, for instance, that refugees are culturally given to duplicity, are generally not to be believed, and are not as honest as are Canadians.[35] Ironically, although Transport Canada advised Air India in 1984 and in February 1985 that it was actively monitoring and evaluating the airline's security programme, the CATSA advisory panel found that no such monitoring was undertaken.[36] For example, Air India proposed the use of the PD-4 explosive scanning device, but in a test at which a Transport Canada official was present, the device did not work. As former RCMP security officer Mattson testified at the inquiry, at no time did regional civil aviation officials register a concern with Air India's security arrangements.[37]

The RCMP gave no indication that they took Air India's warnings seriously. Decisions made to send most dog handlers away to a conference on June 22, 1985, for instance, may well have been influenced by the idea that Indians were not to be believed and that no real threat against Canadians was imminent. In Montreal, a dog handler had to be contacted to come to the airport to search Flight 182. Air India made the decision to allow Flight 182 to depart before the handler arrived at Mirabel Airport. It is chilling in this regard to listen to Mr. Serge Carignan, the dog handler called to the airport that day, declare that he is confident that his dog would have found the explosives had it been allowed to sniff the luggage.[38] When resources are being considered, it is worth noting that only *one* Air India plane flew out weekly from Montreal. It is easy to agree with the conclusion drawn by *Maclean's* that Canadian agencies seem to have treated Air India with "a suspicion bordering on contempt."[39]

Senator Colin Kenny, chair of the Standing Senate Committee of National Security and Defense, has testified that there is a significant difference in urgency between the responses to the Air India crash and the 9/11 bombings (where proportionally fewer Canadians died). Senator Kenny attributes the difference to the belief that for the Air India bombings, "there was a sense that it wasn't Canadians who were involved."[40] How is this belief manifested in aviation security practices in 1985? The evidence shows that Canadian airports did not practice a generalized screening of checked baggage, and did not do so until 2005. Luggage was screened if there was a specific reason to do so.[41] If we consider as cargo, luggage that is checked without a passenger, as was the fatal suitcase containing the bomb, then cargo, too, was not screened in 1985 and is still not screened.[42] Mail that travels on passenger planes from Canadian airports is also still not properly inspected.[43] Transport officials offer that the appropriate technology is not available to do so, but the inquiry has heard from Dr. Kathleen Sweet that this is in fact not the case.[44] If Air India wanted luggage screened in 1985, it had to make these arrangements itself, as it did in 1985 and for Flight 182.

It is tempting to attribute the problems in luggage screening in 1985, problems that continued until recently, and some of which continue to this day, simply to inexperience with terrorist threats, and to an enduring belief that Canadians are not targeted. This latter is itself racially inflected since it is not widely accepted that Indo-Canadians are Canadians. It is plausible, too, that airlines are too concerned about costs and that failings in 1985 arose from this factor rather than from any racial impulses. These arguments fail when we consider that a heightened security *is practiced whenever circumstances warrant*. Since 1971, the International Civil Aviation Organization security manual has provided guidance for special risk flights, and especially for the correlating of baggage to passengers.[45] Israel's national airline, EL AL, as Dr. Reg Whitaker testified, has practiced an enhanced security for several decades.[46] While transport officials testified that airlines balk at screening cargo, they do, in fact, engage in "risk profiles" and make cargo screening decisions accordingly.[47] Today, for instance, Air Canada currently screens cargo in London and Paris with an X-ray machine, and cargo destined for the United States is manually searched in Toronto, Montreal, and Vancouver.[48]

There are a number of legitimate concerns about risk profiles when they concern individuals, as I have shown in the case of Muslims and Arabs profiled after 9/11.[49] These concerns are echoed by the Canadian Air Transport Security Authority Act (CATSA) Advisory Panel and by the Privacy Commissioner Jennifer Stoddart in her testimony.[50] Representatives of the Airline Pilots Association made the point that "behavioural profiling" can be different from racial profiling. In behavioural profiling, one takes into account factors other than race.[51] Had a behavioural approach been taken with the passengers of CP Air, the behaviour of a Sikh passenger who tried to check his luggage without boarding would have served as a red flag when taken in the context of other factors, as the behavioural approach suggests, notably the payment in cash, the name changes of passengers, and the demand that baggage be checked through to Delhi, even though there was no confirmed booking from the Toronto leg of the trip.[52] There remains a great danger, however, as Dr. Whitaker testified, that profiling of any sort "gets out of proportion."[53] With the example of Maher Arar now in our minds, it is possible to imagine the places one can end up with the profiling of individuals, whether directly racial or behavioural. However, had a firm policy been in place that luggage without passengers had to be removed, the suitcase with the bomb would have been taken off the plane without having to resort to profiling.

Many of the decisions to depart from routine practices (for instance the CP agent's decision to allow interlined baggage to be checked through despite the passenger not having a confirmed reservation) that would later prove fatal were made on the assumption that there was little threat. Both the CATSA Advisory Panel report and the Rae report attributed the flawed threat assessment to poor communication.[54] The decisions made to practice a low level of luggage scrutiny would not have been made if transport and security officials had taken seriously the information received from the government of India, Air India, Indian sources, and the force's own surveillance tapes. Ironically, racial profiling seemed to be operating in the sense that information that came from Indian sources was not taken seriously but instead gave rise to the suspicion of these sources as unreliable. A racial response is discernible in the overall *disinclination* to take seriously the specific threat, and the people of Indian origin who offered warnings of it, and who stood to be the most harmed by it. To put the matter bluntly, one pays attention to the security concerns of London, Paris, Washington, and Tel Aviv, but not those of New Delhi.

Resources around Surveillance

The federal government had concerns about possible Sikh violence in Canada in May 1984 and 1985, and a month before the terrorist attack, the government created an interdepartmental committee on Sikh terrorism that specifically considered the risks associated with the anniversary of the Indian assault on the Golden Temple. Around the same time, plots were uncovered to assassinate Indian Prime Minister Rajiv Gandhi while he was visiting the United States, and the FBI had alerted Canada that Sikh extremists in Vancouver were likely involved. In spite of a heightened awareness of the possibility of a terrorist threat, it appears that neither CSIS, the RCMP, nor the federal government entirely believed in its imminence. It is clear that CSIS ultimately considered Sikh extremism a low priority.[55] This belief was reflected in the amount of resources allocated to it. Few personnel were assigned to monitor Sikh extremist activity in British Columbia and one key investigator went on vacation a month before the Air India bombing. On June 18, 1985, CSIS issued a comprehensive threat assessment in which it was noted that the threat had lessened only slightly with the departure of Rajiv Gandhi. On June 19, a threat assessment was also provided to the

RCMP. As the Security Intelligence Review Committee (SIRC) *Air India Report* noted, however, on the same day, "CSIS Headquarters cancelled its previous requirement for daily situation reports from the regions."[56]

Although it was clearly known that Talwinder Singh Parmar (now believed to be the leader of the conspiracy to bomb Air India flights) was an extremely important target who had been under surveillance for some time by the RCMP and CSIS, surveillance on Parmar was suspended between June 17 and June 22, 1985.[57] There is some evidence of inaccurate or incompetent surveillance on the part of CSIS.[58] It also seems that some surveillance might have continued and that Parmar was observed leaving his home on June 19 to meet with Hardial Johal after a telephone call followed the reservation of the Air India tickets.[59]

Inderjit Reyat, convicted of manslaughter for acquiring materials to make the bomb, was actually observed meeting with Parmar, and later testing a bomb in a wooded area near Duncan, British Columbia, on June 4, 1985. The CSIS agent who heard the noise concluded it was a rifle, but there is conflicting testimony about whether or not CSIS realized the significance of this event. The CSIS surveillants performed a cursory search of the area and found nothing to suggest that a bomb had been detonated. However, in subsequent searches following the bombings, the RCMP ultimately found such evidence.[60] The mistake made about the gun, and later the failure to find evidence of a bomb, could perhaps be written off as due to the inherent difficulties of this kind of work where human error is always a factor. When these incidents are put into the context of the overall CSIS and RCMP understanding of the threat of Sikh terrorism as a low one, and we consider that the officer on surveillance duty that day in Duncan did not trouble to bring a camera with her, mistakes seem less benign.[61] They had important consequences, among them, that Reyat and Parmar were not arrested until November 7, 1985. Charges against Parmar were stayed and Reyat was convicted of possessing an explosive substance.[62]

In reading the events leading up to the bombing, it is hard to believe that the RCMP and CSIS knew so much about a possible bombing of Air India and were not spurred to expend greater efforts at surveillance. It seems, however, that once Rajiv Gandhi had departed the United States and the actual anniversary of the assault on the Golden Temple had passed, there was disagreement about how high a threat existed. In 1992, SIRC concluded that the threat assessment was not specific at the time to warrant different practices.[63]

Translation

Perhaps no evidence indicates the presence of an ethnocentric, if not a racist, approach to threat assessment than the issues surrounding translation of surveillance tapes. Although Parmar's phone was tapped beginning March 27, 1985, there were lengthy delays in obtaining translation. Prior to June 8, when a Punjabi translator was hired, tapes were sent to Ottawa to be translated. In Ottawa, there were so many delays that the Ottawa office did not transcribe any tapes after April 9, 1985. The Ottawa translator was not briefed as to the nature of the information on the tapes and had little time to devote to them. Clearly, the Parmar tapes were not a priority. When the BC translator finally began her work, there were eighty-two tapes waiting to be transcribed. Current tapes were given priority and were read/played and loosely paraphrased, rather than transcribed. No notes were taken from June 21 to 29, 1985, owing to the fact that the transcriber was on leave.[64]

With the benefit of hindsight, the difficulties around translation are especially disturbing. If the tapes revealed information that could have prevented the Air India bombings, CSIS was clearly not in a position to obtain it. Although CSIS makes note of the tremendous difficulty of finding translators, and the complications that arise because translators from within the Sikh community might feel (and might actually be) at risk, the slowness of their efforts indicates the lack of a sense of urgency surrounded the threat. Certainly, translators could have also been recruited from outside the Sikh community since Punjabi speakers include Hindus, Muslims, and others not of Sikh background.

Both CSIS and the RCMP were agencies removed from the Sikh community not only by virtue of their own homogeneity but more crucially because they did not see the need to compensate for it. Few steps appear to have been taken to improve their understanding of the Sikh community. Seen from this angle, the threat assessment of Sikh terrorism as low is due to something more than serendipity. The Vancouver police department acknowledged to the inquiry that in 1984 and 1985, the majority of the department was Caucasian and did not understand what is described as "cultural diversity that was within the community itself."[65] Mr. Norm Inkster, a former RCMP commissioner, also admitted that at the time of the investigations into possible Sikh terrorist activity, the force was "ill-equipped" to deal with the language and cultural features of the Sikh community. He undertook to remedy this problem in the years following the crash.[66] As he put it forcefully in testimony, in 1985, "the face of Canada had changed significantly, and the RCMP had not changed with it."[67] The unwillingness to establish procedures and practices that would compensate for the force's shortcomings (no translators, few Indo-Canadians, no sustained links with the community) may in part reflect a force that had simply not kept up, but it betrays an ethnocentrism that in the end had enormous racist impact as individuals, caught in these systems, were unable to respond appropriately to the context in which they found themselves.

Response to the Bombing

Immediately following the bombing, there is little to suggest that governmental agencies were gripped by a strong sense of urgency. The loss of 331 lives, the majority of whom were Canadian, did not disturb the routine practices and rivalries between CSIS and the RCMP, for example. Although the RCMP appointed two hundred investigators, the SIRC *Air India Report* found that the RCMP and CSIS had no plan to cooperate immediately following the bombing.[68] The possibility exists that CSIS had a structure that isolated the director,[69] but it is clear that he did not provide any forceful direction within CSIS for so important a case. In his *Reasons for Judgment* in *R. v. Malik and Bagri*, Mr. Justice Ian Josephson found that there had been a sharing of information. He based his finding on a memo from the director of CSIS that he had advised his officers to cooperate with the RCMP.[70] Nonetheless, there is considerable evidence that following the crash, CSIS and the RCMP remained preoccupied by their own jurisdictional issues. CSIS worried, for example, that if the RCMP enjoyed unfettered access to its raw data, it would be reduced to playing a supporting role.[71] In 1986, when the RCMP wanted access to the CSIS files, it took seven months before access was provided.[72]

The bombings clearly did not prompt either agency to overcome their conflicts. Nothing illustrates this more than the destruction of surveillance tapes. Between March 27, 1985, and July 1, 1985, the force collected 210 tapes; only fifty-four still exist.[73] CSIS did not inform the RCMP that it had obtained a warrant in March to intercept Parmar's communications. The RCMP did not get access to tapes until October 1985, when it learned that several tapes had been erased.[74] Horrifyingly, the information about the booking of tickets on the Air India flight and the arrangements for the suitcase with the bomb are all contained on intercepted communications for June 20–22.[75] Although it is impossible to gauge, one cannot help but wonder whether prosecutions would have been more successful if the evidence on the tapes had not been destroyed, and the suspicion exists that the tapes were destroyed precisely because they might have indicated that CSIS ought to have known about the bombings.

It is hard to make sense of CSIS destroying some of the Parmar tapes and even more so to understand a memo by CSIS director Archie Barr that CSIS was not in the business of collecting evidence and so had no need to retain the tapes.[76] Another memo by the director general of communications advised the contrary.[77] In view of the agency's position on the retention of tapes, it is not surprising that CSIS personnel would see no need to retain the tapes.[78] While established practices around the destruction of tapes (for example, destroying tapes that contain information about innocent third parties) suggest that the destruction of tapes was not necessarily a deliberate act of sabotage of evidence, the enormity of the Air India bombings would have surely given most institutions pause about the impact of their regular practices. One cannot imagine relevant material for the World Trade Center bombings being casually or inadvertently erased *after* the Twin Towers fell. A strange inattention to the event of the bombings prevails. For example, following the bombing, BC CSIS director Randy Claxton still did not request an inventory of the Parmar tapes and an accounting of the tape erasure process.[79] Tapes were mysteriously lost, including one of a conversation on June 22 of Parmar calling the residence of Air India suspect Ajaib Singh Bagri.[80] There are missing minutes of meetings and confusion as to policies around tapes.

Perhaps nothing conveys the limited impact of the Air India bombings on the consciousness of Canadian officials than the few changes made in aviation security. Although some changes were implemented following the bombings (notably that checked luggage without a passenger had to be removed), and Canada participated in international consultations on aviation safety, Transport Canada continued to allow carriers to assume full responsibility for screening passengers and their baggage. Screening remained something that was contracted out to private security agencies, even though it had become clear with the Air India bombings that poorly trained and poorly paid security personnel did not result in proper security. It took the events of 9/11 to galvanize Canada to create the Canadian Air Transport Authority (CATSA) for the purpose of managing the screening of baggage and passengers.[81]

Federal Government Response

To many, when Prime Minister Brian Mulroney delivered his condolences to the government of India, he was simply acting in accordance with the government's perception that Indians and not Canadians had been the major victims of Flight 182. In keeping with the sentiment that the bombings were not intrinsically a Canadian affair, the government sent only a small team of seven Canadians to Cork, Ireland, the site of the recovery of the bodies and wreckage; no member of the team spoke Punjabi or was trained to offer religious or grief counselling.[82]

The Canadian response stands in stark contrast to the response of the Indian government. A large Indian team arrived at Cork, Ireland, on June 24, 1985. By July 13, 1985, the government of India had appointed Mr. Justice B.N. Kirpal, a judge of the Delhi High Court, to head a formal investigation of the incident. Lata Pada, who lost her husband and two daughters in the crash, describes being met at the airport in Cork by the Indian ambassador and his wife, who escorted them to the hotel.[83] In Cork, the Indian government took care to decorate the viewing rooms for the bodies with flowers and incense burning, and they established a room where families could grieve in private. It appears that no effort was spared to ensure that the arrangements provided were as near as possible to those observed in the communities of the families. As Mr. Justice B.N. Kirpal noted in his report of the Indian court's investigations, victims' families felt that these special arrangements "conveyed a deep and individual response to the dignity of each victim which might otherwise be lost with such a large number of bodies."[84]

It is striking how little assistance the families of victims received from the Canadian government. Testimony from Mr. Kalwant Mamak, for instance, who lost his wife in the bombing, recalls that when he first landed in Cork, there were no Canadian officials available to help; Canadians had to rely on Air India for help with accommodations.[85] When they met with Mr. Mamak, Canadian officials responded to his concerns by saying that as yet they had no instructions from Ottawa as to what kind of help could be given.[86] Unable to access any help at a time when he was deeply distraught, Mr. Mamak made a decision he was later to deeply regret, to have his wife cremated in London rather than bringing her body back to Canada for his children to view their mother one last time.[87]

As one of the seven consular officials sent to Cork testified, the Canadian team tried to offer comfort and solace but felt that "there wasn't a great deal we could do in terms of achieving the immediate result that they all sought which was to have access to the recovered bodies."[88] Unable to communicate to some of the families, and in the absence of formal religious assistance or grief counselling, there was indeed little that the team could do. Although individual team members did as well as they could, for example, Mr. Stewart had served in Delhi and had a passing familiarity with diverse Indian burial customs,[89] the team could only rely on such informal experiences. Their superiors in Ottawa, however, who determined the resources to be allocated to activities in Cork, could surely have put into place more appropriate resources, as many family members have attested.

Instead, the Canadian government appears to have been concerned by "hordes descending" on Cork, a careless and disturbing characterization of the families of the victims.[90] They were also concerned by the prospect of having to foot the hotel bill if Air India discontinued its payment of the hotel bills of the families of the victims. The government determined that it would advance funds to the victims' families but on a repayable basis.[91] Families have commented on the minimal availability of Canadian officials. A week after the tragedy, Dr. Bal Gupta, who lost his wife, commented to a journalist that he had not been contacted by a single Canadian representative.[92]

It is important to stress that for the families of victims, the effects of the bombings did not end once they left Cork. Mr. Mamak noted that even at the one-year anniversary in Cork, the Canadian government met with only a few selected families. He was not among those the government met with. He testified about the enduring effects of the loss of his wife, the heart attack he suffered, and his difficulties in bringing up three children alone. In all of this time, he heard from the RCMP once, one month following the crash when they asked him about whether he had life insurance for his wife.[93] Other family members describe the descent into illness they feel was precipitated by the trauma of the crash and note that in the midst of all their pain and suffering, they did not receive a single letter of condolence from the federal government.[94] "Do I not matter?" Satrajpal Rai asked the inquiry.[95] He recalled the tremendous outpouring of support for the families of the victims of 9/11 and wondered if he would have received some of this had he been white.[96] Lata Pada, a family member, commenting that 80 per cent of the passengers held Canadian passports, put the matter of the government's failure to respond poignantly:

> *Imagine the overwhelming sense of betrayal that it took fifteen years before the government of Canada decided to proceed with the trial and imagine again the loss of faith in a system where the incompetence of*

the RCMP and CSIS was singularly responsible for averting a tragedy of such magnitude and devastating consequence. Imagine that an entire nation cannot begin to visualize the horror of this tragedy, their collective memory of this event dulled by years of public amnesia and cross sensationalization of more exciting news.[97]

It has puzzled some observers why the Canadian government did not respond to the Air India bombings as a major terrorist act. A terrorism expert of the time has suggested that to himself and others in the community of terrorism experts, the Air India event merited considerably more attention than it received from Canada. Mr. Bruce Hoffman described the incident as "the most lethal terrorist incident in history for that era."[98] He speculated on why the Canadian government did not view the bombings in this light: "I think, perhaps, people dismissed or diminished the impact of Air India 9/11 because it was in the context of the raid on the Golden Temple at Amritsar, and of basically a vengeance and motivation between militant Sikhs and the Indian government in particular, the Ghandi [*sic*] regime and that of her son."[99] The view that the violence was an exclusively Indian affair prevailed over the fact that 280 Canadians lost their lives. We should find in this position the evidence that anything connected to India could not, by definition, be Canadian, a position that left Indo-Canadians standing outside the nation.

The horrific loss of life notwithstanding, it took ten years for the federal government to approve a reward for information leading to the arrest of anyone connected with the bombing. The significance of this delay is highlighted by the fact that by July 6, 1985, Mark Kingwell reported in the *Globe and Mail* that members of Toronto's Indian community were already pooling money to offer a reward for clues in the crash.[100] Finally, any idea that the Air India bombings were understood to be a Canadian tragedy can be dispelled by the fact that for more than twenty-one years there was little interest on the part of the government in conducting a national inquiry. Certainly, the tardy Canadian response does not compare to the hundreds of American and British investigators who descended on Lockerbie, Scotland, to investigate the bombing of an aircraft, a difference in response that some have attributed to the belief that the Air India bombings were an internal affair between Indians and not one that involved North Americans or Europeans.

Internal documents reveal that the federal government was aware that the victims' families were alleging racism in view of the lack of governmental interest, but the government was equally aware that there was limited public interest and media attention on the bombings.[101] It is also possible that further inquiry stood a chance of revealing the shortcomings of the federal response to the bombings, revelations that potentially made the Government of Canada civilly liable. Civil litigation invites a legalistic approach to compensation, however, that does not allow the families' broader issues to surface. These political considerations cannot be discounted when we assess the federal government's explanation that it did not consider an inquiry while a criminal investigation was ongoing. Such considerations have not affected the tainted blood inquiry in Canada, nor did it stop inquiries into the 9/11 bombings in the United States.

Inquiries are important symbolic acts. A political and media framing of the Air India bombings as one in which there was a *Canadian* loss of life would have gone a long way toward acknowledging to Indo-Canadians their place in the nation. Such an inquiry early on would have also indicated that the government was taking steps to ensure that it not happen again. In its absence, policies and practices that contributed to the racist responses remain unchanged. As a Canadian government official testified, there is as yet no written policy on the appropriate response to terrorist acts of this kind.[102]

The Red Flags: Reading for Race

Each red flag highlighting indifference on the part of Canadian agencies and the Canadian government to the Air India bombings can be explained by incompetence and also by the very real complexities and difficulties of intelligence and national security work. It is true that it is only with the benefit of hindsight that one can even see some of these events as red flags. However, the factors above, when taken altogether, suggest that race influenced the minimizing of the threat of terrorism, and the extremely muted Canadian reaction to the loss of life of more than two hundred Canadians. Although there was clearly considerable intelligence about the threat of Sikh extremist terrorism, particularly in the early part of 1985, CSIS, the RCMP, Department of Transport, and airport officials seemed not to make the threat a priority.

Once the terrible events of the bombings unfolded, there was still no sense of urgency, certainly not the kind that one would expect given that so many *Canadians* had died in the biggest terrorist bombing to date. This is surely a powerful indicator that racism influenced events both before and after the bombings. If we can see little evidence of care *after* the loss of so many Canadian lives, we must reasonably conclude that the value of those lives affected practices prior to the bombings as well. To what else might we attribute the lack of urgency before and after? Why did CSIS, the RCMP, and the nation appear to not care as much as they might? Indeed, why did they not care as much as when far fewer Canadians lost their lives in the World Trade Center bombings? What can we say about successive federal governments that made no public space for inquiry into the bombings, could not bring themselves to even express condolences, and were not moved to commemorate the Canadian lives lost that day until more than twenty years after?

The evidence leaves a powerful impression that race was a factor in pre-bombing threat assessment and in post-bombing responses. First, white Canadians appear to have felt that Sikh terrorism was a problem among Indians, not Canadians. The conflict originated in India and the intended targets were Indian. This could easily have led to the belief that Canadians, read only as white, were not directly involved. When information came that indeed a terror threat was imminent, it came from Indian officials who were likely perceived as less rational and competent than white Canadians. One has only to recall the racist characterization of "banana republics," and, of course, the long history of colonialism in India, to believe that India in the Canadian national imagination was not to be taken to be a "developed" country capable of rational responses.

Neither CSIS nor the RCMP had many Canadians of colour among their ranks and, more significantly, neither appears to have considered the limitations that their homogeneity posed. These agencies could not immediately undertake practical tasks such as translation. They were not in a strong position to assess what they could know and understand about a community about which they knew so little. There is an ethnocentric arrogance in the perception that the routine work of security and policing can be effective when the force lacks personnel and critical training that would enable them to overcome the limitations of being a homogeneously white organization. Certainly, the possibility that individuals could make racist assumptions of Indo-Canadians ought to have been considered in view of the dominant views of Indo-Canadians as different from the norm, outsiders to the nation, and members of an inferior culture. There is nothing inevitable about racism, but the power of dominant groups to narrate the world as their material interests dictate cannot be contested and confronted unless it is first recognized.

The federal government's post-bombing response can only be described as uncaring. There is nothing to indicate that the government considered the crash as a Canadian tragedy and its victims primarily Canadian.

Conclusion

Perhaps the most compelling evidence that racism is a part of the responses to the Air India bombings comes from the families of the victims and from Indo-Canadians generally. Almost without exception, Indo-Canadians, and South Asians more generally, experienced the Air India bombings as the kind of event where you remember what you were doing when you first heard the news. From moderate Sikhs such as Ujjal Dosanjh, who sounded warnings about the explosive atmosphere around Sikh extremists in his community and were ignored; to family members who felt that "the families have been treated like dirt the majority of the last 21 years";[103] and others who feel strongly that "had this been a tragedy that affected mainstream white Anglo-Saxon Canadians...the response would have been very different;"[104] and, finally, those like Mr. Bedi, who lost his wife and two kids, and feels that "I should never want to be an Indian-born Canadian, because nobody cares for you";[105] Indo-Canadians have named racism as a factor in the pre-bombing threat assessment and the post-bombing response. We can choose to see their responses as simply born of grief or we can pay attention. An Angus Reid poll from May 9 to 10, 2007, shows that a third of all Canadians, and 41–43 per cent in British Columbia and Ontario, agree that race played a factor in the Canadian response to the Air India bombings.[106]

Notes

1. *The Impact of Systemic Racism on Canada's Pre-Bombing Threat Assessment and Post-Bombing Response to the Air India Bombings* was originally submitted to the Commission of Inquiry into the Investigation of the Bombing of Air India Flight 182 in 2007.
2. Toni Williams, "Racism in Justice: The Report of the Commission on Systemic Racism in the Ontario Criminal Justice System," in *(Ab)Using Power: The Canadian Experience*, ed. Susan C. Boyd, Dorothy E. Chunn, and Robert Menzies (Halifax, NS: Fernwood Publishing, 2001), 209.
3. Ibid., 208.
4. Sherene Razack, ed., *Race, Space and the Law: Unmapping a White Settler Society* (Toronto: Between the Lines, 2002).
5. Himani Bannerji, *The Dark Side of Nation: Essays on Multiculturalism, Nationalism and Gender* (Toronto: Canadian Scholars' Press, 2000).
6. Sherene Razack, "'Simple Logic': The Identity Documents Rule and the Fantasy of a Nation Besieged and Betrayed," *Journal of Law and Social Policy* 15 (2000): 183–211; Sherene Razack, "Making Canada White: Law and the Policing of Bodies of Colour in the 1990s," *Canadian Journal of Law and Society* 14, no. 1 (Spring 1999): 159–184; Sunera Thobani, *Exalted Subjects: Studies in the Making of Race and Nation in Canada* (Toronto: University of Toronto Press, 2007).
7. Sherene Razack, *Dark Threats and White Knights: The Somalia Affair, Peacekeeping and the New Imperialism* (University of Toronto Press, 2004).
8. Pat McNenly, "Eggleton Asks All Toronto to Share Indian Sorrow," *Toronto Star*, June 25, 1985, A9.
9. *Saskatoon Star-Phoenix*, "One-Third of Minorities Face Discrimination," September 30, 2003, B6.
10. Sherene Razack, *Looking White People in the Eye: Gender, Race and Culture in Courtrooms and Classrooms* (Toronto: University of Toronto Press, 1998).
11. Doreen Indra, "South Asian Stereotypes in the Vancouver Press," *Ethnic and Racial Studies* 2, no. 2 (1979): 164–187.

12. Minelle Mahtani, "Representing Minorities: Canadian Media and Minority Identities," *Canadian Ethnic Studies* 33, no. 3 (2001): 93–133.
13. Yasmin Jiwani, *Discourses of Denial: Mediations of Race, Gender, and Violence* (Vancouver: UBC Press, 2006), 47.
14. Gladys L. Symons, "Police Constructions of Race and Gender in Street Gangs," in *Crimes of Colour: Racialization and the Criminal Justice System*, ed. Wendy Chan and Kiran Mirchandani (Peterborough, ON: Broadview Press, 2002).
15. Jiwani, *Discourses of Denial*, 50.
16. Ibid., 36.
17. Teun A. van Dijk, *Elite Discourse and Racism* (Newbury Park, CA: Sage Publications, 1993).
18. Williams, "Racism in Justice," 208.
19. Wayne Douglas quoted in Government of Canada, *Commission of Inquiry into the Investigation of the Bombing of Air India Flight 182: Public Hearing Transcripts*, May 28, 2007 (Ottawa: Minister of Public Works and Government Services, 2006–2007), 4109.
20. Warden quoted in *Saskatoon Star-Phoenix*, "Seeming Coverup of Air India Mess Worst Revelation," May 11, 2007, A12.
21. Bob Rae, *Lessons to Be Learned: The Report of the Honourable Bob Rae, Independent Advisor to the Minister of Public Safety and Emergency Preparedness on Outstanding Questions with Respect to the Bombing of Air India Flight 182* (Ottawa: Air India Review Secretariat, 2005).
22. CAA 1086, CSIS, "Report to Bob Rae," Air India Review, 3 of 12, in Government of Canada, *Commission of Inquiry into the Investigation of the Bombing of Air India Flight 182: Dossier on Terrorism, Intelligence and Law Enforcement—Canada's Response to Sikh Terrorism*, February 19, 2007 (Ottawa: Minister of Public Works and Government Services, 2007).
23. Superintendent Axel Hovbrender quoted in Government of Canada, *Public Hearing Transcripts*, May 24, 2007, 3921.
24. Ken MacQueen and John Geddes, "Air India Inquiry Reveals Intelligence Faults," *Maclean's*, May 28, 2007, accessed November 23, 2007, http://www.macleans.ca/article.jsp?content=20070528_105308_105308&source=srch.
25. Government of Canada, *Dossier on Terrorism*, 11.
26. Government of Canada, *Commission of Inquiry into the Investigation of the Bombing of Air India Flight 182: Dossier on Civil Aviation Security*, presented on October 23, 2007 (Ottawa: Minister of Public Works and Government Services, 2007), 23–25.
27. Ibid.
28. Government of Canada, *Dossier on Terrorism*, 11.
29. Government of Canada, *Dossier on Civil Aviation Security*, 20.

30. Dale Mattson quoted in Government of Canada, *Public Hearing Transcripts*, May 16, 2007, 3235.
31. St. John quoted in Government of Canada, *Public Hearing Transcripts*, May 29, 2007, 4231.
32. Government of Canada, *Dossier on Civil Aviation Security*, 40–41.
33. CAA 1086, CSIS, "Report to Bob Rae," Air India Review, 3 of 12.
34. CAC 0517, Memo: Minutes of Warren Sweeney, NCIB Coordinating Centre, 2 of 5, January 9, 1986, in Government of Canada, *Commission of Inquiry into the Investigation of the Bombing of Air India Flight 182. Background Materials* (Ottawa: Minister of Public Works and Government Services, 1965, 1985, 1986, 1987, 1989, 1992, 1995, 1998).
35. Razack, "'Simple Logic.'"
36. Government of Canada, *Dossier on Civil Aviation Security*, 38.
37. Mattson quoted in Government of Canada, *Public Hearing Transcripts*, May 15, 2007, 3389.
38. Carignan quoted in Government of Canada, *Public Hearing Transcripts*, May 9, 2007, 2671.
39. MacQueen and Geddes, "Air India Inquiry."
40. Kenny quoted in Government of Canada, *Public Hearing Transcripts*, June 1, 2007, 4700.
41. Jean Barrette quoted in Government of Canada, *Public Hearing Transcripts*, June 4, 2007, 4785.
42. Pierre Cyr quoted in Government of Canada, *Public Hearing Transcripts*, June 4, 2007, 4825–4826.
43. Dr. Kathleen Sweet quoted in Government of Canada, *Public Hearing Transcripts*, June 6, 2007, 4988.
44. Ibid., 4990.
45. Government of Canada, *Dossier on Civil Aviation Security*, 14.
46. Whitaker quoted in Government of Canada, *Public Hearing Transcripts*, June 1, 2007, 4606.
47. Stephen Conrad quoted in Government of Canada, *Public Hearing Transcripts*, June 13, 2007, 5212.
48. Yves Duguay quoted in Government of Canada, *Public Hearing Transcripts*, June 14, 2007, 5290.
49. Sherene Razack, *Casting Out: Race and the Eviction of Muslims from Western Law and Politics* (Toronto: University of Toronto Press, 2007).
50. Government of Canada, *Dossier on Civil Aviation Security*, 40; Stoddart quoted in Government of Canada, *Public Hearing Transcripts*, November 6, 2007, 9090.

51. Captain Craig Hall quoted in Government of Canada, *Public Hearing Transcripts*, October 23, 2007, 8028–8029.
52. Government of Canada, *Dossier on Civil Aviation Security*, 40.
53. Whitaker quoted in Government of Canada, *Public Hearing Transcripts*, June 1, 2007, 4606.
54. Government of Canada, *Dossier on Civil Aviation Security*, 40.
55. Daryl Zelmer quoted in Government of Canada, *Public Hearing Transcripts*, May 4, 2007, 2368–2369.
56. Government of Canada, *Dossier on Terrorism*, 12.
57. Ibid., 12.
58. Ibid., 7.
59. Ibid., 13.
60. Ibid., 9–10.
61. Lynne Jarrette quoted in Government of Canada, *Public Hearing Transcripts*, May 3, 2007, 2197–2198.
62. Government of Canada, *Dossier on Terrorism*, 11.
63. SIRC Review entitled, "CSIS Activities in Regard to the Destruction of Air India Flight 182," in "Report to Bob Rae," Air India Review, 9, CAA1086, in Government of Canada, *Background Materials*.
64. CAA 0609, Cover Letter and Enclosed 3 Letters, Ron Atkey, Chairman, CSIS to J.R. Morden, Director, CSIS, December 18, 1987, in Government of Canada, *Background Materials*.
65. Don McLean quoted in Government of Canada, *Public Hearing Transcripts*, May 1, 2007, 2022.
66. Inkster quoted in Government of Canada, *Public Hearing Transcripts*, November 22, 2007, 10314.
67. Ibid.
68. Government of Canada, *Dossier on Terrorism*, 15.
69. Ibid.
70. Ibid., 16.
71. CAB 0821, CSIS HQ Telex regarding cooperation with RCMP, November 20, 1989, in Government of Canada, *Background Materials*.
72. CAB 0861, Memo, Margaret Purdy, Director Security to Air India Working Group, June 27, 1992, in Government of Canada, *Background Materials*.
73. CAA 0609, Cover Letter and Enclosed 3 Letters, Ron Atkey, Chairman, CSIS to J.R. Morden, Director, CSIS, December 18, 1987.
74. Government of Canada, *Dossier on Terrorism*, 37.
75. Ibid., 39.
76. Ibid., 28.

77. Ibid., 29.

78. CAD 0184, Section 21 CSIS Act Intercept Procedure Circa 1985, August 28, 1998, employee B46, in Government of Canada, *Dossier on Civil Aviation Security*.

79. Government of Canada, *Dossier on Terrorism*, 33.

80. Ibid.

81. Government of Canada, *Dossier on Civil Aviation Security*, 40.

82. Gavin Stewart, Daniel Molgat, and Scott Heatherington quoted in Government of Canada, *Public Hearing Transcripts*, November 6, 2006, 1163–1165.

83. Lata Pada quoted in Government of Canada, *Public Hearing Transcripts*, September 25, 2006, 64.

84. B.N. Kirpal, *Report of the Court Investigating Accident to Air India Boeing 747 Aircraft VT-EFO, "Kanishka" on June 23 1985*, High Court of Delhi, February 26, 1986, 13.

85. Mamak quoted in Government of Canada, *Public Hearing Transcripts*, September 26, 2006, 143.

86. Ibid., 145.

87. Ibid., 147.

88. Gavin Stewart quoted in Government of Canada, *Public Hearing Transcripts*, November 6, 2006, 1165–1166.

89. Ibid.

90. CAE 0219, Minutes, Air India Disaster Meeting, June 24, 1985, 1 of 2, in Government of Canada, *Background Materials*.

91. CAE 0261, Minutes, Air India Disaster Meeting, June 27, 1985, 2 of 2, in Government of Canada, *Background Materials*.

92. Gupta quoted in Michael Farber, "Canada Fails Us: Air-India Mourners," *Montreal Gazette*, June 28, A1.

93. Mamak quoted in Government of Canada, *Public Hearing Transcripts*, September 26, 2006, 148–153.

94. Satrajpal Rai quoted in Government of Canada, *Public Hearing Transcripts*, September 25, 2006, 103–105.

95. Ibid., 103.

96. Ibid., 107.

97. Pada quoted in Government of Canada, *Public Hearing Transcripts*, September 25, 2006, 72.

98. Hoffman quoted in Government of Canada, *Public Hearing Transcripts*, March 9, 2007, 1851.

99. Ibid.

100. Mark Kingwell, "Indian Community Pooling Money to Offer Reward in Air India Crash," *Globe and Mail*, July 6, 1985, 15.

101. CAA 0923, Draft Aide-Memoire, sent to Jim Concoran, SIRC from Paul Dubrule, Director General, National Security, October 11, 1995, 7 of 9, in Government of Canada, *Background Materials*.

102. Robert Desjardin quoted in Government of Canada, *Public Hearing Transcripts*, November 8, 2006, 1310–1311.

103. Rattan Mall, "Bob Rae Fails to See Racism in Reactions to Air India Bombing—Is He Really so DUMB?" *Voice Online*, October 7, 2006, accessed November 23, 2007, http://wwwceonline.com/voice/061007/headline4.php.

104. Lata Pada, who lost her husband and two children, quoted in *Canadian Broadcasting Corporation*, "Calls Mount for Air India Inquiry as Racism Alleged," March 18, 2005, accessed November 23, 2007, http://www.cbc.ca/canada/story/2005/03/17/families-air-india050317.html.

105. Bedi quoted in Ajit Jain, "21 Years Later, Bedi Believes Daughter Survived Kanishka Bombing," *Rediff.com*, September 27, 2006, accessed November 23, 2007, http://rediff.com/cms/print.jsp?docpath=//news/2006/sep/27ai.htm.

106. Angus Reid Strategies, " Terrorism: Canadians Assess Blame in Air India Bombing," May 15, 2007, accessed November 23, 2007, http://web.archive.org/web/20071021233321rn_1/angus-reid.com/polls/view/15745.

Works Cited

Bannerji, Himani. *The Dark Side of Nation: Essays on Multiculturalism, Nationalism and Gender*. Toronto: Canadian Scholars' Press, 2000.

Government of Canada. *Commission of Inquiry into the Investigation of the Bombing of Air India Flight 182: Background Materials*. Ottawa: Minister of Public Works and Government Services, 1965, 1985, 1986, 1987, 1989, 1992, 1995, 1998.

———. *Commission of Inquiry into the Investigation of the Bombing of Air India Flight 182: Dossier on Civil Aviation Security*. Presented on October 23, 2007. Ottawa: Minister of Public Works and Government Services, 2007.

———. *Commission of Inquiry into the Investigation of the Bombing of Air India Flight 182: Dossier on Terrorism, Intelligence and Law Enforcement—Canada's Response to Sikh Terrorism*. February 19, 2007. Ottawa: Minister of Public Works and Government Services, 2007.

———. *Commission of Inquiry into the Investigation of the Bombing of Air India Flight 182: Public Hearing Transcripts*. Ottawa: Minister of Public Works and Government Services, 2006–2007.

Indra, Doreen. "South Asian Stereotypes in the Vancouver Press." *Ethnic and Racial Studies* 2, no. 2 (1979): 164–187.

Jiwani, Yasmin. *Discourses of Denial: Mediations of Race, Gender, and Violence*. Vancouver: UBC Press, 2006.

Kirpal, B.N. *Report of the Court Investigating Accident to Air India Boeing 747 Aircraft VT-EFO, "Kanishka" on June 23 1985*. High Court of Delhi. February 26, 1986.

Mahtani, Minelle. "Representing Minorities: Canadian Media and Minority Identities." *Canadian Ethnic Studies* 33, no. 3 (2001): 93–133.

Rae, Bob. *Lessons to Be Learned: The Report of the Honourable Bob Rae, Independent Advisor to the Minister of Public Safety and Emergency Preparedness on Outstanding Questions with Respect to the Bombing of Air India Flight 182*. Ottawa: Air India Review Secretariat, 2005.

Razack, Sherene. *Casting Out: Race and the Eviction of Muslims from Western Law and Politics*. Toronto: University of Toronto Press, 2007.

———. *Dark Threats and White Knights: The Somalia Affair, Peacekeeping and the New Imperialism*. University of Toronto Press, 2004.

———. *Looking White People in the Eye: Gender, Race and Culture in Courtrooms and Classrooms*. Toronto: University of Toronto Press, 1998.

———. "Making Canada White: Law and the Policing of Bodies of Colour in the 1990s." *Canadian Journal of Law and Society* 14, no. 1 (Spring 1999): 159–184.

———, ed. *Race, Space and the Law: Unmapping a White Settler Society*. Toronto: Between the Lines, 2002.

———. "'Simple Logic': The Identity Documents Rule and the Fantasy of a Nation Besieged and Betrayed." *Journal of Law and Social Policy* 15 (2000): 183–211.

Symons, Gladys L. "Police Constructions of Race and Gender in Street Gangs." In *Crimes of Colour: Racialization and the Criminal Justice System*, edited by Wendy Chan and Kiran Mirchandani, 115–125. Peterborough, ON: Broadview Press, 2002.

Thobani, Sunera. *Exalted Subjects: Studies in the Making of Race and Nation in Canada*. Toronto: University of Toronto Press, 2007.

Van Dijk, Teun A. *Elite Discourse and Racism*. Newbury Park, CA: Sage Publications, 1993.

Williams, Toni. "Racism in Justice: The Report of the Commission on Systemic Racism in the Ontario Criminal Justice System." In *(Ab)Using Power: The Canadian Experience*, edited by Susan C. Boyd, Dorothy E. Chunn, and Robert Menzies, 200–213. Halifax, NS: Fernwood Publishing, 2001.

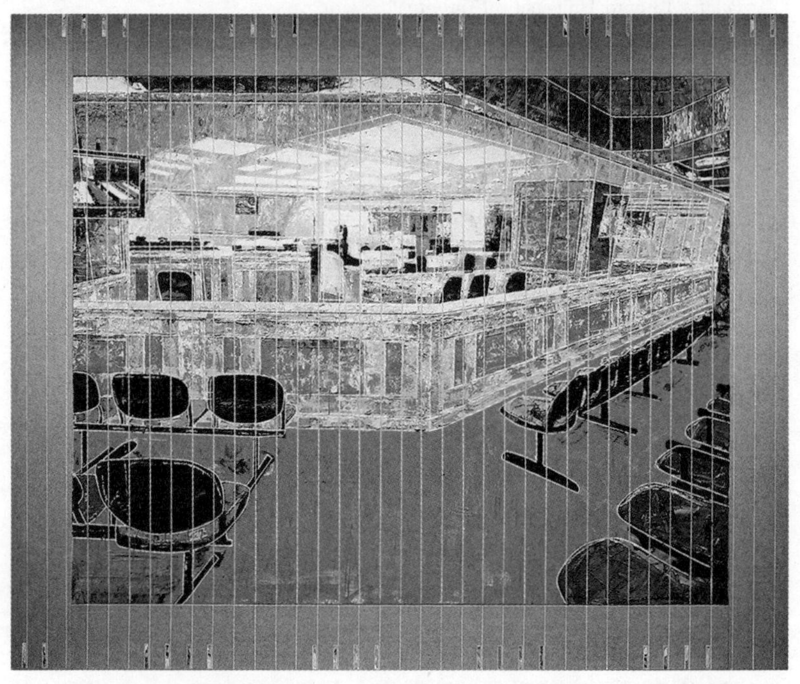

Deon Venter, Courtroom #1 *from the* Flight 182 *series, 2007. Oil on linen. 82" x 100".*

■

In the Vestibule of the Nation

SHERENE H. RAZACK

AS THE EXPERT WITNESS on racism at the Inquiry into the Investigation of the Bombing of Air India Flight 182, I learned first-hand about my place in the nation. Summoned to Ottawa to be cross-examined on my report on the role that racism played in the events before and after the bombing, I was struck by the extent of the disrespect shown to me by the lawyer representing the Attorney General of Canada, Barney Brucker. Of course, belligerence is par for the course in cross-examinations, but I was nevertheless surprised, not only at what I experienced as Brucker's brutish manner but by the fact that he could approach the task at hand armed only with innuendo and wildly inaccurate summaries of my political and academic views. Seeking to establish that I was an activist rather than a bona fide academic with more than twenty years of work on racism and the law, Brucker addressed my participation at the World Conference against Racism in Durban, South Africa, in 2001, an event he characterized as one where there was a great deal of anti-Semitism. Guilty by association, he triumphantly proclaimed that I was more of an activist than an academic, and possibly an anti-Semitic one to boot. This was followed by a shot at my strange belief that Canada was a colonial society. In a voice that seemed to me to be dripping with sarcasm, Brucker asked, " The white settler society as I understand the way you express it has certain connotations and is there—is that a universally held view among sociologists or is it a view that's held by you and a number of authors that you cite?"[1] Momentarily thrown by this stunning and yet predictable response of the Canadian government to the argument that racism exists in Canada, I replied that white settler colonialism was a well-established fact that few academics would dispute. While I imagine that many legal analysts would see in this interaction merely an example of crude lawyering, I am sure that few people of colour will miss the point of the performance. Whether as academic or complainant, if we dare to say that racism exists in Canada, we will be met with contempt. If, under the watchful gaze of the commissioner of the inquiry, the expert witness meets with such contempt, how will the families of the victims be treated? That day, my Brown skin and theirs seemed to mean the same thing. Outsiders to the nation, we learned that skin was the limit point of citizenship.

In her essay, Maya Seshia recounts the ways that victims' families articulated their eviction from the nation. As they tried to deal with the trauma of identifying the bodies recovered from the sea, they found they could not turn to their state for help. Speaking of the limited role of Canadian officials at Cork, Ireland, the site where the bodies were brought for identification, one man's words summed up the families' experience: "It's almost like we never existed. I'm a Canadian citizen."[2] Treated as outsiders to the nation at the time, a small shift occurred following 9/11 and, crucially, after vigorous lobbying efforts by victims' families. From a tragedy not of Canadian making to a Canadian experience of terrorism, the shift in the government's response, Seshia suggests, was more likely due to the state's need to win support for its anti-terrorism initiatives than it was due to any genuine acknowledgement that Canadians of Indian origin are, in fact, Canadian. Indeed, the recognition that Canadians died in the crash came at a cost: new anti-terrorism legislation that targets anyone with Brown skin.

It is not surprising that the inquiry concluded that racism was not a factor either in the events leading up to the bombings or in the treatment of families following the bombings. It is, however, instructive. Brown Canadians are served notice that we do not exist as citizens. Nothing committed against us can be considered a crime, an observation Giorgio Agamben made about the inmates of concentration camps, airport detention centres, and camps for illegal migrants that proliferate in the First World under the banner of emergency. Agamben noted that in such spaces, law has authorized its own suspension. It becomes legal to deny fundamental rights to anyone in such spaces, all in the interest of national security.[3] The camps' inmates are thus inside and outside the law, a space of indeterminacy that Deon Venter captures brilliantly in his depiction of *Courtroom #1*, from the *Flight 182* series.

In Venter's painting, we see the boundaries of law. There is a wood-panelled inner sanctum closed off from the spectators. The painting shows the empty chairs bordering the sanctum. The spectators are absent, invisible, and therefore not witness to the legal proceedings. We should remember that secret evidence is a cornerstone of much anti-terrorism legislation. The chairs are the kind one finds in airport lounges. The airport, of course, resembles the space of indeterminacy of the camp; it is a kind of no man's land in which security concerns trump individual rights. It is not hard to imagine who might fill the seats on the outside of the wood-panelled inner room. The painting invites us to see those who wait for entry into the nation as the same ones who wait for justice. We can imagine refugees seeking asylum or new immigrants entering Canada for the first time and learning at the airport that their status is an indeterminate one, neither in the nation nor outside of it. The floor of this waiting room is red; it is a place where blood flows. I am reminded of the work of African American theorist Hortense Spillers, who has described African slaves as evicted from humanity, bodies who wait in the vestibule of modernity, a place where the slave owner knows that violence against the slave is entirely legal.[4]

The Canadian citizens who died in the Air India bombings were symbolically and materially evicted from the category of citizens (the prime minister at the time saw them as Indian nationals), stranded outside the nation, in this case literally, in the ocean or at Cork, Ireland. These bodies are not grievable, to use Judith Butler's term. She asks, "Who counts as human? Whose lives count as lives? And, finally, what *makes for a grievable life?*"[5] States often reply to these questions by asserting that non-citizens' lives are not as grievable as citizens' lives. In viewing the victims of the bombings as Indian nationals, the state was asserting the limits of its care and grieving. Evictions from the nation are spatial events, as Venter's painting shows. The bodies of the victims were abandoned to the care of the Irish state (by all accounts, a generous state at the time), and to the care of their families. Canada offered only grudging help, as all the victims' families attested during the inquiry. Insisting on legal personhood, the families spoke of their experiences of racism. Racism, the commissioner of the inquiry concluded, was not helpful to describe how the families were treated. The seats of *Courtroom 1* were filled by nonpersons, those whom the law does not recognize.

Notes

1. Government of Canada, *Commission of Inquiry into the Investigation of the Bombing of Air India Flight 182: Public Hearing Transcripts* (Ottawa: Minister of Public Works and Government Services, 2008), 12734.
2. See Seshia in this volume.
3. Giorgio Agamben, *Homo Sacer: Sovereign Power and Bare Life*, trans. Daniel Heller-Roazen (Palo Alto, CA: Stanford University Press, 1998).
4. Hortense Spillers, "Mama's Baby, Papa's Maybe: An American Grammar Book," *Diacritics* 17, no. 2 (1987): 65–81.
5. Judith Butler, *Precarious Life: The Powers of Mourning and Violence* (London: Verso Books, 2004), 20.

Works Cited

Agamben, Giorgio. *Homo Sacer: Sovereign Power and Bare Life.* Translated by Daniel Heller-Roazen. Palo Alto, CA: Stanford University Press, 1998.

Butler, Judith. *Precarious Life: The Powers of Mourning and Violence.* London: Verso Books, 2004.

Government of Canada. *Commission of Inquiry into the Investigation of the Bombing of Air India Flight 182: Public Hearing Transcripts*. Ottawa: Minister of Public Works and Government Services, 2008.

Spillers, Hortense. "Mama's Baby, Papa's Maybe: An American Grammar Book." *Diacritics* 17, no. 2 (1987): 65–81.

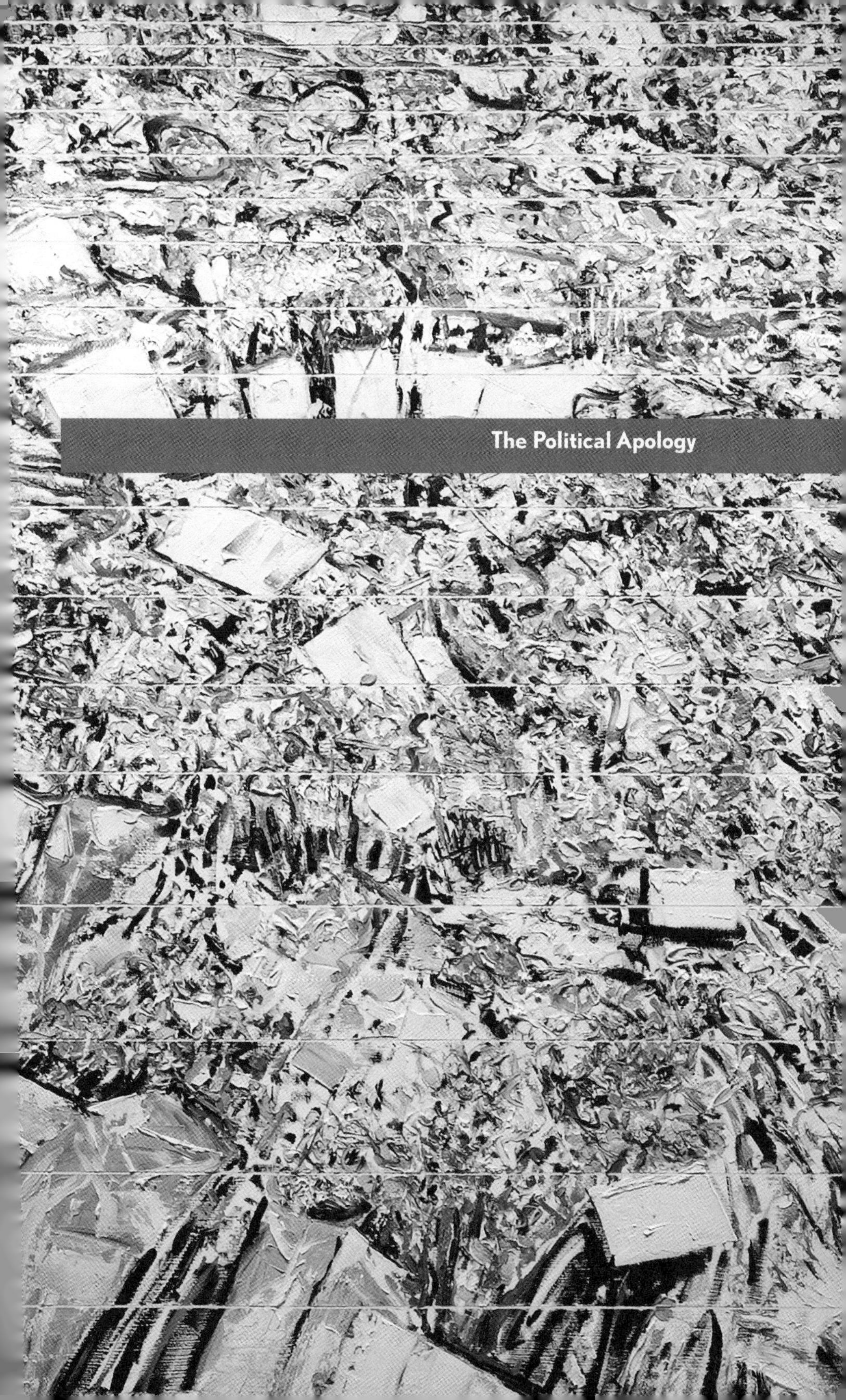

The Political Apology

Overleaf: Deon Venter, King's Cross #1, Flower Memorial *(detail) from the* Flight 182 *series, 2008. Oil on linen. 39" x 73". Copyright © Deon Venter, reprinted by permission of the artist. Photo by David Borrowman.*

Politics of (Im)moderation

The Production of South Asian Identities in the Canadian Apology for Air India Flight 182

CASSEL BUSSE

Introduction

"Everything in moderation" is a phrase that we are used to hearing applied as a standard for anything from state governance to spending and personal diet. Although "moderation" has arguably become the bedrock for the formation of a racialized, gendered, and classed democratic imaginary, the term itself seems neither solid nor immutable.[1] Tracing the social and political use of moderation to Aristotle, one of the originary and most influential philosophers on the subject, reveals this inconstancy.[2] In his *Nicomachean Ethics*, Aristotle asserts that to be moderate is to be affected "at the right times, with reference to the right objects, towards the right people, with the right motive, and in the right way."[3] The modern definition of moderation according to the *Oxford English Dictionary* is to exert an "avoidance of excess or extremes in behaviour" and exhibit "temperateness, self-control, [and] restraint."[4] From these definitions, which invoke avoidance, *self*-control, and affect, it seems that moderation in both its classical roots and contemporary usage is a judgement shaped by the atmosphere or context one currently resides in or experiences, not an objective rule or measure one may draw upon. To choose what is right in the interest of moderation is to orient or align oneself with the norms, values, affects, and politics of the community, society, or nation-state in which one resides.

While such a concerted effort against the excessive may seem like nothing more than "common sense," this essay will examine moderation as a means of encapsulating what makes Others Other, particularly those perceived as outside of a Western epistemological and ontological frame. More specifically, I would like to draw attention to the racialized characterizations of moderate and immoderate behaviour in the discourse surrounding former Prime Minister Stephen Harper's apology for the failure of the Canadian government to recognize Air India Flight 182's tragic end on June 23, 1985, as a Canadian loss. This flight had departed Montreal *despite* the warnings of several parties—including Air India and the Indian government—that there was a risk of explosives on board. Flight 182's final destination would have been Delhi, India, had it not exploded over the Atlantic Ocean in Irish airspace due to a bomb that had escaped the attention of luggage security, killing 329 passengers who were predominantly of South Asian descent.[5] The suspected perpetrators were three Indian Sikh separatists, whose political motives were used by criminal investigators and the Government of Canada to dismiss the "Air India bombings and their resultant deaths as matters of national urgency."[6] As a result, twenty-two years passed before the government launched an official inquiry in 2006; by this time, two of the accused had been acquitted.

In what follows, I will critique the political agenda of the Canadian government's framing of the attack on Air India Flight 182 by analyzing the racialized binary of liberal moderation/political immoderation in Prime Minister Stephen Harper's 2010 apology. Such a binary produces an ideological apparatus of state power in two ways. First, state power is produced in relation to the ways in which the nation-state of Canada becomes depoliticized through the discourse of tolerance, the removal of the "culture" that makes an individual or community ethnically, religiously, or politically marked, and the overarching structure of progressive modernity in the Canadian social landscape. Second, it is produced through the delineation of the borders of liberalist Canada and its project of white ascendancy through the dichotomization of "model" and "terrorist" South Asian populations. In this formation, the former subject is made to support dominant Canadian claims of inclusion and tolerance while the latter is made an object for the displacement of state power manipulations such as the everyday exclusions of racial, religious, gendered, and sexualized Others, and the economic gains of a predominantly white, male minority. Simply put, the "terrorist" configuration of South Asian identity in the aftermath of the attack on Flight 182 comes *to inhabit the political* as a figure of immoderate, fundamentalist ethnicity.[7]

My analysis interrogates a single political address at a specific historical moment and thus cannot claim to fully represent the complexities of the relationship between multicultural states and their "minorities," or the demonization of certain subjects as "terrorists." Indeed, even a historical moment as specific as the bombing of Flight 182 is deeply connected to a multitude of other histories of discrimination and violence that exceed the scope of a singular nation, political speech, or academic perspective; however, an analysis of Harper's 2010 apology might reveal *some* of the racist inner workings of Canadian multiculturalism and state governance, and serve to question the xenophobic identity formations implicit in the construction of a "moderate" Western political culture.

The Feeling of Multicultural Nationhood

Canada is a nation that prides itself on its moderate political climate, democratic neutrality, and vision of progressive futures. While Canada's claim to moderation is built upon an array of national concerns, including economics and a neutral, even "lenient," style of governance and peacekeeping abroad, the nation is frequently associated with multicultural diversity and the tolerance of Others, especially in comparison with the American assimilationist "melting pot."[8] That the nation evokes a feeling of liberalism and political moderation brings us back to Aristotle's theorization of good social behaviour as contingent upon environmental and emotional contexts; just as moderation is dependent upon the right time, persons, occasions, and objects, so, too, does a national feeling or affect depend upon *who*, *when*, and *where* one is. In *The Cultural Politics of Emotion*, Sara Ahmed argues that "emotionality as a claim *about* a subject or a collective is clearly dependent on relations of power, which endow 'others' with meaning and value."[9] To *feel* included in a national character and therefore a national "we" is to have acceptance into a "form of racial kindred,"[10] particularly in nations such as England (Ahmed's locus of analysis) or Canada, which are regarded as predominantly white nations that have become open to non-white immigration. As cultural theorist Himani Bannerji argues, the *feeling* of Canadian "open-mindedness" depends upon "visible minorities" to provide an image of liberalism. Yet, despite this dependence on difference for the good feelings of Canadian pluralism, cultural difference also "denotes the power of definition that 'Canadians' have over 'others.'"[11] This is an unequal power that manifests in many ways, from the racial "segmentation of the labour market in Canada" to the poor quality of life on Indigenous reserves, to the lack of diversity in seats of governance.[12] Moreover, the common characterization of Canada's international relations through peacekeeping and foreign aid is questionable in light of many incidents such as the torture of innocent captives in a military mission in southern Afghanistan in 2006 and 2007,[13] and former Prime Minister Harper's freezing of funds for foreign aid and women's health rights in 2010.[14] Thus, the synonymity of cultural neutrality, nonviolence, and "Canadian-ness" can be revealed as a complex ideology that becomes specifically *felt* and discursively supported by a dominant white population with relation to its so-called Others. A narrative of Canadian liberal governance and peaceful diversity exists in spite of the realities of systemic racism that occur nationally and internationally; a narrative of multicultural nationhood denies any accusations of violence, discrimination, and power manipulation on behalf of the nation or its government. This ideology has been maintained by the Canadian government's public expression of political neutrality and liberal conduct, even though Canada has been presently and historically involved in colonization, war, and globalized economic exploitation. This contradiction between narratives of Canadian cultural tolerance and the reality of the nation's ongoing legacy of colonial occupation and violence is particularly evident in Harper's multiple addresses to various marginalized communities in the form of the state apology.

An apology is itself an act of moderation. It is an extension of a hand or a gesture of humility toward a subject or party the apologizer has previously opposed, injured, or excluded. We might say that an apology is an effort to "meet in the middle," an act that admits the wrongs of previous acts of injury. For the Harper Government, the subjects of apology varied from Indigenous victims of residential schools to the Chinese Head Tax, examples of Canada's ongoing history of overt and systemic racial violence in and of themselves. For the purposes of this inquiry, I will now turn to the 2010 apology for the delayed Canadian response to the Air India Flight 182 tragedy.

The Rhetoric of the Apologetic: Maintaining a Blameless Nation

The purpose of the Canadian government's apology to its South Asian community was to recognize the shameful delay in response to the Air India tragedy of 1985, and then Prime Minister Brian Mulroney's inability to conceive of these attacks as a Canadian crime that victimized its citizens. Yet, as many theorists—Jacques Derrida, Elizabeth Povinelli, and Sara Ahmed, to name a few—have noted, national apologies frequently function not only as platforms from which to acknowledge historical trauma but also as sites of political rallying and the alignment of citizen affect with state interest. In *On Cosmopolitanism and Forgiveness*, Derrida writes,

> *when the body of the nation can, without risk, support a minor division, or even finds its unity reinforced by trials, by opening the archives, by the lifting of repression...it is always the same concern: to see to it that the nation survives its discords, that the traumatisms give way to the work of mourning, and that the Nation-State not be overcome by paralysis.*[15]

By exposing the error of a previous government, an apology has the power to bring the addressed victims to the same side of history that the state envisions itself to be on through shared mourning. As Harper iterated in his 2010 apology, "your pain is our pain. As you grieve, we grieve."[16] In this superficial and rhetorical unification of the state and its South Asian minority, Canada's history of discrimination against South Asians was elided, if not altogether forgotten. Indeed, the infamous 1914 turning away of the *Komagata Maru*—a ship filled with 376 Indian immigrants of Sikh, Muslim, and Hindu ethnicity—was not even a century behind us, and was followed by a series of quota restrictions on South Asian immigration to Canada that were not abandoned until the 1960s.[17] In 2008, the Sikh community in Surrey, British Columbia, rejected Harper's apology for the racism of the *Komagata Maru* incident. According to Jaswinder Singh Toor, president of the Descendants of Komagata Maru Society at the time of the attempted apology, Harper ignored requests to apologize officially in Parliament, as he had done in his apology for the Chinese Head Tax and the forced assimilation of Indigenous children in Canada's residential school system.[18] During Harper's leadership, no formal resolve was reached that satisfied the Indo-Canadians who received this apology, making clear the fact that national reconciliation for Harper was only a performance. It is problematically the state, and not its victims, that dictate the reparations of traumatic histories.[19]

In his apology for the treatment of Air India victims, Harper made a distinction between the "scant respect and consideration" of Indo-Canadians in Canada's *past*,[20] and the conciliation and shared mourning of the *present* in his public apology for Air India Flight 182, an assertion of state racism as historical that breaks down in his 2008 dismissal of the validity of many South Asian Canadians' disputation of the Surrey address. The very rhetorical structure of the statement "as *you* grieve, *we* grieve" seems to reiterate the ethnic and national divisions that Harper's apology supposedly attempts to denounce.[21] Although the "you" of this excerpt is clearly directed toward the friends and families of those lost in the Air India catastrophe, the insinuation of "we" is far more opaque, particularly as it is immediately followed by Harper's insistence that "*Canadians* now understand that this atrocity was conceived in Canada [emphasis added]."[22] Who counts as "we," or as Canadian? Does this pronoun claim a kind of origination or nonhyphenation of Canadian identity? Is it the "we" who bestow either racism or tolerance onto Others and are thus a perceived white Canadian majority? Though these questions cannot be definitively answered, it would seem that the opposition of "you" and "we" reveals a point of ongoing binary opposition, of a tenuousness of national belonging and a narrative of Othering that is not reconciled even in the public act of "truth and reconciliation."

That previous *and* present examples of racism and failed reconciliation are evaded in the attempt to gain political support from present-day minorities is in keeping with Derrida's observation that national apology is not actually a space of retrospect but of calculated forward momentum. Histories of racism are not recognized as lengthy narratives of systemic and objective violence against Indo- and other South Asian Canadians that continue in the present but are rather used to reinforce a rift between the arcane, violent past and the already occurring egalitarian future. As Failler notes in her important work on Harper's speech at the 2007 unveiling of Toronto's Flight 182 Memorial, the commemoration of the bombings is actually more about *forgetting* than *remembering*, and so comes to be less about the "loss and losses of South Asian Canadians" and more focused upon "the project of maintaining a blameless nation state."[23] Although I will return to Failler's notion of forgetting in the rhetorical production of South Asian identities, I would like to move now to the depoliticization of racism and the elision of state responsibility at work in Harper's 2010 Flight 182 apology.

Depoliticizing State Violence

The concept of tolerance, defined as the "action or practice of tolerating" and the "*disposition* to be patient with or indulgent to the opinions or practices of others [emphasis added],"[24] is frequently a corollary of political moderation; just as moderation involves "temperateness" and self-restraint in one's actions and emotions, tolerance requires restraint and control in one's judgements and feelings toward others. Discourses of liberalism—written into the charters of many Western nations such as Canada's Charter of Rights and Freedoms—conjure images of moderate governance and tolerance toward "diverse" communities. Yet, as Wendy Brown points out in *Regulating Aversion*, tolerance is often a means of "distinguishing 'us' from 'them,'" contributing to the construction of the West as politically and culturally exceptional when compared to the supposedly anachronistic attitudes of non-Western nations.[25] This logic of exceptional tolerance is asserted by Harper in the 2007 address at the unveiling of Toronto's Flight 182 Memorial, when he claims "there is no doubt all of us, no matter where we came from, are among the most fortunate people in the world. We share a country that is strong and united."[26] The language of fortune—that is, of outstanding good circumstance or exception—presents a uniqueness of Canadian social harmony that defines itself comparatively through the insinuated misfortune, strife, and dissonance of other nations.[27] Thus, moderation and its emergent trait of tolerance produce depoliticizing and de-culturing effects capable of shoring up the non-Western Other as *over*-politicized and laden with "culture" and "ethnicity." As part of a white Western "civilization discourse," cultural and political moderation operates under the "conceit of neutrality,"[28] positioning the ethnic, religious, or political Other as diametrically opposed and threatening to white liberal peace and progressive sociality.

The conceit of Canadian cultural neutrality and depoliticized governance, conferred onto the nation through images such as the multicultural "mosaic," allowed Harper to assert in his Air India apology that the real lesson to be learned from Flight 182 is that politicized violence is not found within Canada but beyond its borders. In his apology for the government's response to the Air India crisis, Harper did attend to the "disdain" and "sanitization" of the Canadian government's response to the Indian government's warning of potential attack, and lack of resolve in the aftermath of the bombing. He even went so far as to declare that the 1985 bombing was "conceived in Canada, executed in Canada, by Canadian citizens."[29] However, this seemingly forthright concession is emptied of any reparative function that it may at first glance perform. Despite Harper's criticism of the "disdain" toward minorities demonstrated in the Air India tragedy, many of the victims' families accused the Harper Government of disrespect with regards to the low amount of compensation offered (CAD $20–25,000) and the purposeful exclusion of family members and their legal representatives from inquiry meetings.[30] Moreover, that the Harper Government admitted to the wrongdoing of all "the years during which [the victims' families'] legitimate need for answers and indeed, for empathy, were treated with administrative disdain"[31] but did not address the racism behind the state's lack of action is revealing of a continued desire to keep Canada's multicultural record untarnished *over and above* the need to address differential treatment of racialized subjects in Canada. To return to Derrida's criticism of state apology, the prime minister ensured the unity of the nation through a careful opening of the archives and a calculated bearing of faults achieved by proclaiming the bombing of Air India Flight 182 a "Canadian tragedy," while simultaneously destabilizing the Canadian-ness of its perpetrators through the focus on external political motivations. Although Harper began his apology by foregrounding the importance of recognizing the attack as an act of terrorism within Canadian borders, the ultimate line of action described in the apology and in the 2010 final report makes no mention of an inquiry into state-sanctioned discrimination in Canada and its relationship to the laxity of security measures and the absence of governmental action after the bombing. All measures described in the 2010 apology identify the problem of Flight 182 as one of *external* terrorist threat. Harper asserted that what must be done in the aftermath of this national crisis is not an address of the *present-day* racial and xenophobic discrimination that bear upon the state's relationship with its diverse communities; rather, he declared that alongside the fortification of airline security, we must "marginalize, carefully and systematically marginalize, those extremists who seek to import the battles of India's past here and then export them back to that great and forward-looking nation."[32]

In the context of the entire apology delivered by the then prime minister, this statement contains a number of ironies and contradictions. By describing the political aims of the Sikh separatist bombers as "imported" and "exported" extremism from "India's past," these figures are made to appear as perverse free radicals wandering between, but disenfranchised from, the "forward-looking" India and Canada of the here and now. One might question how an India invested in futurity and "progressive" modernity produces what Harper sees as anachronistic citizens, particularly considering that Sikh separatism is not only a product of modern geopolitics arising from the British government's 1947 Partition of India but is also an ongoing conflict in India and Canada.[33] Harper's relegation of Sikh separatism to the past and his representation of an India emptied of its citizens and present political climate certainly warrant investigations of their own, but for the purposes of this discussion I will be focusing on the contradictory elision of racism as a form of political violence in Harper's address. What I seek to question is this: If the bombing of Air India Flight 182 "was not a foreign act of violence" but an "outrage...made in Canada,"[34] then why are Canadians focusing their anti-terrorism vigilance on Indian "extremists" alone? Within the logic of Canadian tolerance and moderate political attitudes, acts of terror are posited as part and parcel of an "ethnic" (read non-Canadian) identity that belongs to the archaism of India's past. This reasoning, in the language of Derrida, is the function of "ontopology," or the ontological value ascribed to "the phantasm of the sovereign nation" and its production of a false relationship between so-called national character and native soil.[35] With this assertion of Canadian ontopology, violence is codified as ethnically Indian and the racism against Indo-Canadians in the aftermath of the Air India tragedy can be couched in the language of "institutional failings" and general "disrespect."[36] Harper could say, without a trace of irony, that Canadians must *marginalize* South Asian Canadians who bear signs of extremism in spite of the fact that it was the marginalization of South Asian Canadians by the Canadian government that begot Harper's apology in the first place.

The depoliticization of the Canadian government and the investment of ethnic or national difference with the sign of extremism are further used to elide any inquiry into state-sanctioned racism through a kind of victimization of the nation. Repeating the conjured image of a white Canadian "majority," Harper declared, " We fear that when we invite from around the world, those who share our aspirations for a better life, others also come, those who see in our Canada, not new bridges to a hopeful future but only another chance to travel the old roads to the blood-feuds of the past."[37] Here Canada is positioned as a nation free of political motives or extremist actions, a nation that welcomes those who recognize the "better life" it offers. The comparative statement presents a binary in which immigrant Others come bringing violent hostility from somewhere else. What is introduced is the narrative of a nation that is exploited for the advantages it offers; Canada is, paradoxically, represented as being *too* moderate in its policies and attitudes. Indeed, as Ahmed argues in *The Cultural Politics of Emotion*, there is a conception that "the nation is made vulnerable to abuse by its very openness to others...to 'take in' is to be 'taken in.'"[38] In the persuasive structure of Harper's apology, the focus on specific citizens in the form of the many Indo-Canadians who perished in the bombing of Flight 182 is broadened to include Canada as victim. This conception of national victimization is problematic not only for what Failler identifies as the capitalization of white-dominated economies upon "racial grief"[39] but also for the diffusion, even elision, of responsibility for the loss and then dismissal of so many lives in the bombing of Flight 182. Through this discursive formation of Canada as a victim of foreign political violence, the sovereignty of the state is reasserted by the full transference of blame onto racialized, and thus externalized, "extremists."

Discourses of Terror

It is important to recognize that the discourse of "too open" or "too tolerant" is not necessarily unique to Canada; in fact, the rhetoric of a society antagonized for its democracy is directly linked to the language of the US " War on Terror." Just as George W. Bush had declared that the United States was attacked by a Middle Eastern militia group because it is "the brightest beacon for freedom and opportunity in the world,"[40] so, too, did Stephen Harper attribute the attack on Flight 182 to Canada's desire to welcome others into its "better life" and "hopeful future."[41] Despite the difference of national politics and motivations invested in 9/11 and the bombing of Air India Flight 182, it is certainly significant that the inquiry into the latter was reopened after the Taliban's attacks on the United States. As Failler argues, the bombing of Flight 182 "and its still-emerging legacy must be recognized for its impact on the Canadian national imagination in terms of how Canadians conceive of themselves...in the post-9/11 era of 'war on terror.'"[42] In other words, it is crucial to acknowledge how the dominant narrative of anti-terrorism vigilance and heightened xenophobia that has been adopted in 9/11's aftermath has affected the way in which the Air India disaster has been reconceptualized.

Of course, the argument has been made that in Canada's desire to include the upstanding and forward-thinking aspiration of Others, it was ultimately caught off guard by the Air India bombing. In this line of thought, the logical lesson to be learned is to strengthen surveillance and increase the policing of borders, even if the cost is a heightened suspicion toward those who bear the North American cultural signifier of terrorism: a non-white body.[43] There are a number of criticisms of this seemingly intuitive "logic," but in the context of Canada's dismissal of the Air India disaster and subsequent state apology, I would like to argue two points. First, this line of thought assumes that before the bombing of Flight 182, the surveillance and exclusion of non-white—specifically South Asian—immigration was not already systemically exercised. It follows from a false logic that insinuates that racialized outsiders have abused the trust the Canadian state extended toward them; in other words, "the nation was good to you, tolerated your differences and accepted you, and now look what has happened." The nation that *once* opened its doors will close them if it has learned its lesson properly; it is now forced to "carefully and systematically marginalize" Others, in the words of Prime Minister Stephen Harper.[44] I have called this logic false because it is clear from the history of Canadian racism outlined above that the marginalization of racial, ethnic, and religious minorities in Canada is not an emergency decision made only in the context of terrorism. It must be recognized that Air India Flight 182 was allowed to embark from Montreal with explosives in its cargo not simply because the Canadian government and airport administration had become lax on all flight security measures but because these Canadian officials elected to ignore the warnings of a potential attack on a flight that was bound to India, full of citizens who failed to fully qualify as "Canadian." The increased suspicion toward what Harper called "extremists who seek to import the battles of India's past" is a transformation—or perhaps merely a facet—of the conception of the already-marginalized non-white Other.[45] Thus, the increased marginalization of non-white Canadians and the tightening of xenophobic immigration policy after the bombing are in actuality justifications of existing racist power manipulations by the Canadian government that redirect "resources back towards the very institutions in question."[46] This justification maintains the conception of Canadian governmentality as moderate and rational, and formulates exclusion and domination as necessary, reasonable steps in the protection of all citizens. I would also like to point out that the "blown chance" logic of increased racialized exclusion and surveillance is contradictory to Harper's initial chronology of Canadian race relations in his 2010 apology: that the Canada of the past treated its Indo-Canadian population with disrespect but has progressed to recognition and inclusion in the present. This highly rhetorical line of reasoning also calls upon the vigilant efforts of Canadians ("it is incumbent upon us all") to take up a similar suspicion of Others on the "home front,"[47] translating citizenship "into a form of Neighbourhood Watch."[48] This suspicious citizenship differs vastly from Harper's encouragement to all Canadians to acknowledge the loss of Indo-Canadian lives as losses of "their own" at the beginning of his address.[49] The 2010 apology for the Air India tragedy thus puts forward two dissonant past/present binaries of the state's relationship with its minority populations. In these opposing temporalities of Canadian tolerance, a common element is reflected: the racism of the nation toward non-white Others, whether at home or abroad.

I am by no means suggesting that these attacks should be valourized and their aggressors exempted. Rather, I hope that in my critique of the depoliticization of Canadian governance and the displacement of the political onto the figure of the South Asian fundamentalist, I might describe the ways in which the construction of Canadian political moderation and tolerance can become a shifting, contingent "justification of [Western] imperial and colonial adventures" and motives.[50] Rather than acknowledge any connection between the colonial history expressed in the desire for a separate Sikh state in India and the suggestion by Indo-Canadians that their losses are differently and unequally treated by Canada,[51] political dissent and dissenting bodies are completely refigured by Harper as inhabiting an ontological state of being stuck in the rut of "old roads to the blood-feuds of the past,"[52] *facing backward* and against the grain of democratic moderation. This deflective discourse in the apology for the bombing of Flight 182 works to keep the construct of ethnic tolerance and political moderation in Canada untainted, and allows for the continued dismissal of racist politics in Canada in favour of the "grander narrative" of potential terror from the unknown.

"Model Minorities" and the Construction of Multicultural Nationhood

It is important to acknowledge that this portrayal of politicized actions and persons as always racialized, "culturalized," backward-facing, and external is not necessarily universally applied to all South Asian immigrants or citizens of South Asian ancestry. Indeed, as Bannerji explains in her work on the power structures inherent within Canadian "diversity," the continued sovereignty of a specific white masculine class of state officials and leadership depends upon the inclusion of some "visible minorities."[53] Thus, the typifying of the terrorist as irrational and anachronistic not only creates a dichotomy between white democratic Canada and "transient" South Asian terrorism but also polarizes the identity of South Asian immigrants between the extremes of terrorist and "model minority." In Virinder Kalra's sociological study on British stereotypes of South Asian masculinity, he notes the frequent oscillation between these two discursive figures: "one emphasizing patriarchy and aggression, and the other effeminacy and academicism."[54]

This binary is also exercised in narratives of nation-building new citizens versus "backward," dangerous immigrants in the United States. Jasbir Puar and Amit Rai note the "increasing polarization of model-minority diasporic populations and discourse, and those who may complicate or contaminate such discourses."[55] The authors define the "model minority" as a construct "applied to Asian American populations, with particular reference to South Asian Americans," who perform "economic exceptionalism, upward class mobility [and] educational excellence."[56] Puar and Rai note that model South Asian minorities are hierarchized on a scale of proximity to identities associated with "Osama bin Laden and other terrorist figures," placing more visibly "cultured" or "ethnic" South Asians such as Sikhs and Muslims with beards or turbans as "fringe" model minorities.[57] What these models expose is not simply a fear of terrorism or state interest in protecting the lives of its citizens; as we have witnessed in the dismissal of Flight 182 as not a Canadian concern, these discourses of "good" immigrants support the state's care for certain lives over others, a mode of preference tied to ongoing histories of colonialism, imperialism, and white ascendancy.

In his analogies of progressive versus regressive cultural politics, Harper's vision of "new bridges" functions according to Ahmed's concept of "happy objects," which project "good" migrants toward the promise of "happy futures," if they are ready to "leave the past behind them, where pastness is associated with the custom and the customary."[58] The subject who migrates to Canada is therefore rewarded for jettisoning an Indian past and embracing "a common culture that is already given";[59] this citizen can then be brought into the national fold when Canadian cultural identity is recognized as an opportunity for renewal, prosperity, and a future. Therefore, the upstanding immigrant disposes of any cultural or ethnic signifiers in identification with and support of white neoliberal values.[60]

This alignment, with "axes of privilege,"[61] occurs not only in the forgetting of a specifically Indian past but also in the forgetting of historical and/or current acts of white racism toward certain South Asian individuals and communities.[62] Harper's apology—not to mention previous commission reports and speeches—encourages a desire to forget Canadian racism alongside the "blood-feuds" of deepest, darkest Indian history. As Puar tells us, "the seduction by the global capital is conducted through racial amnesia, among *other forms of forgetting* [emphasis added]."[63] The induction to forgetting in Harper's apology is most visible in its structure, as it begins with a recognition of Canada's lack of care for its South Asian communities *in the past*; as the narrative of Harper's address progresses to the Canada of the present and future, the nation simply becomes a welcoming and modern space for "aspiring" immigrants,[64] making the apology itself a monument to Canada's own problematic but no longer present history. Interestingly, a similar amnesia about racism was repeated only a few days after this address in a parliamentary speech celebrating "Canada–India relations."[65] Unifying the political moderation and social advancement of Canada and India through the mutual bearing of "the scars of terrorism" and the "common cause against it," Harper further connected the interests of these two nations as "inheritors of the centuries-old and proven traditions of the Westminster system of parliamentary democracy."[66] In this statement, Harper effaced the unequal historical relationship Canada and India have had with the British Empire, evoking a shared history of progressive civilization that sanitizes the horrors of India's fight for independence from England, and the unresolved ethnic and territorial conflicts left in the wake of the British Partition of India in 1947.

Although there is not enough space here to delve deeply into the politics of Harper's celebration of renewed relations with India, it is important to briefly comment on the pervasiveness of the "progressive" national imaginary beyond a white, Canadian perspective. In claiming a celebration of "Canada–India relations," then Indian Prime Minister Manmohan Singh also enacted an elision of current and historical political tension, as his recrimination of Sikh terrorism avoided a long history of discrimination in India that continues to demonize Sikhs as radical fanatics.[67] Although Singh, himself a Sikh, may not have claimed that practicing Sikhs are "the enemy within," as other Indian leaders have,[68] he was frequently under scrutiny by the Sikh community for his inadequate treatment of anti-Sikhism in India and abroad in the Sikh diaspora. A series of protests by Sikh communities in Canada and the United States addressed Singh's protection of Indian Congress members who were involved in the Sikh massacre of 1984 in Amritsar,[69] as well as Singh's allegation that Canadian Sikhs are of particular concern for national safety.[70] In an interview with Canadian journalist Haroon Siddiqui, Singh recommended "vigilance and close cooperation between [Canadian and Indian] governments" in order to "crack down" on "Sikh extremism, separatism, and militancy."[71] When asked if Singh felt this threat from the Sikh diaspora had anything to do with the way the Indian government has treated Sikh populations in India, Singh responded by claiming that this was a false accusation.[72]

My inclusion of Singh's depoliticization of racial violence is not intended, in its symmetry with Harper's actions, to absolve Canada or normalize state elision of racialized trauma. Rather, the collusionary nature of both leaders' idealized projection of nations freed from the baggage of old wounds and the unrest of marginalized communities displayed an alarming complicity toward the erasure of public memory. It is evident through Harper and Singh's shared stance on the continued threat of "extreme" Sikh behaviour as an abnormal limit case in otherwise "well-governed" nations that this erasure is empowered by the "celebration" of class-based economic relations.[73] For Harper, this renewed relationship with India acted as a continuation of the narrative of Canada's internationally diverse and peaceful character, which, in turn, masks the complex hierarchies of "freedom" and power that gird liberal Canadian politics.[74] As Bannerji writes,

> *In the ideology of multicultural nationhood...difference is read in a power-neutral manner rather than as organized through class, gender, and race. Thus at the same moment that difference is ideologically evoked it is also neutralized, as though the issue of difference were the same as that of diversity of cultures and identities, rather than those of racism and colonial ethnocentrism.*[75]

Therefore, in Harper's address to the Indian prime minister on June 27, 2010, and his address to Indo-Canadian citizens on June 23, it becomes clear that the right to a protected life is only guaranteed in the forgetting of certain histories and the "consciousness of racism" in favour of the continued support of white liberal hegemony.[76] In developing a fissure between Indians "who share our aspirations for a better life" and "those extremists who seek to import the battles of India's past,"[77] Harper was able to secure and solidify the image of Canadian political and cultural neutrality, not to mention cleanse the ongoing history of India's colonial oppression. This cleansing occurs through the acceptance of exceptional "model minorities" alongside the displacement of political extremism onto an always-racialized, irrational Other. Thus, the governmental discourse of moderation or tolerance "inevitably articulate[s] identity and difference, belonging and marginality" without drawing attention to its own racist and political agendas.[78] Indeed, these agendas are masked through a conceit of political temperance and "colour-blind" nationalism.

To conclude, I reassert that I am not suggesting that acts of terrorism or known terrorists should be accepted by nations with open arms, nor that acts of violence such as the bombing of Flight 182 should be discounted. However, I do believe these acts of violence should not be seen as "mere" examples of criminality arising from arcane and arbitrary ethnic sentiments, as the nation's tendency toward an interpellative amnesia may have us believe. Rather, they must be seen as grounded in the complexities of recent and ongoing histories of colonial and state violence. Further, the racialization of danger and the primitivization of non-Western cultures, coupled with the masking of white Western political agendas and systemic racisms, raises disconcerting questions about the so-called liberal multiculturalism and equal rights mandates propagated by societies such as Canada, *particularly* after instances of state indifference such as the actions before and after the explosion of Flight 182. As a final meditation, I would like to return to Aristotle's argument that moderation hinges upon emotional, political, and social contexts in conjunction with the problematic matrix of the racialized/deracialized and politicized/depoliticized identities formulated in Canadian politics and governance. If, as Kalra notes, the development of model minorities emerges alongside certain "modes of governance" and national affects,[79] then what can be made of the article "Too Asian?" published in the national magazine *Maclean's*?[80] The article flagged a number of Canadian universities as having a high ratio of Asian students, which purportedly threatens white performance (not to mention the pleasure of a traditional, white image of university life). As one student relates, "many white students simply believe that competing with Asians—both Asian Canadians and international students alike—requires a sacrifice of time and freedom they're not willing to make."[81] This unwilling sacrifice translates to an anxiety over the loss of white students' privilege, thereby making the once-model academicism of Asian Canadians a threat to continued white ascendancy.

How do moments such as these relate to, or even support, the notion of a universal code of Canadian diversity and "tolerance"? Where does "Too Asian?" fit with Harper's declared stamp of approval on "aspiring" immigrants, or indeed the greater constellation of model versus radically marginalized, terrorist Others? As I have attempted to argue here, it is moments such as these that expose the instability of multicultural promises and immoderate governmentality, which the red-and-white flag of Canada attempts to disguise. Indeed, what becomes apparent is that systemic racism, like Aristotle's moderation, is an assemblage of shifting contexts and influences, as innocuous and inclusive as it is deceitful, oppressive, and even fatal.

Source

This is a revised and updated version of the article, "Politics of (Im)moderation: The Production of South Asian Identities in the Canadian Apology for Air India Flight 182," by Cassel Busse. Copyright © 2012, TOPIA: *Canadian Journal of Cultural Studies*, originally published in TOPIA: *Canadian Journal of Cultural Studies* 27 (2012): 233–251, reprinted by permission of TOPIA and by permission of the author.

Notes

1. See Seyla Benhabib, *The Claims of Culture: Equality and Diversity in the Global Era* (Princeton, NJ: Princeton University Press, 2002); David Theo Goldberg, *The Racial State* (Oxford: Wiley-Blackwell, 2002); Glen Newey, *Virtue, Reason, and Toleration: The Place of Toleration in Ethical and Political Philosophy* (Edinburgh, Scotland: Edinburgh University Press, 1999).

2. For example, see Aristide Tessitore, *Aristotle and Modern Politics: The Persistence of Political Philosophy* (Notre Dame, IN: University of Notre Dame Press, 2002).
3. Aristotle, *The Nicomachean Ethics*, trans. David Ross and Lesley Brown (Oxford: Oxford University Press, 2009), 30.
4. *Oxford English Dictionary Online*, 3rd ed., s.v. "moderation," accessed June 30, 2011, http://www.oed.com/view/Entry/120606.
5. Government of Canada, Commission of Inquiry into the Investigation of the Bombing of Air India Flight 182, last modified July 17, 2010, vol. 1, chap. 1, accessed June 30, 2011, http://epe.lac-bac.gc.ca/100/206/301/pco-bcp/commissions/air_india/2010-07-23/www.majorcomm.ca/en/reports/finalreport/volume1/default.htm.
6. Angela Failler, "Remembering the Air India Disaster: Memorial and Counter-Memorial," *Review of Education, Pedagogy, and Cultural Studies* 31 (2009): 151.
7. Where the "political" is a derogatory term used to denote radicalism in the interest of gaining or overthrowing power, particularly through immoral or unprincipled means, as opposed to neutrality, moderation, and liberal democracy.
8. For scholarship on this conception of Canada, see Sherene Razack, *Dark Threats and White Knights: The Somalia Affair, Peacekeeping, and the New Imperialism* (Toronto: University of Toronto Press, 2004) and Himani Bannerji, *The Dark Side of the Nation: Essays on Multiculturalism, Nationalism, and Gender* (Toronto: Canadian Scholars' Press, 2000).
9. Sara Ahmed, *The Cultural Politics of Emotion* (New York: Routledge, 2004), 4.
10. Ibid.
11. Himani Bannerji, " The Dark Side of the Nation: Politics of Multiculturalism and the State of 'Canada,'" in *Canadian Cultural Studies: A Reader*, ed. Sourayan Mookerjea, Imre Szeman, and Gail Faurschou (Durham, NC: Duke University Press, 2009), 328.
12. Ibid., 336.
13. Steven Chase, "Canada Complicit in Torture of Innocent Afghans, Diplomat Says," *Globe and Mail*, November 18, 2009, accessed June 30, 2011, http://www.theglobeandmail.com/news/politics/canada-complicit-in-torture-of-innocent-afghans-diplomat-says/article1369069/.
14. Jeffrey Simpson, "Solving Our Problems on the Backs of the Poor," *Globe and Mail*, March 29, 2010, accessed June 30, 2011, http://www.theglobeandmail.com/globe-debate/solving-our-problems-on-the-backs-of-the-poor/article4312785/; for more on the contradictory notion of Canadian peacekeeping, see Razack, *Dark Threats and White Knights*.
15. Jacques Derrida, *On Cosmopolitanism and Forgiveness* (New York: Routledge, 2001), 41.
16. Stephen Harper, "Prime Minister Stephen Harper's Air India Memorial Speech," *Canadian Television News*, June 23, 2010, accessed January 24, 2017, http://www.ctvnews.ca/prime-minister-stephen-harper-s-air-india-memorial-speech-1.525828.

17. Citizenship and Immigration Canada, "Forging Our Legacy: Canadian Citizenship and Immigration, 1900–1977," last modified July 1, 2006, accessed June 30, 2011, http://www.cic.gc.ca/english/resources/publications/legacy/chap-6.asp#chap6-3.
18. *Canadian Broadcasting Corporation*, "Harper Apologizes in BC for 1914 *Komagata Maru* Incident," August 3, 2008, accessed June 30, 2011, http://www.cbc.ca/news/canada/british-columbia/story/2008/08/03/harper-apology.html.
19. Since this time, Prime Minister Justin Trudeau has made a formal apology for the rejection of the *Komagata Maru* in the House of Commons. However, at the time of my writing this essay, Harper was still prime minister.
20. Harper, "Air India Memorial Speech."
21. Ibid.
22. Ibid.
23. Failler, "Remembering the Air India Disaster," 151.
24. *Oxford English Dictionary Online*, 3rd ed., s.v. "tolerance," accessed June 30, 2011, http://www.oed.com/view/Entry/202979.
25. Wendy Brown, *Regulating Aversion: Tolerance in the Age of Identity and Empire* (Princeton, NJ: Princeton University Press, 2008), 17; for more on Western exceptionalism, see Jasbir K. Puar, *Terrorist Assemblages: Homonationalism in Queer Times* (Durham, NC: Duke University Press, 2008).
26. Stephen Harper, Prime Minister Unveils Memorial Dedicated to Victims of Air India Flight 182. Public address in Toronto, 23 June 2007.
27. That there are indeed potential reasons for citizens of other nations to immigrate is not being contested here. Rather, it is the concept put forth by the Canadian government that Canada is not productive of, and is thus superior to, the "unfortunateness" of the extreme fundamentalism and power manipulations of non-Western nations that requires a political rather than ethnic, racial, or cultural analysis. It is thus the illusion that Canada is free of discrimination against others, and is an "arbiter of appropriate ethics, human rights, and democratic behaviour" that is being questioned. Puar, *Terrorist Assemblages*, 8.
28. Brown, *Regulating Aversion*, 7.
29. Harper, "Air India Memorial Speech."
30. Terry Milewski, " The Air India Families: Shut Out Again," *Canadian Broadcasting Corporation*, December 6, 2010, accessed June 30, 2011, http://www.cbc.ca/newsblogs/politics/inside-politics-blog/2010/12/air-india-the-pilots-son-hits-the-roof.html.
31. Harper, "Air India Memorial Speech."
32. Ibid.; Harper's recommendation to "marginalize extremists" as a preventative against further terrorist attacks mirrors, but also exaggerates, the language of the final report on the 2010 government inquiry into Flight 182, which lists the "establishment

of a culture of security awareness and constant vigilance." Government of Canada, Commission of Inquiry, vol. 1, chap. 7, 204.

33. For example, former prime ministers Manmohan Singh and Stephen Harper had been actively working since 2010 to form an anti-separatist alliance. *Times of India*, "Canada 'Committed' to Curb Sikh Separatism," April 27, 2010, accessed June 30, 2011, http://timesofindia.indiatimes.com/world/indians-abroad/Canada-committed-to-curb-Sikh-separatism/articleshow/5862158.cms?referral=PM; for a more populist expression of the presence of the Khalistan or Sikh separatist movement, see Raveena Aulakh, "Sikh Separatism: Still Alive and Festering in Canada," *Toronto Star*, May 3, 2010, accessed June 30, 2011, http://www.thestar.com/news/gta/article/804021--sikh-separatism-still-alive-and-festering-in-canada.html.
34. Harper, "Air India Memorial Speech."
35. Jacques Derrida, *Specters of Marx* (New York: Routledge, 1993), 103.
36. Harper, "Air India Memorial Speech."
37. Ibid.
38. Ahmed, *Cultural Politics of Emotion*, 2.
39. Failler, "Remembering the Air India Disaster," 158.
40. George W. Bush, Text of September 11th Speech, *Cable News Network*, September 11, 2001, accessed June 30, 2011, http://articles.cnn.com/2001-09-11/us/bush.speech.text_1_attacks-deadly-terrorist-acts-despicable-acts?_s=PM:US.
41. Harper, "Air India Memorial Speech."
42. Failler, "Remembering the Air India Disaster," 153.
43. The homology between race and terrorism is openly admitted in the CSIS statement release on Canada's increased security since 9/11. In Reid Morden's official commentary on Canadian intelligence efforts, he states, "It is no secret that the communities most vulnerable to being listed [as terrorist threats] are those which are visibly identifiable as racial, ethnic, and religious minorities." He dismisses any "misgivings" on this racial profiling by suggesting that opposition can be taken up by "civil libertarians" in court. Reid Morden, "Spies, Not Soothsayers: Canadian Intelligence after 9/11," Commentary No. 85 (Fall 2003), Canada Security Intelligence Service, accessed June 30, 2011, http://www.csis.gc.ca/pblctns/cmmntr/cm85-eng.asp.
44. Harper, "Air India Memorial Speech."
45. Ibid.
46. Failler, "Remembering the Air India Disaster," 159.
47. Harper, "Air India Memorial Speech."
48. Ahmed, *Cultural Politics of Emotion*, 78.
49. Harper, "Air India Memorial Speech."
50. Brown, *Regulating Aversion*, 8.

51. As Failler analyzes, accusations that the neglect of this event by the government was based upon systemic racism were immediately shut down by the attorney general. Failler, "Remembering the Air India Disaster."
52. Harper, "Air India Memorial Speech."
53. Bannerji, *Dark Side of the Nation*, 328.
54. Virinder S. Kalra, "Between Emasculation and Hypermasculinity: Theorizing British South Asian Masculinities," *South Asian Popular Culture* 7, no. 2 (2009): 115.
55. Jasbir K. Puar and Amit Rai, "The Remaking of a Model Minority: Perverse Projectiles under the Specter of (Counter)Terrorism," *Social Text* 22, no. 3 (2004): 81.
56. Ibid., 77.
57. Ibid., 82.
58. Sara Ahmed, *The Promise of Happiness* (Durham, NC: Duke University Press, 2010), 137.
59. Ibid., 138.
60. While in a Canadian context the removal of ethnic signifiers such as the turban or Dastar is seen as a move toward a progressive (white) sociality, this stigmatization of religious—and particularly Sikh or Muslim—markers also occurs outside of the production of Western model subjecthood. As Brian Keith Axel notes, long beards and turbans have become part of a Sikh terrorist profile in India. Brian Keith Axel, "The Diasporic Imaginary," *Public Culture* 14, no. 2 (2002): 417.
61. Puar, *Terrorist Assemblages*, 28.
62. I stress "certain" here because I do not want to portray a homogenized South Asian or Indian ethnic identity, nor a homogenized experience of racism. In Canada, South Asian and/or Indo-Canadians may be differentiated and discriminated against not only through physical ethnic markers (such as the turban and beard noted by Puar) but also economic and political class differences. I would also like to take the time here to acknowledge that vastly different Indian histories and memories are also dependent on class and ethnicity and so cannot be equally "forgotten." There is, however, a homogenization of differing pasts, identities, and relationships between India and Canada in Harper's assertion of the need to put "the past" aside. Harper, "Air India Memorial Speech."
63. Puar, *Terrorist Assemblages*, 25.
64. Harper, "Air India Memorial Speech."
65. Stephen Harper, Statement Delivered at the House of Commons, "PM Celebrates Canada–India Relations," June 27, 2010, accessed June 30, 2011, http://www.pm.gc.ca/eng/news/2010/06/27/pm-celebrates-canada-india-relations.
66. Ibid.

67. For more on this topic, see Axel, "Diasporic Imaginary," and Veena Das, *Life and Words: Violence and the Descent into the Ordinary* (Berkeley: University of California Press, 2007).
68. Darshan S. Tatla, " The Morning After: Trauma, Memory, and the Sikh Predicament since 1984," *Sikh Formations* 2, no. 1 (2006): 66.
69. *Canadian Broadcasting Corporation*, "Sikhs Protest Visit from India MP," March 23, 2008, accessed June 30, 2011, http://www.cbc.ca/news/canada/toronto/sikhs-protest-visit-from-india-mp-1.974447.
70. Amrik Singh, "Sikh Genocide and 'Sikh Extremism' Roil Canada," *Panthic*, June 30, 2010, accessed January 24, 2017, http://www.panthic.org/articles/5265.
71. Quoted in Haroon Siddiqui, "Manmohan Singh Is King at G20," *Toronto Star*, June 26, 2010, accessed June 30, 2011, http://www.thestar.com/news/gta/g20/2010/06/26/siddiqui_manmohan_singh_is_king_at_g20.html.
72. Quoted in ibid. Although I have cited a Canadian news agency, I would like to point out that there is much coverage in the Indian press on these issues, as well as diverse commentary on various Indian and Indo-Canadian organization websites. For examples, see TheIndiaTribune.com, Panthic.org, Sikhnn.com, and IndiaTimes.com.
73. Singh quoted in Siddiqui, "Manmohan Singh"; in this interview, Singh speaks predominantly of Canada's compatibility with India in terms of regulatory banking strategies, financial growth, and contribution to the world economy, as well as joint interests in nuclear business "ventures" in Africa.
74. Historically, Canadian and Indian governments have not been so amicable. Issues surrounding India's development of nuclear weapons in the aftermath of the Cold War put a considerable strain on its relationships with Canada, not to mention, of course, the Sikh separatist threats of the 1980s. India's economic reform in the 1990s proliferated Canada's political interest in this nation and a desire to resolve previous tensions. Ryan M. Touhey, "A New Direction for the Canada–India Relationship," *Canadian International Council*, No. 5 (August 2009), accessed June 30, 2011, http://www.opencanada.org/wp-content/uploads/2011/05/A-New-Direction-for-the-Canada-India-Relationship-Ryan-M.-Touhey1.pdf.
75. Bannerji, "Dark Side of the Nation," 328.
76. Ahmed, *Promise of Happiness*, 143.
77. Harper, "Air India Memorial Speech."
78. Brown, *Regulating Aversion*, 10.
79. Kalra, "Between Emasculation and Hypermasculinity."
80. Stephanie Findlay and Nicholas Kohler, " Too Asian?" *Maclean's*, November 10, 2010, accessed June 30, 2011, http://oncampus.macleans.ca/education/2010/11/10/too-asian/.
81. Ibid.

Works Cited

Ahmed, Sara. *The Cultural Politics of Emotion*. New York: Routledge, 2004.

———. *The Promise of Happiness*. Durham, NC: Duke University Press, 2010.

Aristotle. *The Nicomachean Ethics*. Translated by David Ross and Lesley Brown. Oxford: Oxford University Press, 2009.

Axel, Brian Keith. "The Diasporic Imaginary." *Public Culture* 14, no. 2 (2002): 411–428.

Bannerji, Himani. *The Dark Side of the Nation: Essays on Multiculturalism, Nationalism, and Gender*. Toronto: Canadian Scholars' Press, 2000.

———. "The Dark Side of the Nation: Politics of Multiculturalism and the State of 'Canada.'" In *Canadian Cultural Studies: A Reader*, edited by Sourayan Mookerjea, Imre Szeman, and Gail Faurschou, 327–343. Durham, NC: Duke University Press, 2009.

Benhabib, Seyla. *The Claims of Culture: Equality and Diversity in the Global Era*. Princeton, NJ: Princeton University Press, 2002.

Brown, Wendy. *Regulating Aversion: Tolerance in the Age of Identity and Empire*. Princeton, NJ: Princeton University Press, 2008.

Das, Veena. *Life and Words: Violence and the Descent into the Ordinary*. Berkeley: University of California Press, 2007.

Derrida, Jacques. *On Cosmopolitanism and Forgiveness*. New York: Routledge, 2001.

———. *Specters of Marx*. New York: Routledge, 1993.

Failler, Angela. "Remembering the Air India Disaster: Memorial and Counter-Memorial." *Review of Education, Pedagogy, and Cultural Studies* 31 (2009): 150–176.

Goldberg, David Theo. *The Racial State*. Oxford: Wiley-Blackwell, 2002.

Kalra, Virinder S. "Between Emasculation and Hypermasculinity: Theorizing British South Asian Masculinities." *South Asian Popular Culture* 7, no. 2 (2009): 113–125.

Newey, Glen. *Virtue, Reason, and Toleration: The Place of Toleration in Ethical and Political Philosophy*. Edinburgh, Scotland: Edinburgh University Press, 1999.

Puar, Jasbir K. *Terrorist Assemblages: Homonationalism in Queer Times*. Durham, NC: Duke University Press, 2008.

Puar, Jasbir K., and Amit Rai. "The Remaking of a Model Minority: Perverse Projectiles under the Specter of (Counter)Terrorism." *Social Text* 22, no. 3 (2004): 75–104.

Razack, Sherene. *Dark Threats and White Knights: The Somalia Affair, Peacekeeping, and the New Imperialism*. Toronto: University of Toronto Press, 2004.

Tatla, Darshan S. "The Morning After: Trauma, Memory, and the Sikh Predicament since 1984." *Sikh Formations* 2, no. 1 (2006): 57–88.

Tessatore, Aristide. *Aristotle and Modern Politics: The Persistence of Political Philosophy*. Notre Dame, IN: University of Notre Dame Press, 2002.

■

Statement by the Prime Minister of Canada at the Commemoration Ceremony for the 25th Anniversary of the Air India Flight 182 Atrocity

PRIME MINISTER OF CANADA

---

23 June 2010
Toronto, Ontario

Ladies and gentlemen, distinguished guests, friends and families, thank you for being here this evening.

A quarter century has gone by since the terrible event for which we are gathered today, namely the destruction of Air India Flight 182, which killed 329 people, most of them Canadians.

The destruction of Air India Flight 182 on June 23, 1985, was, and remains, the single worst act of terrorism in Canadian history. It cost the lives of 329 men, women, and children. They perished that day, when a bomb planted in the hold of their aircraft exploded. Meanwhile, a similar bomb intended for another Air India flight, detonated at Tokyo's Narita airport, killing two baggage handlers.

Around the world, it was a dreadful day.

Let us picture it once more. Most of those on Flight 182 were our fellow citizens, Canadians going to India for business or pleasure or family reunions. Eighty-two of those aboard were children, no doubt to be received and shown off with happy pride. Activities familiar to all of us, then, a journey begun with excitement and hopeful expectations.

But, that day the innocence, the pleasure, the anticipation, all of it was snuffed out by an act of grotesque violence and malevolence. And you who are left, you were handed this heartbreaking loss, the burden of which it is all but impossible to calculate, severed bonds that still ache with the burning sadness of love remembered in empty silence.

This was evil, perpetrated by cowards, despicable, senseless, and vicious. I will make no attempt to make any sense of it. Nor will I speak of roads to healing. Some wounds are too deep to be healed even by the remedy of time. What I can tell you is this.

Your pain is our pain. As you grieve, so we grieve. And, as the years have deepened your grief, so has the understanding of our country grown. Canadians who sadly did not at first accept that this outrage was made in Canada, accept it now. Let me just speak directly to this perception. For, it is wrong, and it must be laid to rest. This was not an act of foreign violence.

Canadians now understand that this atrocity was conceived in Canada, executed in Canada, by Canadian citizens, and its victims were themselves mostly citizens of Canada. We wish this realization had gained common acceptance earlier.

However, it is this understanding which guides the actions of our Government today. So, we have encouraged the building of more memorials such as the original one in Ireland that I had the honour of visiting in 2005, and this one here in Toronto.

It is why the Government of Canada made June 23 the National Day of Remembrance for Victims of Terrorism. And it is why four years ago, in one of the very first acts of our new government, we appointed retired Justice John Major to scrutinize without limit the investigation of the bombing of Air India Flight 182.

I come now to a difficult place. Commissioner Major reported on the first phase of his inquiry, in December 2007. In it, he recorded many personal stories, some that I have heard first-hand from families of victims. I found their words deeply moving.

Six days ago, Commissioner Major issued his second report. It is, finally, a thorough examination of events, and deeply disturbing. For although Commissioner Major's report runs to 3,000 pages, although it summarizes the testimony of hundreds of witnesses, although it shines a light on institutional processes that Commissioner Major referred to in some cases as a "dysfunctional focus on self justification," and in others as "slow, intermittent, and acrimonious," it can still be reduced to a few words: this should not have happened.

This should not have happened. And 329 people should not have perished in the sky that day in June, south of Ireland.

It is not enough to say that the system failed. It did of course. But, this is to sanitize with words a succession of woeful inadequacies that Commissioner Major calls "a cascading series of errors."

No. That is not enough.

Commissioner Major delivered a damning indictment of many things that occurred before and after the fact. Things, ladies and gentlemen, that this Government of Canada cannot defend, has no wish to defend.

And, Commissioner Major finds that, to make matters worse, the families of the victims were for years after treated with scant respect or consideration by agencies of the Government of Canada.

These are things for which honour and duty require that the Government of Canada, the government that called this inquiry, now apologize.

I stand before you therefore, to offer on behalf of the Government of Canada, and all Canadians, an apology for the institutional failings of twenty-five years ago and the treatment of the victims' families thereafter.

The protection of its citizens is the first obligation of government.

The mere fact of the destruction of Air India Flight 182 is the primary evidence that something went very, very wrong. For that, we are sorry. For that, and also for the years during which your legitimate need for answers and indeed, for empathy, were treated with administrative disdain.

Ladies and gentlemen, Commissioner Major has made many important recommendations. We are in the course of reviewing them and have already begun the vital work of improving safety and security at our airports. It is a matter of the utmost importance to our government that such a thing never happens again.

Sadly, we have no way of knowing when, if, or how we may once more be attacked, or by whom. We know only that terrorism is an enemy with a thousand faces, and a hatred that festers in the darkest spots of the human mind. And we fear that when we invite from around the world, those who share our aspirations for a better life, others also come, those who see in our Canada, not new bridges to a hopeful future but only another chance to travel the old roads to the blood-feuds of the past.

And let me address, as the families have asked me to do, my fellow political leaders of every stripe: it is incumbent upon us all, not to reach out to, but rather to marginalize, to carefully and systematically marginalize, those extremists who seek to import the battles of India's past here and then to export them back to that great and forward-looking nation.

We must have none of it. Just as we must continue the struggle against destroyers and murderers of all kinds. And it will, with energy and urgency. Whatever the threat, we must anticipate it. Wherever it comes from, we must be ready for it.

Whoever would lift up a perverse ideology by casting down the innocent, we must learn how to thwart them.

The greatest legacy we can leave to your loved ones is to make the skies safe for travel.

Let me say that again: the finest memorial we can build to your loved ones is to prevent another Flight 182. This is our duty to you, and to all Canadians. I want to thank the victims' families for inviting me here today.

Thank you very much.

God bless you all.

And God keep our land glorious and free.

Source

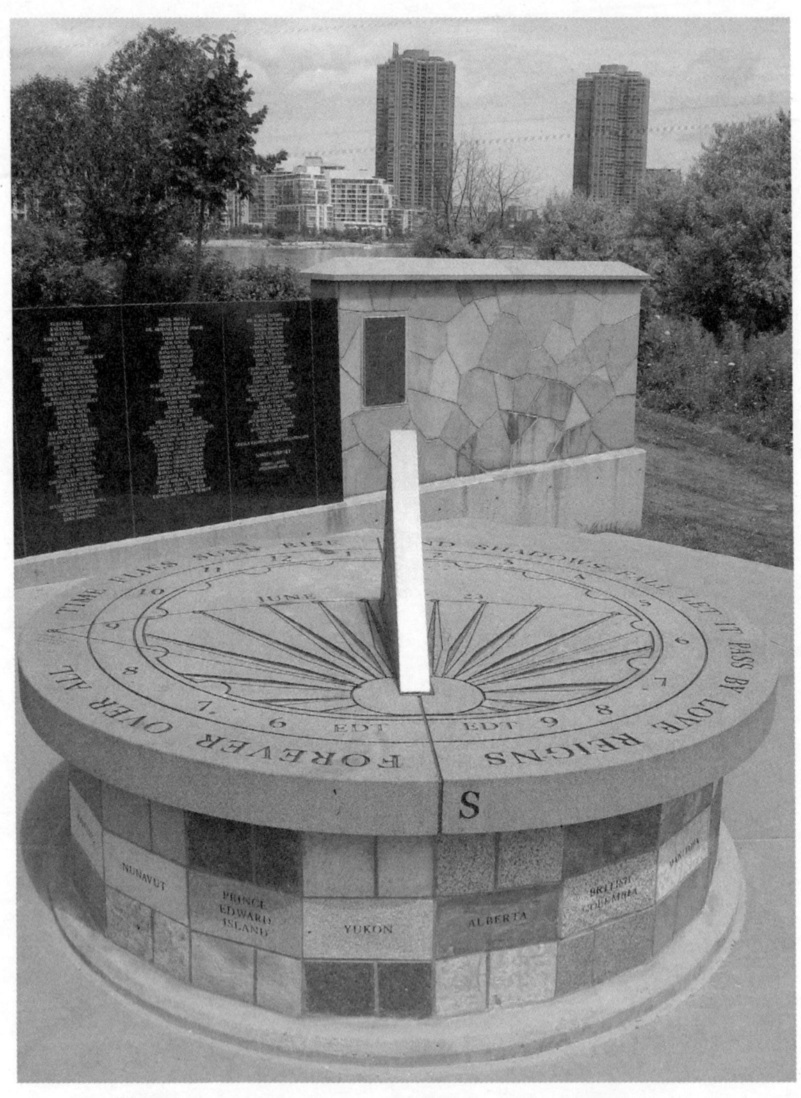

Air India memorial at Humber Bay Park, Toronto. Photo courtesy Amber Dean.

The Canadian Government's Apology to the Victims and Families of Air India Flight 182

KAREN SHARMA

HOW DO WE RECOUNT the event of Prime Minister Stephen Harper's apology to the families of those killed in the bombing of Air India Flight 182? We might choose a starting point—a place from whence to begin an account. In some records, the story of Stephen Harper's apology opens with the moment when he ascends the podium to deliver his address to those gathered at the Air India memorial site in Humber Bay Park, Toronto, Ontario. The narrative begins on June 23, 2010, and describes the prime minister's words, his contritions and commitments, his mood and affect. We hear about the apology's meaning—its significance, potency, and shortcomings. We may learn of those present during his address, and perhaps even of those deemed absent from its proceedings.

But what of the many moments that led up to his apology, those that come after, and those yet to come? What of the (ongoing) labour of families, activists, and communities to garner official response and redress—their persistence in the face of this traumatic history; the insidious racism and institutional neglect that marred their relations with Canada before and after the loss of their loved ones on June 23, 1985? How do we tell the story of Harper's apology in ways that recognize the complexities that surround and shape its delivery?

Perhaps the challenge in recounting political apologies lies in their tendency to reduce long, emotional, and tumultuous histories of sorrow, activism, solidarity, and discord into a single moment in time. The apology's affective force shifts our focus from those who have fought for and against its address to those performing the ritual act. Through the apologizer's enactment of repentance, we are directed away from the complex and, at times, conflicting histories that necessitate the apology itself, and are left instead with the apologizer's unequivocal account of events. As with the Air India apology, these speech acts are often delivered by senior politicians, and, as such, their narrative accounts of the past have the tendency to be understood as official, true, and legitimate (re)tellings of history. In this way, political apologies create the conditions for a univocal recounting of our past, with the beginning and ending of the story resting with the apologizer—in this case, Prime Minister Stephen Harper—whose descent from the podium on June 23, 2010, supposedly closes this "sad chapter of our collective history."[1]

Political apologies not only reframe and reduce their referential histories (and their attendant complexities). As Cassel Busse notes, the affective quality of the Air India apology—and its claim upon the grief and pain of its victims—works to elide Canada's persistent legacy of racism and marginalization toward South Asian residents. Busse's critical reading of the Air India apology reveals its multiple and, at times, contradictory ends. While the apology seeks to reflect upon the Canadian government's failure to adequately address the systemic failures that rendered the bombing possible, it also operates verdictively to construct the nation as the ultimate victim of tragedy, whose safety and security is under the constant threat of "those who see in Canada, not new bridges to a hopeful future but only another chance to travel the old roads to the blood-feuds of the past."[2] Hence, the political apology's emotive roots exist alongside, nay bolster, its strategic ends—Canada's apology to the families of those killed in the Air

India bombings seeks to preserve its interests by rewriting an official record of the past, closing it to other narrative accounts and critical engagements.

But it is not simply its narrative and affective qualities that help us understand the political apology's character and impact. As political scientist Matt James notes, the location of its delivery shapes its reception as well.[3] What, then, might we make of the issuance of the Air India apology at a small commemorative event in front of a memorial site erected in Humber Bay Park in honour of those killed in the bombings? While the issuance of the apology at a site dedicated to its public memory holds certain symbolic value (and perhaps also intimate importance for the families of those lost to the bombings), James urges us to understand how delivering political apologies outside of Parliament, and its official record, has the perhaps unintended consequence of writing it in a kind of "disappearing ink."[4] Although the Air India apology was available by searching (with some effort) the archives of former Prime Minister Stephen Harper's website and is captured in fragments in news media reports from the time of its delivery, the actual text is liable to vanish over time, compromising the ability of communities to return to and hold accountable the assertions and promises contained therein. Moreover, the disappearance of political apologies makes it increasingly difficult to read them within their historical context. As such, the immortalization of the apology in its written form—as is accomplished in this volume—becomes a political act in and of itself, challenging a framework of delivery that structures its eventual fading from public memory.

It might seem that the eventual disappearance of some political apologies stands in sharp contrast with memorial sites, which are etched in stone and cast into the earth as enduring symbols of historical wrong. But some of the Air India memorial sites may challenge this analysis. When I first visited the Air India memorial site in Stanley Park, Vancouver, I was struck by how difficult it was to locate. The structure itself stands as a stone retaining wall, built into a mound of slightly raised earth. Accompanied by a bench and plinth, the retaining wall memorializes those killed in the bombings, with their names inscribed along the upper stones. The architectural design of the memorial structure conveys a kind of symbiosis between nature and monument, making it easy to overlook as simply a landscaping feature of the park. Since the memorial site was unveiled in 2007, it has weathered with time and its once distinguishable text is slowly being overtaken by oxidation and rust. In this way, the site not only conveys a relationship to the land but is slowly returning to it and, in so doing, risks our loss of the history it was meant to memorialize.

The delivery of the Air India apology at the memorial site in Toronto is not only significant for how it shapes our remembering of the apology but also for how the memorial itself contains and constrains other forms and sites of public memory. It is noteworthy that the delivery of the Air India apology coincided with the Toronto Police and Royal Canadian Mounted Police services' suppression of civil liberties of thousands of protestors who had gathered in response to the G-20 Summit being hosted by the Canadian government in downtown Toronto.[5] Within this context, Harper's call for greater state securitization (under the looming threat of terrorist others) with the Air India apology both distracts from and reveals a strategic investment in mobilizing the tragedy as a means for supporting an "insidious" and "dangerous" agenda of unconstitutional civil rights violations in its present context.[6]

While the Air India apology may illustrate the problematics associated with political apologies, it does not necessarily follow that we should abandon the speech act altogether. Indeed, critical engagements with political apologies must hold in tension their shortcomings with the tremendous emotional and physical work communities have undertaken to bring about their issuance by state officials. The efforts of families and communities toward recognition and redress raise the analytical and political imperative that we envision the conditions and features necessary for political apologies to achieve their conciliatory potential. What, then, might an effective political apology look like?

A better political apology might recognize the impossibility of forgiveness, contesting a focus on the future by accepting that not all harms can be healed. Instead, the apologizers might commit to remaining open to the pain they have caused, while recognizing that this pain cannot be known or understood. Moreover, a more just political apology would be committed to public record, challenging modes of address that would see it eventually fade from public memory. This does not necessarily mean that the delivery of all political apologies must occur in Parliament, or provincial/territorial legislatures, particularly if those wronged desire more intimate ceremony, but rather that the apologizer finds ways of preserving their act through multiple and accessible mediums. Finally, political apologies might challenge their preferential focus on the apologizer by recognizing the importance of hearing the reactions, stories, and even rejections of those to whom they are addressed. Rather than understanding these responses as after-effects of the apologetic speech act, we might instead recognize them as integral to its offering *and* a key component of its historical record. In so doing, perhaps a more diverse, engaged, and sustained reflection of our national past might be rendered.

Notes

1. Public Safety Canada, Remembering Air India Flight 182, April 3, 2014, accessed January 24, 2015, http://www.publicsafety.gc.ca/cnt/ntnl-scrt/cntr-trrrsm/r-nd-flght-182/index-eng.aspx.
2. Stephen Harper, Statement Delivered at the Commemoration Ceremony for the 25th Anniversary of the Air India Flight 182 Atrocity, June 23, 2010, accessed January 24, 2015, http://pm.gc.ca/eng/news/2010/06/23/statement-prime-minister-canada-commemoration-ceremony-25th-anniversary-air-india.
3. Matt James, "Wrestling with the Past: Apologies, Quasi-Apologies and Non-Apologies in Canada," in *The Age of Apology: Facing Up to the Past*, ed. Mark Gibney, Rhoda E. Howard-Hassmann, Jean-Marc Coicaud, and Niklaus Steiner (Philadelphia: University of Pennsylvania Press, 2008), 137–153.
4. Ibid., 146–147.
5. André Marin, *Caught in the Act: Investigation into the Ministry of Community Safety and Correctional Services' Conduct in Relation to Ontario Regulation 233/10 under the Public Works Protection Act* (Toronto: Ombudsman of Ontario, 2010).
6. This language reflects Ombudsman of Ontario André Marin's conclusion regarding the legislative authorities invoked to detain protestors during the G-20 Summit.

According to Marin, there is "a real and insidious danger associated with using subordinate legislation, passed behind closed doors, to increase police authority." Ibid., 101.

Works Cited

James, Matt. " Wrestling with the Past: Apologies, Quasi-Apologies and Non-Apologies in Canada." In *The Age of Apology: Facing Up to the Past*, edited by Mark Gibney, Rhoda E. Howard-Hassmann, Jean-Marc Coicaud, and Niklaus Steiner, 137–153. Philadelphia: University of Pennsylvania Press, 2008.

Marin, André. *Caught in the Act: Investigation into the Ministry of Community Safety and Correctional Services' Conduct in Relation to Ontario Regulation 233/10 under the Public Works Protection Act.* Toronto: Ombudsman of Ontario, 2010.

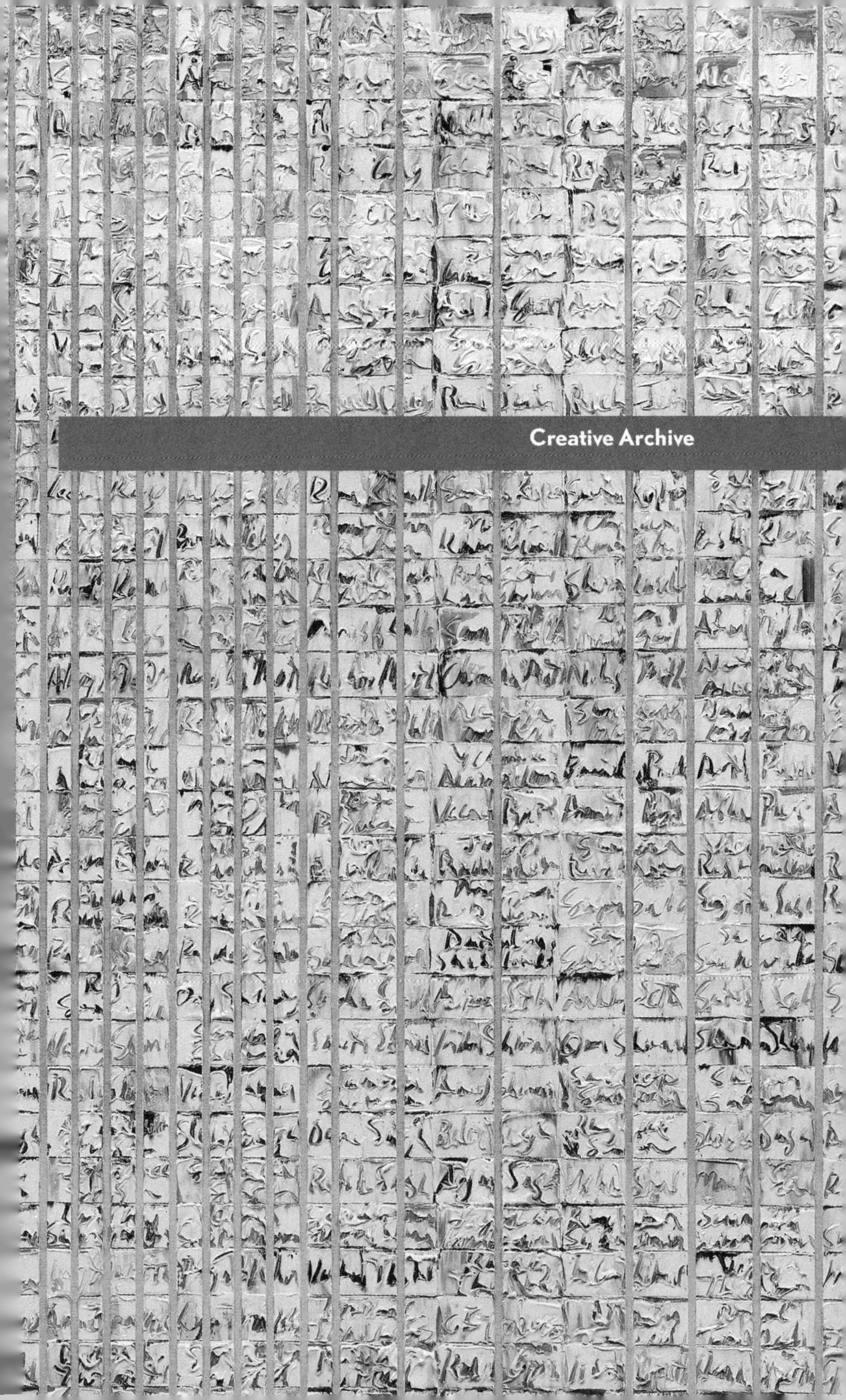
Creative Archive

Overleaf: Deon Venter, Names #2 *(detail) from the* Flight 182 *series, 2007. Oil on linen. 58" x 70". Copyright © Deon Venter, reprinted by permission of the artist. Photo by David Borrowman.*

Mediating Memories of the 1985 Air India Bombings

A Critical Dance with Lata Pada's Revealed by Fire

ELAN MARCHINKO

LINKING ARMS, the dancers engulf her like suffocating flames. They shame her with pointed fingers then push her to the ground. Their feet stamp the floor in time with the music's ominous rhythm. She is left alone on the stage in a crumpled heap. Numbly, her fingers trace the stage. Her hands ball into fists that beat the floor in anguish. On huge rice paper panels is projected a close-up of her upper body and face blurring and twisting in slow motion. Through these technological manipulations, the progressions of her facial muscles are magnified and make palpable her intensities. Her hands flutter frenetically as she plunges into her metaphorical test of fire, facing her traumatic past. Meanwhile, back on the stage, she pulls herself along the floor with her arms and rolls toward a strip of light that illuminates the farthest upstage panel. She gazes into its glare and crawls backwards. She pulls herself up to standing, illuminated by a white square of light. She moves jerkily forward and runs upstage to balance on the balls of her feet, on the precipice between life and death. A crossroads. She repeats this pattern in several directions as if trying to find a way out of her pain. She falls to the ground. But, slowly and steadily, she wills movement into her frozen body and rises from the floor. Her arms expand outwards from her chest and will her knees into a deep bend. She begins to dance.

Sampradaya Dance Creations' 2001 contemporary *bharatanatyam* dance production, *Revealed by Fire: A Woman's Journey of Transformation*, chronicles the voyage of South Asian Canadian dance artist Lata Pada through the loss of her husband, Vishnu, and daughters, Brinda and Arti, in the 1985 bombing of Air India Flight 182.[1] The scene above is but one of several multilayered representations of her story of tragedy, grief, and recovery. A scene of struggle, it connotes Pada's coming to terms with, and healing from, her catastrophic loss. During this scene, the deceleration of her image reveals her body's every incipiency. Blurring across the screen, Pada stirs in me a quickening, an *affect*. Even though I am watching the DVD recording of the live performance, my heart pounds and chills crawl at the back of my neck. Through my body, I, the viewer, am summoned into Pada's story. I am moved by her, and I move with her.

I have been moving with *Revealed by Fire* since 2010 while working as a research assistant on a broader research program with Dr. Angela Failler at the University of Winnipeg titled "Building Communities of Memory: Remembrance Practice after the 1985 Air India Bombings." A main contribution of this project has been to identify the value of artistic responses in the formation of public memory of the bombings, which has otherwise been dominated by official accounts that rely on War on Terror framings of remembrance and redress implemented by the former Harper Government.[2] As an extension of this project, and to further explore the potentiality of what I shall refer to as the "creative counter-archive" (as opposed to the "official" archive of state-sponsored monuments and performances by government officials, and the "mainstream" archive of news media coverage and press photography circulating in the public sphere), I had the opportunity to view *Revealed by Fire* with Pada herself, in 2012. As she talked me through the production, I was struck by its powers as an intermedial dance performance to summon me kinesthetically as a witness to Pada's painful past; to make visible and visceral her integration of personal tragedy into self-repair, and to highlight the dancing body as a portal to those we have loved and lost.

My dance with *Revealed by Fire* proceeds through the following framing concepts and sections: first, through glosses of theories of art, performativity, and movement by queer theorist Eve Kosofsky Sedgwick and art historian Simon O'Sullivan, I analyze how Pada's performance gestures toward a reparative shift away from dominant modes of reception and critical analysis; next, moving with theorists of affect and queer studies, Mike Featherstone and Joshua Chambers-Letson, I parse the ways in which video technology makes visible Pada's splitting, undoing, and putting herself back together as a reparative feminist act; then, moving with ideas surrounding "the archive" put forth by dance scholar André Lepecki, I reimagine Air India's archives as shifting bodies in motion and dialogue, co-existing instead of colliding, where we, as settler Canadians, and as kinesthetic witnesses to this unfinished past, can send breath into their extremities, as to create a more nuanced picture of Air India's history as it unfolds within the global climate of anti-brown racism and white supremacy.

This essay is intended as a new entry point into the rich textures of *Revealed by Fire*, and is in conversation with the existing literature on *Revealed by Fire*, which spans across the fields of dance criticism, dramaturgical analysis, anthropology, and Pada's self-reflexive essays.[3] My embodied experience as a dancer and researcher allows me to curate theories of affect, dance, and performance, and to put these various disciplines and practices in dialogue with one another. I frame this essay as a dance with Pada to ground myself in my white settler body and to ethically position myself as a scholar-artist in relation to the victims and their families.

Affect, Art, and Reparative Reading

Revealed by Fire, the performance, begins quite informally. The lights fade up to illuminate a backdrop of giant rice paper panels draped with saris in red, orange, and yellow, the colours of fire. In a long white dress and simple purple sash (*pallu*), Lata Pada, as "Lata," enters the stage. As if humming music inside her head, she snaps her fingers, marking the movements with her hands as if turning inward to her mind's eye. Background noises of Hindi film scores and traffic are punctuated by the ominous roar of an airplane. The sound effects foreshadow rations of what is to come and slowly draw the audience into *Revealed by Fire*. Pada lays out the conventions of a typical rehearsal, of what was supposed to be an ordinary day in her life. She stands up and proceeds to map out a box-like pattern on the stage floor, a movement phrase she will repeat at the very end of the performance. Palms pressed together and hips gently swaying, Pada dances to classical Indian music. Her eyes open wide out to the audience she is imagining in rehearsal; the audience viewing the live performance of *Revealed by Fire*. She executes several sprightly phrases while travelling through the deep classical *bharatanatyam* knee bend as her arms and hands carve the air. Her movements are of strictly classical syntax, another indication this scenario represents the rehearsal of June 23, 1985, when a telephone call informed Pada of the deaths of her husband and daughters.

Suddenly, the ringing of the telephone smashes through this pleasant scene. The moment the telephone rings, the videographer has treated the DVD recording such that Pada's image is doubled so it appears as if there are two Padas dancing alongside each other, as if she is beside herself with grief. Her/their dance comes to a halt. Pada's face contorts into a pained expression. And when her image is slowed down, as in the first scene described, we can discern "the affect thresholds which cannot be perceived in the normal choreography of face-to-face interactions, but can be felt."[4] Pada's slow-motion body image becomes what Mike Featherstone calls a "body without image"; an open, affective body.[5] The magnification of Pada's facial expressions externalizes the qualitative displacements of her body in space, where her dancing body as the art "object/the dance" becomes an *event* beneath the surface of consciousness and language.[6]

Affect, that sense of being moved and/or moving something or someone, offers a way to move past a reading of the world as "encoded" or "mediated," whereby theory "decodes" or "extracts" meanings and truths.[7] Opening up one's awareness to experiencing-then-thinking-through affect is to surrender to a temporal shift in exploring how the body, movement, affect, and theories of such may provide radical new avenues to think through remembrance, mourning, and subjective experience. But how does one reach this level of receptivity? I am a dancer and, thus, assume I possess keen body awareness, but I have also been formally trained to privilege what is rational and quantifiable. Thinking through *Revealed by Fire*, and the entire creative counter-archive, beckons a shift in cognitive energies toward something queer theorist Eve Kosofsky Sedgwick calls "reparative reading."[8] Sedgwick thinks that paranoia, as a "hermeneutics of suspicion," has become the major paradigm for interpreting the world and objects of analysis, even though it is but one of many cognitive practices.[9] Consequently, dominant critical approaches have become anticipatory, seeking always to "reveal" the truth, "uncover" the real structures of hegemonic power, and ward off any bad surprises. Although these approaches are effective, paranoia thwarts alternative possibilities for making sense of the world.[10] Far-reaching and reductive, paranoia is about exposure via narrative, visibility, and detection.[11] For Sedgwick, interpretation needs to move past determining whether a piece of knowledge is true, or how can we reveal "truth," to what knowledge *does*; how it is performative and how best to move among its causes and effects.[12]

We must protect ourselves against certain threats to survive, but, as Sedgwick surmises, more often than not, paranoia reveals little to us about what to *do* with said fear other than to remain locked in a cycle of trying to stop it, and, in doing so, generating more of it.[13] In a similar tenor, art historian Simon O'Sullivan thinks we are caught on a certain "spatio-temporal" register where we see only what we have already seen and, thus, what we are already interested in. In the push to deconstruct, as is the dominant way of thinking about art and ourselves, we foreclose the possibility of accessing art as an *event* that is both of the world, as a made thing, and apart from the world. It is art's "apartness," or *affect*, that is of value over and above its occupation as a cultural object.[14] Instead of theorizing affect as some ethereal, transcendent thing, O'Sullivan suggests thinking about the aesthetic power of art in an *immanent* sense—as within the scope of our experience.[15]

Put differently, it is *transhuman*: "It is that which connects us to the world. It is the matter in us responding and resonating with the matter around us."[16] For O'Sullivan, art is indeed a portal to another world—our world, just "experienced differently," as "a world of impermanence and interpenetration, a molecular world of becoming."[17] Thus, if art has a function, it is to reconnect us with the nonhuman world around us; to re-access that which was there all along, and, with that, an understanding of *ourselves* as events and affects.[18]

Following the shrill ring of the telephone, recorded playtext spoken by Pada states,

> *It was an ordinary day. I was rehearsing. The phone rang. The phone rang on an ordinary day when I was rehearsing. On an ordinary day the phone rang. I was rehearsing when the phone rang. It was an ordinary day. I was rehearsing. It was an ordinary day. The phone rang. The phone rang. The phone rang.*[19]

In this stanza, written by playwright Judith Rudakoff, the repetition and permutations of a limited number of words invokes trauma's shattering of coherent communication, one of the prerequisites of intelligible subjecthood. This opening scene is the first of many occasions through which Pada draws the viewer in at a visceral, extra-linguistic level. In the absence of words, the splitting of Pada's image externalizes how the social and psychical fracture along trauma's fault lines. The two Padas are connotative of how the traumatized subject may, quite literally, be beside one's self in shock, something that cannot be fully realized in words. Unpacking affect further, O'Sullivan thinks affects are independent from knowledge or meaning and occur on a different, *asignifying* register, something that differentiates art from language.[20] (However, he points out that language does have an affective register whereby signification itself might be understood as just as complex an affective function, where meaning is the effect of affects. As I am, ultimately, doing here, writing about affects, attempting to translate affects into an essay, language is what makes affect meaningful.) Put differently by dancer and affect theorist Erin Manning, "Words are an extra component of the experience of articulation, not its final form."[21] My point is that the telephone poem exposes the instability of the linguistic utterance, bringing it onto an equal plane with nonverbal communication.

Dancing the Archive, Transforming Memory

Ocean waves crash across the rice paper screen as two dancers enter the stage playing Pada's daughters Brinda and Arti. Photographs of the lost girls float in water across the screen to connote their floating in the Atlantic Ocean—images of them as children, images of them as they were before they perished. The sounds of children laughing ripple over the soundscape as if to remind us of the many children whose lives and innocence were lost on board Flight 182. Pada enters the stage, spinning around with the two dancers. Their hands break apart and they slowly turn away from each other; the memory dissolves. The recorded playtext says, "There are stories of Vishnu and Brinda and Arti splashing in the swimming pool, the three of them bobbing up and down in the water. So long in the water."[22] A picture of Pada and her daughters as teenagers floats in water, to which von Tiedemann added black dye to connote the murkiness of these memories. Pada sits on the stage. One girl kneels down, resting her head on Pada's lap, then the other. Suddenly, a phone message, a message Brinda left on a friend's answering machine right before the fateful flight plays over the soundscape. They each kiss her on the cheek. She touches her cheeks with her hands, savouring the memories, the sensation on her skin. Then she opens her eyes, her arms and hands miming a tearing motion, tearing the fabric of memory. Pada hugs the girls close to her. Brinda's voice says, "Bye. Have a nice summer."[23] The dancers slowly get up. Pada is resistant to let go of their hands, to let go of the comfort and suspension within these fleeting memories.

Dance theorist André Lepecki shifts notions of archiving as only preserving the past toward Foucault's treatment of the archive in *The Archeology of Knowledge* (1972) as "a system of *transforming simultaneously* past, present, and future."[24] Writing about choreography specifically, Lepecki reframes the archive's ontology, or state of being, as a permeable membrane "where all sorts of onto-political 'rewritings' take place, including the rewriting of movement, including the rewriting of the archive itself."[25] In so doing, Lepecki understands dance "as that which passes away (in time and across space)"; "as that which passes around (between and across bodies of dancers, viewers, choreographers)"; and "as that which also, always, *comes back around.*"[26] Choreography "founds a particular economy, where bodies inter-twine, or intermingle, across time—in an endless chain of reciprocal emissions, transmissions, receptions, and exchanges of times, gestures, steps, affects, sweat, breathing, and historical and political particles."[27] It is Lepecki's notion of the dancer's body as an infinitely changeable archive or "archival-corporeal system" that I apply to the dancers in *Revealed by Fire*, where they offer Pada passage back to her family.

Another dancer joins her onstage. They mirror each other, caressing each other's faces. The dancer could be Vishnu, conjuring the memory of his presence and touch. " There are stories of falling in love and falling out of the sky. Falling leaves and falling out of favour. There are stories about falling forward and falling backwards. There are stories of falling into winter and falling into depression."[28] Pada and her partner curve over, supported on each other's backs. " There are stories about falling away and falling in to, in a tiny black box the final moments recorded. How do I unlock the box? What's the combination? I sleeplessly turn left turn right."[29] A picture of Vishnu and the two little girls smiling out at the camera appears. " Turn left. We never recovered his body. I dream and in the dream again and again Vishnu comes back as if at the end of a long business trip but Brinda and Arti aren't with him."[30] Pada and the dancer, joined together, lunge together, enveloped in each other's arms. "No one took a photograph at the airport. What were they wearing? I don't even know what they were wearing that day."[31] Alone, Pada makes slow, curving motions. The photographs disappear into stain, ink, murkiness.

Representing Pada's husband and two daughters, the dancers' bodies become the mediums between "Lata" and her loved ones. Through the dancers' likenesses, flashes of their memories take tangible form, an occurrence also expressed in Shelley Saywell's 1999 film *Legacy of Terror: The Bombing of Air India*, which documents the personal narratives of Pada and Sarojini Laurence, whose teenage daughters Shyamala and Krithika, acclaimed South Asian dancers and friends of the Padas, were also killed in the bombing.[32] There is a scene in Saywell's film where Laurence watches Pada's dancers in rehearsal. Later, she reflects, "When this girl was doing [all] these movements she reminded me of Shyamala so much. I began to see her there and then...I saw Krithika there." To this Pada responds, "I see Brinda and Arti in many of them and sometimes it's just amazing. It might even just be a physical characteristic. It might just be a way a girl tosses her hair, the perfume that one of them wears and it just brings back all these memories."[33] The dancers' moving bodies and likeness to the women's murdered daughters allow them to conjure and superimpose their traces onto the dancers' bodies. The girls are physically absent but never lost. Through their conjuring of Pada's loved ones, the dancers' sculpting of time and space with their bodies makes room for the memories of Vishnu, Brinda, and Arti. And, if dance is that which comes back around, though never the same as before, her dancers enable Pada to savour memories, though always indirectly, of her family in new and unexpected ways.

Transforming Loss, Performing Self-Repair

As the performance continues, each re-enactment of one of Pada's memories: her childhood, arranged marriage, immigration to Canada, and the bombing of Flight 182, which another loss materializes, is a foreclosure of some other entity, dream, or desire within: lost homeland, lost dreams, lost illusion of Canada as a peaceful country, lost husband, lost role as a wife, lost children, lost motherhood. In light of all of these losses, it would appear that, like her family on board Flight 182, Pada has also fallen off the radar, so to speak. In her new social role as a widow, her imbrications within these lost people and objects blur her being and render her an impossible subject, evidenced by Rudakoff's playtext: "Widow. Black cat. I stain the world around me."[34] There is a poignant scene near the end where Pada, as "Lata" the widow, kneels on the stage floor, shrouded in a white veil. The "veil" is a large white cloth covered in red handprints. Pada pulls it over her shoulders, holding it up like a wall behind her to represent a wall in Rajasthan, India, that still bears the handprints of Hindu widows who, in fear of the Muslim invasion during the Post-Vedic and Epic periods, jumped into their husbands' funeral pyres instead of suffering rape and the social ostracism of widowhood. The dancers crouch in front of the white sheet. They place their hands over the red handprints for several moments. Then, hands gyrating, they lift them off the fabric. This sequence is symbolic of the widows' rubbing of their hands in vermilion and marking them on the wall before committing *jauhar*. A powerful image, this scenario connotes a sense of connecting to the past, of the dancers, in the present, touching the lives and stories of the women who came before them. Wrapped in the stories of the widows, "Lata," literally and figuratively, carries the past.

Later, Pada joins her dancers in a colourful, hopeful dance that lasts several minutes. The phone rings again, but this time it is followed by her recorded message about Sampradaya Dance Creations' performance of *Revealed by Fire*, signifying a sense of continuum. Savoury memories of her family envelope and sustain her. "Lata" re-maps the box-like pattern she traced at the beginning of the performance. The stage floor is like flesh upon which she has etched her story. Although the scab has healed, it remains a shiny palimpsest-like patch on the skin of her life. Through the recorded playtext, Pada speaks:

> *All my mothers a line through me. The sounding of voices calling in colours. Who am I? I am the journey. Arc across my sky. All my mothers a line through me. An ocean of faces carried inside. Who am I? I am the journey. The only way out is through. All my mothers a line through me. Beginning with ending. End of all beginnings. Who am I? I am the journey. I have always been here. The only way out is through.*[35]

This scene provides a reparative sense of "wholeness," where Pada does not suppress her past wounds, but, instead, integrates them into her self-healing in the present and future.[36] Further, in Pada's framing of herself as a hybrid subject, her journey through grief undoes racist framings of the victims' families as eternally melancholic subjects that relegate their "South Asianness" and "brownness" to a register of abjectness and subalternaiety, even though many are Canadian citizens. In doing so, Pada liberates grief from its popular designation as a negative emotion and illuminates its powers as a creative force, constitutive of her nuanced positionality as a South Asian Canadian woman. Her embrace of her wounds activates her trauma and grief not as pathology but as a creative means with which to (re)mediate memories and self-knowledge. Pada carries her past both literally and figuratively. Her dancing body is her archive, the vessel of her personal genealogy, the history of her present. Her energy radiates in infinite vectors from her strong centre core, puncturing the spokes of her kinesphere, puncturing the guise of "truth" cloaking "official" and "mainstream" representations and bending the frames of cultural representation, such as news media photographs that freeze the victims' families in their expressions of lingering grief, as melancholic "affect aliens" in their apparent "failure" to "get over" their loss.[37]

To conclude, then, *Revealed by Fire* takes us outside of paranoid hermeneutics and into alternative, reparative spaces of resistance—openings where mourning and grief may remain unfinished and where seemingly "negative" emotions are, instead, different paths to illumination. But we also catch a glimpse of something else; the body in flux—that which escapes cultural grids and semiotic encapsulation. It materializes before our eyes like a handprint on fogged-up glass, for, as O'Sullivan puts it, the moment, the event, is inaccessible to consciousness and all we ever have is its trace.[38] Instead of covering up the wound, *Revealed by Fire* materializes, if only partially, the imprint of psychic scars, the violence of neo-colonialism in a post-9/11 era. Reframed through affect theories, *Revealed by Fire* incites us to practice epistemic humility regarding the objects persons may attach to affects of grieving and remembering those lives lost. It empowers us to ask different questions, such as how emotions may be politicized and pragmatic forms of reparation discovered. As an entity, the creative counter-archive unsettles paranoid hermeneutics, facts, hard evidence, and anti-terrorist legislation—attempts at redress that, ultimately, lead to racial profiling and further discrimination against minoritized subjects. It dances in and around narratives of liberal multiculturalism and tolerance that regulate national feelings and perform Canada as a benevolent country. On a final and more hopeful note, the creative counter-archive reminds us of the various lenses through which to make sense of the world and that there are different frequencies of understanding and awareness with which to forge a re-membering of Air India in its future becomings. Through the gauge of affect, even dances predicated on the most horrific of events, as *Revealed by Fire* is, actualize the possibilities of life.

Author's Note

I would like to thank Angela Failler for introducing me to *Revealed by Fire*. This essay is fondly dedicated to Margaret E. Toye, who introduced me to affect theory, and with whom I developed the idea of the creative counter-archive. I would also like to thank Lata Pada for her generosity and for guiding me through her art. Finally, I would like to thank the editors for their patience and rigorous constructive criticism of this essay.

Notes

1. Lata Pada, *Revealed by Fire: A Woman's Journey of Transformation*, directed and choreographed by Lata Pada, composition by Timothy Sullivan and R.A. Ramamani, visual design by Cylla von Tiedemann, dramaturgy by Judith Rudakoff (Mississauga, ON: Sampradaya Dance Creations, 2001), DVD.
2. This program was originally funded by a grant from the Social Sciences and Humanities Research Council of Canada (SSHRC). See Angela Failler, "'War-on-Terror' Frames of Remembrance: The 1985 Air India Bombings after 9/11," *TOPIA: Canadian Journal of Cultural Studies* 27 (Spring 2012): 253–269; Angela Failler with artwork by Eisha Marjara, "'Remember Me Nought': The 1985 Air India Bombings and Cultural *Nachträglichkeit*," *Public: Art/Culture/Ideas* 42 (2010): 113–124; Angela Failler, "Remembering the Air India Disaster: Memorial and Counter-Memorial," *Review of Education, Pedagogy, and Cultural Studies* 31, no. 2–3 (April 2009): 150–176.
3. Bonnie Kim, " The Divine Within: Lata Pada and Cylla von Tiedemann," *The Dance Current* 3, no. 10 (2001): 21–23; Judith Rudakoff, *Revealed by Fire: Backgrounder* (Mississauga, ON: Sampradaya Dance Creations, 2001); Judith Rudakoff, "Shifting Boundaries and Crossing Borders: Dramaturging Lata Pada's *Revealed by Fire*," *Theatre Forum: An International Journal of Theatre Performance* 20 (2002): 13–20;

Susan McNaughton, "Revealed by Fire: One Woman's Journey of Transformation," *InTensions* 4 (2010): 1–35; Susan McNaughton, "Revealed by Fire: Lata Pada's Narrative of Transformation," in *Fields in Motion: Ethnography in the Worlds of Dance*, ed. Dena Davida (Waterloo, ON: Wilfrid Laurier University Press, 2011), 381–402; Lata Pada, "Revealed by Fire: From the Personal to the Universal," *Canadian Theatre Review* 146, no. 1 (2011): 45–49.

4. Mike Featherstone, "Body Image/Body without Image: Body, Image and Affect in Consumer Culture," *Body & Society* 16, no. 1 (2010): 199.
5. Ibid.
6. Ibid.
7. Brian Massumi, *Parables for the Virtual: Movement, Affect, Sensation* (Durham, NC: Duke University Press, 2002), 2.
8. Eve Kosofsky Sedgwick, "Paranoid Reading and Reparative Reading, or, You're So Paranoid, You Probably Think This Essay Is about You," in *Touching Feeling: Affect, Pedagogy, and Performativity* (Durham, NC: Duke University Press, 2003), 123–154.
9. Ibid., 125.
10. Joshua Chambers-Letson, "Introduction: Reparative Feminisms, Repairing Feminism—Reparation, Postcolonial Violence, and Feminism," *Women and Performance: A Journal of Feminist Theory* 16, no. 2 (July 2006): 172.
11. Ibid., 138.
12. Ibid., 124.
13. Chambers-Letson, "Introduction," 172.
14. Simon O'Sullivan, " The Aesthetics of Affect: Thinking Beyond Art Representation," *Angelaki Journal of the Theoretical Humanities* 6 (2001): 127.
15. Ibid., 126.
16. Ibid., 128.
17. Ibid., 128.
18. Ibid.
19. Rudakoff, *Revealed by Fire.*
20. O'Sullivan, "Aesthetics of Affect," 126.
21. Erin Manning, *Relationscapes: Movement, Art, Philosophy* (Cambridge, MA: MIT Press, 2009), 215.
22. Rudakoff, *Revealed by Fire.*
23. Ibid.
24. André Lepecki, " The Body as Archive: Will to Re-Enact and the Afterlives of Dances," *Dance Research Journal* 42, no. 2 (2010): 30.
25. Michel Foucault quoted in ibid., 38.
26. Ibid., 42.
27. Ibid.

28. Rudakoff, *Revealed by Fire.*
29. Ibid.
30. Ibid.
31. Ibid.
32. *Legacy of Terror: The Bombing of Air India*, directed by Shelley Saywell (Toronto: Bishari Films, 1999), DVD.
33. Ibid.
34. Rudakoff, *Revealed by Fire.*
35. Ibid.
36. Chambers-Letson, "Introduction."
37. Sara Ahmed, *The Promise of Happiness* (Durham, NC: Duke University Press, 2010), 133.
38. O'Sullivan, "Aesthetics of Affect," 126.

Works Cited

Ahmed, Sara. *The Promise of Happiness.* Durham, NC: Duke University Press, 2010.

Chambers-Letson, Joshua. "Introduction: Reparative Feminisms, Repairing Feminism—Reparation, Postcolonial Violence, and Feminism." *Women and Performance: A Journal of Feminist Theory* 16, no. 2 (July 2006): 169–189.

Failler, Angela, with artwork by Eisha Marjara. "'Remember Me Nought': The 1985 Air India Bombings and Cultural *Nachträglichkeit.*" *Public: Art/Culture/Ideas* 42 (2010): 113–124.

———. "Remembering the Air India Disaster: Memorial and Counter-Memorial." *Review of Education, Pedagogy, and Cultural Studies* 31, no. 2–3 (April 2009): 150–176.

———. "'War-on-Terror' Frames of Remembrance: The 1985 Air India Bombings after 9/11." TOPIA: *Canadian Journal of Cultural Studies* 27 (Spring 2012): 253–269.

Featherstone, Mike. "Body Image/Body without Image: Body, Image and Affect in Consumer Culture." *Body & Society* 16, no. 1 (2010): 193–221.

Kim, Bonnie. " The Divine Within: Lata Pada and Cylla von Tiedemann." *The Dance Current* 3, no. 10 (2001): 21–23.

Legacy of Terror: The Bombing of Air India. Directed by Shelley Saywell. Toronto: Bishari Films, 1999. DVD.

Lepecki, André. " The Body as Archive: Will to Re-Enact and the Afterlives of Dances." *Dance Research Journal* 42, no. 2 (2010): 28–48.

Manning, Erin. *Relationscapes: Movement, Art, Philosophy.* Cambridge, MA: MIT Press, 2009.

Massumi, Brian. *Parables for the Virtual: Movement, Affect, Sensation.* Durham, NC: Duke University Press, 2002.

McNaughton, Susan. "Revealed by Fire: Lata Pada's Narrative of Transformation." In *Fields in Motion: Ethnography in the Worlds of Dance*, edited by Dena Davida, 381–402. Waterloo, ON: Wilfrid Laurier University Press, 2011.

———. "Revealed by Fire: One Woman's Journey of Transformation." *InTensions* 4 (2010): 1–35.

O'Sullivan, Simon. "The Aesthetics of Affect: Thinking Beyond Art Representation." *Angelaki Journal of the Theoretical Humanities* 6 (2001): 125–135.

Pada, Lata. *Revealed by Fire: A Woman's Journey of Transformation*. Directed and choreographed by Lata Pada. Composition by Timothy Sullivan and R.A. Ramamani. Visual design by Cylla von Tiedemann. Dramaturgy by Judith Rudakoff. Mississauga, ON: Sampradaya Dance Creations, 2001. DVD.

———. "Revealed by Fire: From the Personal to the Universal." *Canadian Theatre Review* 146, no. 1 (2011): 45–49.

Rudakoff, Judith. *Revealed by Fire: Backgrounder*. Mississauga, ON: Sampradaya Dance Creations, 2001.

———. "Shifting Boundaries and Crossing Borders: Dramaturging Lata Pada's *Revealed by Fire*." *Theatre Forum: An International Journal of Theatre Performance* 20 (2002): 13–20.

Sedgwick, Eve Kosofsky. "Paranoid Reading and Reparative Reading, or, You're So Paranoid, You Probably Think This Essay Is About You." In *Touching Feeling: Affect, Pedagogy, and Performativity*, 123–154. Durham, NC: Duke University Press, 2003.

Revealed by Fire

Artist Statement

LATA PADA

IN JUNE 1985, Canadian *bharatanatyam* dancer Lata Pada was rehearsing in a studio in Bombay, India. A devastating phone call informed her of the loss of her husband and two daughters in the midflight explosion of Air India Flight 182. Sixteen years later, Lata created *Revealed by Fire*, a multidisciplinary dance-theatre production, in collaboration with photographer/visual designer Cylla von Tiedemann, dramaturge and playwright Judith Rudakoff, and composers R.A. Ramamani and Timothy Sullivan.

Revealed by Fire is the story of self-discovery, of the artist's triumphant, albeit painful, journey to reclaim her life and a return to wholeness. Dance is the medium for this mythic journey of transcendence of loss and a ritual of transformation that reconciles the classical aesthetic tradition of *bharatanatyam* to express something new.

The tension between perceptions of "tradition" and "contemporary" are heightened by the artistic, aesthetic, and cultural discourses surrounding the practice of *bharatanatyam* outside its place of origin, i.e., India. *Revealed by Fire* also addresses the redefinition of *bharatanatyam* within a diasporic

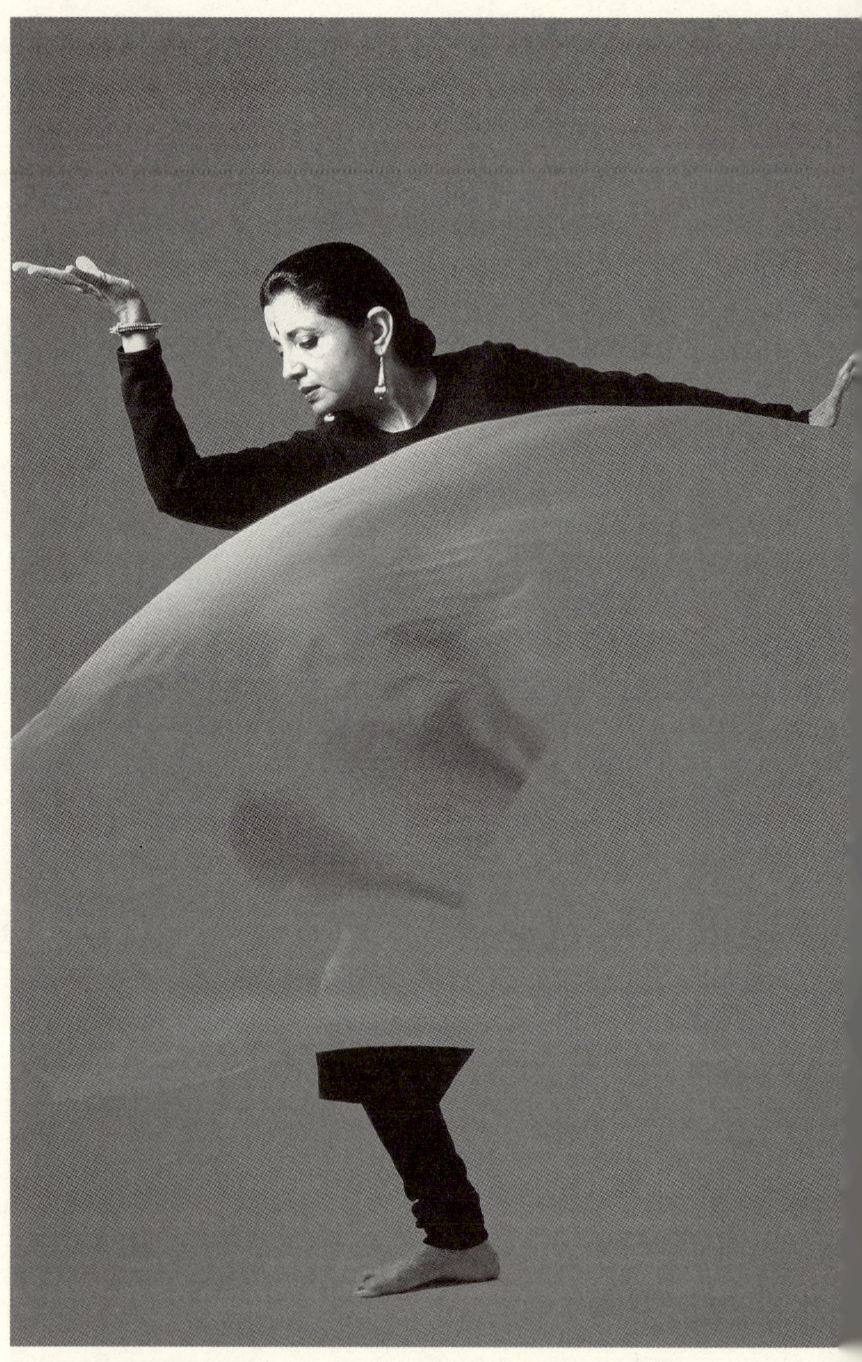

Dance performance still from Lata Pada's Revealed by Fire. *Photograph by Cylla von Tiedemann. Reprinted by permission of the photographer and the artist.*

culture of two worlds and two temporal frames of reference. In claiming the narrative as her own, the artist negotiates and transcends prescribed formal values of "tradition" and "authenticity."

Source

The artist statement has been adapted from "*Revealed by Fire*: From the Personal to the Universal," by Lata Pada. Copyright © 2011 by University of Toronto Press. Originally published in *Canadian Theatre Review* 146 (Spring 2011): 45–49. DOI: http://dx.doi.org/10.3138/ctr.146.45. Reprinted by permission of University of Toronto Press and by permission of the author.

■

An Invocation Dance for Lata

UMA PARAMESWARAN

for June 23, 2000:
15th anniversary of the crash of *Emperor Kanishka*, Air India Flight 182

iii.
An Invocation Dance for Lata

(After five years of withdrawal and meditation, Lata Pada returned to the world of dance, and is now the Artistic Director of Sampradaya Dance Academy in Toronto)

Come, Ambike, to where I stand.
Come, be seated, I pray.
Queen of beginnings,
Whose benediction brings worlds into being,
and in time dissolves them into nothingness.
Goddess lovely as the dawn
and frightening as moonless night.

Wide sea of compassion,
Wielder of sword incarnadine.
Giver of grief greater than any mother should ever have to bear,
Sole comfort in my years of anguished despair.

Ambike, creator of all past worlds,
and of those yet unborn,
Mother, in whom all opposites converge,
help me understand
why you struck down all that was mine,
then raised me to dance exultantly at your side,
to sing in celebration that I am I,
a woman born of woman with woman power
to feel
    joy at the sight of the rising sun,
    rage at my sisters' pitiable plight,
    hope for our children's future
in this lovely land of endless skies.

Source

An Ethics of Remembering

Air India 182 and Its Creative Archive

TERESA HUBEL

SOMETIMES, through a loss that is extraordinary, a human being is pushed beyond the boundaries of the ordinary and into what might be described as the mythic. This is the kind of story that Lata Pada tells in her 2001 *bharatanatyam* dance performance, *Revealed by Fire*. In addition to Pada herself, the main characters in the performance—hinted at through photographic images projected against the back wall of the stage, momentarily embodied in the movements of the young dancers, and mentioned in Judith Rudakoff's dramaturgical text—include her husband, Vishnu, and their two daughters, Brinda and Arti. By the middle of the production, we begin to realize that the narrative of this family involved a migration from India to Canada, from Bombay to Thompson, Manitoba, during the 1970s when many other South Asian families made similar journeys. It is the crash of Air India Flight 182 that severs Pada—whose husband and children all died when that plane went down—from the common, the everyday, and the ordinary.

It is difficult to feel adequate to the task of addressing this dance fashioned from the torn edges and the profound mineshafts of the almost incomparable (literally "without compare") life of Lata Pada. I vividly remember the photographs that first tried to tell the Air India 182 story in the pages of the *Kingston Whig-Standard* in that summer of 1985, when I, too, was a student of *bharatanatyam* and was looking forward to a year-long trip to Madras, where I would study this classical Indian dance form in a well-known school. In shot after 1980s studio shot, page after newspaper page, I saw families, frozen in their wholeness, not ruptured by catastrophe, and then—quite shockingly to me because suddenly the event became intensely personal—an image of two girls in colourful costumes caught in the statuesque poses of *bharatanatyam*. I think now they must have been the daughters of Sarojini Laurence, another woman whose motherhood fell into horrific bewilderment after the crash, which claimed her only children, Shyamala and Krithika. I do not know for certain if these girls were the Laurence sisters, but I remember that the photo's caption read that they had been on their way to India to learn dance. In July 1985, I began the same trip and returned safe, but utterly changed, to Canada a year later. I came home. Perhaps my story doesn't really matter in the face of the inalterable loss that was the Air India tragedy. It is, after all, only a small connection to a more monumental tale, but it is that small connection that has been for me the means through which I have tried, for over thirty years now, to make sense of this almost incomprehensible loss. What makes large events real to us except the ability to touch them, to connect with them, in some way? We touch them so we can begin to understand and incorporate them into our histories.

Revealed by Fire invites us into a personal relationship with an international tragedy. It is one of the many tales, accounts, and chronicles in films, novels, poems, and short stories that have emerged from the Air India crash, a collection that represents the creative archive of Air India 182. What does this archive do? And what do we do with it? Concentrating on Pada's life and performance, Elan Marchinko and Uma Parameswaran offer us possibilities.

For Marchinko, Pada's "embrace of her wounds activates her trauma and grief not as pathology but as a creative means with which to (re)mediate memories and self-knowledge."[1] The perpetrators of the bombing of Flight 182 are not even hinted at in *Revealed by Fire*, though it is the focus on this side of the tragedy—the who-did-it story—that propels "official" memorializations of this singular event in Canadian history. In these "official" records, the victims' families are, she writes, framed as eternally "melancholic 'affect aliens,'"[2] fixed in their roles as "traumatized subjects."[3] Pada's dance production defies this mainstream image by ignoring it, ultimately showing us a woman who is fired by the kiln of grief into something fine and strong and artistically resourceful, into someone not eternally grieving but not *not* grieving either. Pada's art points us toward an ethics of remembering.

For Parameswaran, Pada's return to *bharatanatyam* following years of withdrawal is lovingly envisioned as a prayer for illumination to the goddess Ambike: "creator of all past worlds, / and of those yet unborn, / Mother..."[4] The motherhood of the now childless mother who is Lata Pada after the plane's crash engenders triumph and sisterhood.

These texts speak about what is enabled by Pada's grief and the dance that has emerged from it.

But what is *revealed* by fire?

Is it Lata Pada's potent creative agency, which stands in defiance of and contrast to "official" attempts to cement her—and all the other family members who lost loved ones in the Air India crash—in the abjectified, objectified position of the perpetual mourner, as Marchinko asserts?

Or Pada's own personal connection to a Sita-like, forged-by-fire ideal, where, in impersonation of the goddess, she must, as the voice-over in *Revealed by Fire* observes, "step into the fire" and become the burned-alive woman: "she looked into the fire and the fire was terrifying...and in the moment of greatest pain and burning, she, like Sita, saw that at the heart of the fire was its strength and its weakness and so she embraced it and found that it embraced her."[5] This is the person we see in the photograph reproduced here: a woman, Pada herself, half hidden by a swath of red (a sweep of diaphanous cloth? a wave of crimson water?) against a red background. Her face is composed, but is she burning?

Or is it Parameswaran's revelation of the presence of the female divine in Pada's reclamation and reformation of a self-consciously feminist self in Canada, "this lovely land of endless skies"?[6]

Maybe what is finally revealed to us is that if she can remake herself—as fragmented and contingent as that remaking is—so can we, as individuals and as citizens of a Canada that not only remembers the Air India tragedy of June 1985 but embraces our relationship to it. As extraordinary an event as it was, especially for those who have been personally bereft by it, it was, as bereavement, an event of incontrovertible humanness. The varied creative responses to that bereavement, such as Lata Pada's dance, can lead us toward new, more ethical kinds of connections and commitments.

Author's Note

I would like to thank Nandi Bhatia, Brian Patton, and Julia Emberley for reading earlier drafts of this essay and offering such insightful advice.

Notes

1. See Marchinko in this volume.
2. Ibid.
3. Ibid.
4. See Parameswaran's "An Invocation Dance for Lata," in this volume.
5. Judith Rudakoff, *Revealed by Fire: Backgrounder* (Mississauga, ON: Sampradaya Dance Creations, 2001).
6. See Parameswaran's "An Invocation Dance for Lata," in this volume.

Works Cited

Rudakoff, Judith. *Revealed by Fire: Backgrounder.* Mississauga, ON: Sampradaya Dance Creations, 2001.

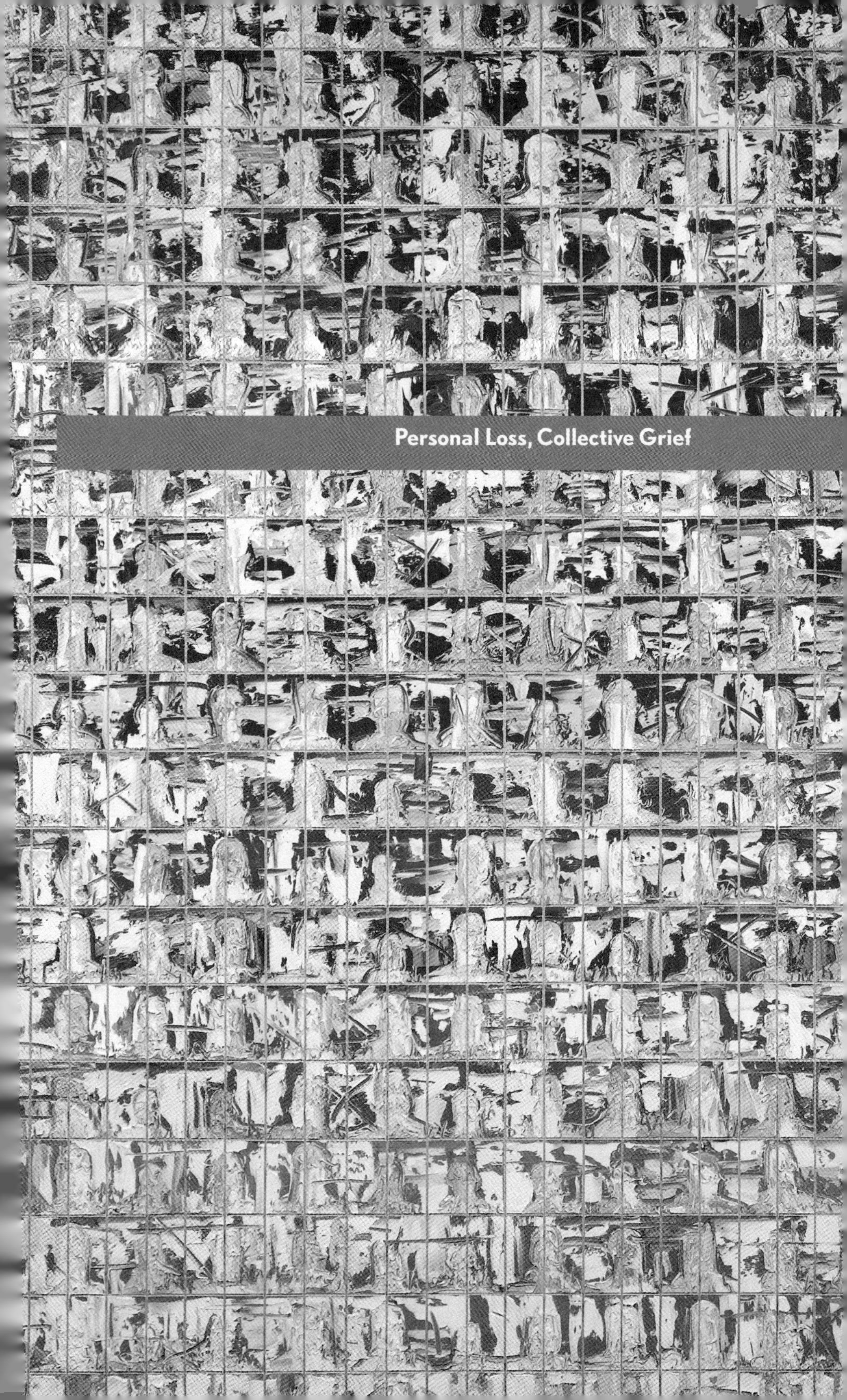

Personal Loss, Collective Grief

Overleaf: Deon Venter, Names *(detail) from the* Flight 182 *series, 2008. Oil on linen. 73" x 87".*

Model Mourning, Multiculturalism, and the Air India Tragedy

CHANDRIMA CHAKRABORTY

Whose lives count as lives? And, finally, what makes for a grievable life?

—JUDITH BUTLER, "Violence, Mourning, Politics," 2003, p. 10

Grief is the thing left over after grievance has had its say.

—ANNE ANLIN CHENG, *The Melancholy of Race*, 2000, p. 172

THE AIR INDIA TRAGEDY represents a clear moment of crisis in Canadian multiculturalism.[1] The numerous—belated—attempts in the last decade to memorialize the June 23, 1985, bombing of Air India Flight 182 that killed 329 people and the explosion of a bomb in Narita International Airport that killed two others can be read as official attempts to "manage" this crisis. Notable examples include a Canadian prime minister's attendance at the annual memorial service held in Ahakista, Ireland, in 2005, the establishment of the commission of inquiry into the bombing of Air India Flight 182 in 2006, and the installation of permanent public memorials for the victims of Air India Flight 182 beginning in 2007. These acts of state memorialization were undoubtedly prompted by the lingering grief and grievances of those who lost family and friends on Air India Flight 182, for as Clark Blaise and Bharati Mukherjee point out, " The failure to acknowledge the victims of the crash as Canadians remains for most of the families the enduring political grief of Air India 182."[2] Canadian government discourse narrativizes the "cascading series of errors" by the Canadian government and official agencies that John C. Major chronicles in his final report of the commission of inquiry as an isolated wrong, an aberration in the Canadian state's long and celebrated lineage of welcoming immigrants.[3] This framing essentially covers up a history of racism: momentous, as in the case of the 1914 rerouting of the *Komagata Maru*, and mundane, as in the discriminations experienced by minorities in their day-to-day living.[4] Through this framing, the Air India story is also made comprehensible as an accidental bump on the road in Canada's acclaimed multicultural journey, while Canadian multiculturalism is reconsolidated with the nation having publicly acknowledged its errors and "come clean" before its aggrieved minorities.[5]

I have discussed elsewhere how highly public(ized) official redressals function as tools of the state to manage and suppress the feelings that linger in the psyche of those who lost loved ones in the Air India bombings.[6] I am interested in exploring here how mourners *continue to grieve*, despite government discourses that encourage closure. If, as Anne Cheng reminds us, a redressal of grievance—"the social and legal articulation of grief"[7]—cannot signal the end of grief and grieving, how can we grapple with the "emotional labour" required of racialized minorities living with loss and managing feelings of grief, anger, rage, helplessness, or frustration?[8] How can we be responsive and responsible to such emotional labour?

For many contemporary Western thinkers interested in the political impact of grieving, Sigmund Freud's "Mourning and Melancholia" is the conventional point of departure. Drawing upon Freud's famous 1917 essay, scholars have viewed mourning as a healthy and normal process of grieving and melancholia as pathological, a type of grieving process that does not seem to end. Freud attributed this interminable pathological affect to the melancholic subject's essentially unfinished relationship with the lost loved object, leading the grieving (melancholic) subject to uncontrollable self-berating and self-devaluation, and withdrawal from the world.[9] Thus, melancholia came to stand for a disassociation from one's everyday social world and the inability to get over the past. Successful completion of the work of mourning entailed accepting loss and the past as finished followed by a reorientation toward the present and future.[10]

Resisting this imperative to see melancholia as only pathological, Judith Butler mobilized Freud's argument about melancholia or the inability or refusal to give up what has been lost as a more productive emotion. She reconceptualized melancholia not as a pathological state that is to be worked through but as the sign of a political, indeed hegemonic, prohibition to be worked against. Instead of an "aberrant form of mourning," in which the mourner is unable to break attachment to the one who is lost, Butler suggests that melancholia be read as the "social regulation of psychic life."[11] Following Butler's lead, José Muñoz, Anne Cheng, David Eng, and David Kazanjian, among others, have urged us to think about what might be gained "from tarrying with grief, from remaining exposed to its unbearability."[12] Cheng and Muñoz, in particular, have examined the fraught process of racialized and heteronormative national subject formation that calls for the recasting of grief. As Muñoz puts it, "for blacks and queers...melancholia [is] not a pathology or a self-absorbed mood that inhibits activism, [but] a mechanism that helps us (re)construct identity and take our dead to the various battles we must wage in their names."[13] Such a conceptualization of melancholia offers us a means to comprehend the grief and loss of the aggrieved not as stasis but "as a dynamic process" with "transformative potentials for political imagination."[14] Engaging with a history of grief that is carried by successor generations who inherit the legacies of sorrow involves facing its intricacies and paradoxes. Rather than an inability to let go of the past, melancholia that involves "a continuous engagement with loss and its remains allows us," according to Eng and Kazanjian, "to gain new perspectives on and new understandings of lost objects."[15] The work of mourning, in fact, becomes possible "through melancholia's continued engagement with the various and ongoing forms of loss" because it necessitates that one remain open to the contradictions produced by loss and resistance.[16] It is the melancholic's painful attachments to the past that keeps the past alive in the present and calls for an ongoing, creative dialogue with history.

The appeal of the turn to melancholia in recent scholarship for me lies in this affect of unfinished grieving and unfinished pasts that alert us to silences, silencing, and other(ed) stories and, in addition, call us to strive for justice and accountability for past injustices. Creative remembrances of the Air India tragedy and its aftermath illustrate how grief persists in and shapes the present for those who lost loved ones in the bombing of Air India Flight 182. I examine two creative texts in this essay, Bharati Mukherjee's 1988 short story " The Management of Grief," and Eisha Marjara's 1998 docudrama *Desperately Seeking Helen*, both of which offer compelling understandings of melancholia as an engagement with loss that refuses closure.[17] Both trace for us a long history of racialized subjects living with loss and struggling to "manage" their grief. They place emphasis on "the constitutive role that grief plays in racial/ethnic subject-formation,"[18] and illustrate how racialized subjects have to suppress their grief and cultivate a "proper" outer display of feelings in order to fit into multicultural Canada. This essay looks toward these two texts in seeking to answer the following questions: What does it mean for racialized subjects to live with loss? How does one "manage" grief while mourning loss? How do mourners continue to grieve in the face of government discourses that direct them toward closure? In answering these questions, I hope to demonstrate how Mukherjee's and Marjara's works bear the burden of excavating elided histories and bringing to the surface the suffering and pain of minoritized subjects who are usually not heard or deemed legible. As they move the reader from the subjective or predominantly privatized conception of grief to a reconceptualization of grief as collective and ongoing, these texts position grief as creative, unpredictable, political, and social.

Managing Grief, Managing Minorities

In *The Managed Heart*, Arlie Hochschild examines the emotional labour or work involved in private and public life as we bridge the gap between what we feel and what we "ought" to feel. She argues that based on our private mutual understanding of "feeling rules,"[19] we constantly manage our outer expressions of feeling. Writing in the Canadian context, Daniel Coleman elaborates for us the feeling rules that Canadians (white and non-white) have to follow.[20] He writes, "Canadians are mythologized as civil" and part of being "civil" is demonstrating "cultivated, polite behaviour."[21] According to Coleman, civility operates as a mode of both internal and external management. Internal management involves subjects "disciplin[ing] their conduct in order to participate in the civil realm, and they themselves gain or lose legitimacy in an internally striated civil society depending on the degrees to which they conform to its ideals."[22] On the other hand, as a "mode" of external management, civility gives "civil subjects a mandate for managing the circumstances of those perceived as uncivil."[23] Evidently, then, these cultural frames of "white civility" work to uphold certain losses as worthy of grieving and certain forms of grieving as emblematic of the "civil" or "model" Canadian citizen ("internal management"). This, in turn, sets limits on mourning *particular* losses and on the specific practices of mourning ("external management"). In the context of the Air India tragedy, Blaise and Mukherjee note that the bombing of Air India Flight 182 en route to Delhi from Montreal via Toronto was initially viewed as a "foreign" tragedy, "an Indian post-colonial tragedy in which newly independent peoples try to redraw provincial boundaries. It was a tragedy affecting only Hindus and Sikhs...A foreign carrier had crashed off foreign seas."[24] In the face of the Canadian state's dismissal of the Air India tragedy as Canada's loss, how could the loss be rendered visible and how could mourning take place? How did Canadian norms of civility work to recognize some mourners as "civil" (i.e., "model") Canadians, while rendering unintelligible the grief of other mourners?

Creative texts such as Mukherjee's and Marjara's allow us to engage with these questions. In Mukherjee's " The Management of Grief," the trauma of those who lost loved ones in the bombing of Air India Flight 182 is reflected through the central protagonist Shaila, whose husband and two sons were on the plane. That the Canadian state's nonrecognition of the tragedy forces grieving families to hide their loss is evocatively portrayed in the first lines of the story: "A woman I don't know is boiling tea the Indian way in my kitchen. There are a lot of women I don't know in my kitchen, whispering and moving tactfully. They open doors, rummage through the pantry, and try not to ask me where things are kept."[25] Peopled by anonymous "whispering" characters who move "tactfully," the story poignantly reproduces the precariousness of minority existence that necessitates the careful "management" of feelings in the context of a tragic loss that does not register *as loss* within the wider community. The depiction of a house full of immigrants from the Indo-Canadian community, who have discreetly gathered at the narrator's home to offer solidarity and support, makes the indifference in the Canadian public realm stand out. This is further clarified for the reader when one of the men in Shaila's house complains that the white preachers on television carry on "like nothing's happened," and Shaila wants to tell him it is because "we're not that important"; "*they* care about nothing [emphasis added]."[26]

Faced with the tragic loss of her family, Shaila's "body is tensed, ready to scream."[27] She hears her husband's and children's voices all around her "and their screams insulate [her]...like headphones."[28] She feels "[n]ot peace, just a deadening quiet."[29] She wishes she "*could scream, starve, walk into Lake Ontario, jump from a bridge.*"[30] But her profound grief resists "being brought into the open"; it is "neither seen nor declared."[31] Melancholia is thus occluded from view and Shaila appears remarkably calm to the young government social worker, Judith Templeton, who concludes that Shaila is "coping very well."[32] The premise behind such an observation is evidently that emotion is dangerous in the first place because it prompts irrational actions; the ability to manage displays of emotion is therefore presumed a good thing. Templeton views Shaila as a model mourner, which, to social service agencies, means someone who can accept the loss and move forward with her/his life. She suggests that Shaila's apparent strength—she is "the strongest person of all,"[33] according to most observers—may be of practical help to those who are "hysterical" (i.e., mourning improperly): "Perhaps if the others could see you, talk with you, it would help them."[34] Templeton believes that Shaila would be able to teach other grieving families how to *feel* properly, *manage* their feelings properly, and *display* their emotions properly in public. Therefore, she asks Shaila's help as an intermediary or cultural translator for other traumatized families. Shaila responds, "By the standards of the people you call hysterical, I am behaving very oddly and very badly, Miss Templeton... They would not see me as a model. I do not see myself as a model."[35]

Hesitantly, however, Shaila accompanies Templeton to meet an elderly Sikh couple who had been brought to Canada just two weeks before their sons were killed in the crash. Shaila doubts if she will be of any assistance because she believes that the Sikh couple "will not open up to a Hindu woman."[36] But when Shaila identifies herself to the Sikh couple as another of the bereaved, another parent who has lost her two boys, grief creates (even if momentarily) a common ground. Here affect emerging out of muddy, paradoxical relatedness makes it possible for Shaila to move beyond her involuntary fear "at the sight of beards and turbans,"[37] a fear arising from her knowledge that "Sikh bomb[s]" were in all likelihood responsible for the death of her family.[38]

We see here how grief both acts upon individuals and spurs them to act. Grief that makes Shaila anxious of Sikh turbans also produces empathy for the turban-wearing Sikh parent. Shared grief allows her to reach out to "terrorist-look-alikes," despite regional, linguistic, class, and religious differences, and despite the generalized fear and suspicion of members of the Sikh community as alleged perpetrators, supporters, or bystanders of the crime. Similarly, on hearing of her loss, the old Sikh lady's "eyes immediately fill with tears,"[39] and her husband mutters, "God provides and God takes away," which, to Shaila, "sound like a blessing."[40] This brief encounter between Shaila and the Sikh couple ruptures consolidated configurations of community to clear space for the remaking and reinvention of community. We see here the potential to produce community not by an appeal to sameness but within difference through the recognition of shared (parental) grief.

The implication is that recognition of mutual suffering and mutual loss might offer a way of thinking beyond violence as what divides communities to reconceptualizing violence as prompting identification across communities. The possibility that myriad others can bond over shared experiences and memories while maintaining distance in effect carries the promise of making communities anew. In the brief encounter between Shaila and the Sikh couple in the story, this framework of communities-in-relation, while never suggesting that positionings are identical, offers us a glimpse of an emergent consciousness of a possible world.

Mukherjee's narrator is also deeply alert to the various ways through which bereaved families strive to cope with their loss. Shaila tells Templeton, "Nothing I can do will make any difference...We must all grieve in our own way."[41] Cheng's observation on the distinction between grief and grievance is instructive here. What happens, Cheng asks, "if grievance understood to be the social and legal articulation of grief" cannot accommodate "those aspects of grief that speak in a different language—a language that may seem inchoate because it is not fully reconcilable to the vocabulary of social formation or ideology?"[42] The elderly Sikh couple's refusal to sign the official documents that would secure them money, lodging, and utilities signifies to Shaila that they have not yet given up hope for their sons' lives, for as Shaila observes, "*[i]n our culture, it is a parent's duty to hope.*"[43] But the Sikh couple's mode of grieving that has "not surrendered hope" is incomprehensible to Templeton.[44] Templeton is not interested in listening to Shaila's perspective, even after she has sought out Shaila as a cultural translator for other grieving families purportedly to ensure that there is "the right human touch"—"We don't want to make mistakes," proclaims Templeton.[45] The model mourner Shaila seems to be enlisted, then, for the sole purpose of assisting the government in its plan to help other family members "accept" loss through helping them to enrol in college or to volunteer with cultural societies.[46] For government officials such as Templeton, "[a]cceptance means you speak of your family in the past tense and you make active plans for moving ahead with your life,"[47] which makes credible Cheng's observation that "we as a society are at ease with the discourse of grievance but terribly ill at ease in the face of grief."[48] Templeton wants to put pressure (socially and officially) on the bereaved Sikh parents to get over their loss. Her push for quick closure risks depriving the grieving parents of the time to grieve and their practice of culturally specific ways of mourning the loss of their children. She wants them to sign the official documents quickly so she can close their file and move on to the next family, the next task on her list.

Templeton posits her irritation with the Sikh couple, whom she deems uneducated and unintelligible, as the problem of multiculturalism—the difficulty of translating "foreign" cultures and cultural differences. "You see what I'm up against? I'm sure they're lovely people, but their stubbornness and ignorance are driving me crazy," she tells Shaila.[49] The refusal to address the social facts of immigration and settlement (how they came, when or why, their age or class) is demonstrated by Templeton's focus on the psychological difficulties of the Sikh couple in accepting the death of their sons and the difficulties of cross-cultural interaction. Templeton's exasperation embodies the Canadian government's impatience with minorities who continue to turn back to or hold on to lost objects (whether a homeland, cultural practices, or memories of dead sons), rather than accept the government's reconciliatory gestures of closure (such as a public inquiry, monetary compensation, or an official apology) and move on. But it is by refusing to be propelled forward—as the Sikh couple in Mukherjee's story refuses to do in pushing back against Templeton's insistence on approximating the mythic figure of the model mourner or the good minority, and as Shaila refuses to do in declining her assistance to Templeton later on in the story—that Air India family members have been able to incorporate their personal stories and memories of the Air India tragedy within a long history of racial grief (dislocation and resettlement, in/visibility of minorities, and the psychic and corporeal effects of racialization).

Managing Displacement, Seeking Belonging

In narrativizing the personal grief of losing family members on Air India Flight 182, Mukherjee's story and Marjara's docudrama illuminate a history of racism and the failures of Canadian multiculturalism. As they reveal how grief is connected to the textures of everyday experiences of racialized minorities, the assumption that social relations prior to the 1985 Air India bombings were "orderly" emerges as a "fantasy." Butler writes, "When grieving is something to be feared, our fears can give rise to the impulse to resolve it quickly, to banish it in the name of an action invested with the power to restore the loss or return the world to a former order, or to reinvigorate a fantasy that the world formerly was orderly."[50] The difficulties of settling down in a "new country" that prompt immigrants from India, despite differences in language, food, religion, and class, to seek out each other is gestured to in "The Management of Grief."[51] This pre-empts the desire to view the period before 1985 in Canada as a multicultural haven. Mukherjee's central character, Shaila, describes relationships between Indian immigrants in Canada in the years before the Air India bombings as "a time when we all trusted each other in this new country, it was only the new country we worried about."[52] The shared fellow feeling that is depicted in the story then becomes a product of diasporic conditions, rather than a shared feeling that pre-existed migration. In documenting the loss of her mother and sister on Air India Flight 182, Eisha Marjara's *Desperately Seeking Helen* opens up an "equally protracted history of physically and emotionally managing...[racial] grief on the part of the marginalized, racialized people."[53] In familial terms, Marjara ties together her unresolved grief at the loss of family members in the Air India bombing with multiple repressed narratives of the diaspora that are intimately connected, making it possible for viewers to recognize the long-term effects of living with loss. The film successfully produces "an archive of emotions," which, for Ann Cvetkovich, is "one of trauma's most important, but most difficult to preserve, legacies."[54]

The story, narrated by the protagonist Eisha, who is played by the filmmaker, Marjara, begins with Eisha arriving in Bombay to begin searching for her childhood idol, Bollywood's renowned vamp, Helen. This quest for Helen, as we discover as the film progresses, is essentially a search for self.[55] We are told that the narrator and her family moved from Amritsar, Punjab, to Trois-Rivières, Quebec, in 1971, with her father being offered a teaching position. They settled in a town with a 99 per cent French-speaking population without anyone who looked like them "for miles around." Marjara recalls that her mother, Devinder, who was trained as a school-teacher, wanted desperately to find a teaching job. She went from school to school with résumé in hand, with the hope of "doing something she wanted in a place where she could belong." But, soon after she found a job, she was replaced by "an English lady who looked the part" and did not speak English with a Punjabi accent. Forced into becoming a housewife, Devinder became deeply unhappy, with Marjara sadly observing of her experience, "the hard part about being a housewife was the house."[56]

The narrator repeatedly draws our attention to not only her mother's isolation from the wider community but also her dissatisfaction with being a housewife. Forced to perform the role of a stay-at-home mom, Devinder could never "get the balance right," Eisha tells us. This is literally encapsulated in Devinder's discomfort on the snow, which ruined her love of walking. Eisha notes that, for her mother, it became a matter of "saving yourself from the next fall." This is in sharp contrast to Eisha and her sisters for whom the snow was their playground and "Quebec was home." The film thus provides viewers with compelling narratives of how the same geographical space can produce very different experiences and histories. Forced indoors without work, without a hospitable community of friends and neighbours, and without a feeling of belonging to the Canadian landscape (whether walking on the snow or driving on the road), Devinder regains her sense of self, to the extent that she can, by focusing her energies into being a "good" housewife (cooking, cleaning, and caring for her husband and her children). Yet, while cooking Indian food enables Devinder to stake a claim to the space of the home, Eisha, who desires a Barbie-doll body, dislikes the fat-inducing foods her mother prepares. Eisha's ideal is the Anglo-Indian-Burmese actor Helen Ann Richardson (popularly known as simply "Helen"), who made her first breakthrough in the Hindi film *Howrah Bridge* (1958), dancing to "Mera Naam Chin Chin Choo." Helen went on to two decades of Hindi film roles but was always cast as a Westernized vamp, the counterpoint to the wholesome Indian heroine (i.e., the good wife and mother). From Eisha's perspective, Helen was everything her mother was not, and most of all, "she had fun"—a wry reminder that Devinder did not enjoy "play[ing] house."[57]

However, Eisha's own teenage struggles with gendered identity and feminine beauty make her oblivious to Devinder's hidden grief and she can only access her mother's grief later through her camera: "From behind the lens I saw my mother wanted to do something in a place that couldn't make her belong," Marjara tells us. This work of melancholia thus enables memories of what is forgotten and repressed from her childhood to surface. By placing her mother on the other side of the camera, the film opens up for discussion the performance of gendered and racialized identity in domestic and public settings. Eisha's mother's experience is a particularly gendered one, as an inhospitable social context pushes her indoors, and in the process she ends up performing a stereotypical Indian feminine identity. Here minority identity is exposed as performative, with dominant (racist) discourse producing the effects that it names. This is similar to Helen, who cannot play any other role in Hindi cinema except that of a vamp, and in the process becomes the stereotypical Westernized woman—the embodiment of immorality in the Indian context. Eisha's mother playing house (similar to the heroines of Hindi cinema) and Helen playing the vamp onscreen converge in more ways than one in the cinematic narrative. The narrator states, " The vamp is always the outsider";[58] Eisha's mother, too, was an outsider, no matter how hard she tried to work her way in. The vamp dies at intermission; Eisha's mother dies early, too.

The "desperately seeking" in the film's title is encapsulated in the narrator's realization that she will never be able to find "Helen," as Helen only exists through her onscreen performances, which are the images imprinted in the minds of the cinematic viewer. Similarly, her deceased mother also exists only in memories, photographs, and home-video footage. In an interview, Marjara says that her "longing for both these women will never cease, and will forever remain unfulfilled—and desperate."[59] The narrator's "unfulfilled—and desperate" longing for her mother becomes particularly poignant when we learn at the end of the film that she lost her mother in the bombing of Air India Flight 182. Eisha states, "She never made it back. She never made it home. The plane blew up between here and there."[60] This statement turns the viewers' attention to the grieving daughter and to a parallel thread of unresolved grief: the unhappy mother having to manage her grief inside the house and Marjara, who, in the absence of any public acknowledgement or mourning, is forced to carry the grief of the loss of her mother within her. It is also telling that while searching for Helen in India, Marjara finds her mother and herself in the haunting spectre of her own childhood home in Canada. The home offers a space for the unassimilated and the transgressive, for the mother and the daughter, to imperceptibly mingle. Eisha's and her mother's separate struggles with normative whiteness seem to produce a desire in Eisha to literally disappear, to become *in*visible. The film offers us a brief glimpse of Eisha's struggle with anorexia, while alerting viewers to the fact that Eisha would have been on that plane along with her mother and sister had she not been kept hospitalized for rehabilitation for having fallen a few pounds short of her weight goal. As Marjara says in an interview, the film reveals "how my mother's life and mine intersected, and how my experience with anorexia was directly linked to my mother's struggle adjusting and trying to belong in a different culture."[61]

Eisha's inability to separate herself from her dead mother, along with her failed attempt to find Helen, captures the lives of those who grieve without "recovery," those who have incorporated their identification of the lost object within themselves, unlike the paradigmatic "model" mourner who can work out of the identification with the lost object. By "tarrying with grief," Eisha brings the ghosts and spectres of the past into the present, while her ability to express multiple losses at once—a key feature of the melancholic, according to Eng and Kazanjian[62]—opens up space for narrativizing pain as psychic.[63] Her personal, individual history of grief opens up to public gaze the everyday grief of minority subjects. This effectively undermines the framing of the Air India tragedy as an exceptional or aberrant moment in Canadian multiculturalism. Throughout the film, we see how different histories of travelling and dwelling produce a network of partially connected histories that point to the intricate meshing of past and present, history and memory, here and there, Canada and India. The narrative makes clear the difference between feeling at home in Canada and declaring Canada as home. This raises important ethical questions: Can racialized subjects such as Devinder stake a claim to Canada as home if they are continuously relegated within discourse to a non-Canadian homeland? And how could those who lost loved ones in the Air India bombing mourn in the face of the Canadian state's non-acknowledgement of their loss?

Desperately Seeking to Challenge the Management of Grief

The Canadian government's discourse on the Air India tragedy is essentially about a particular mode of governing—a means of making the past and the future amenable to intervention and management. Yet Mukherjee's and Marjara's works demonstrate the regulatory effects of Canadian multiculturalism on the minority subject in the everyday. They propose that everyday grief and violence are in need of being recovered, rather than the grief of Air India conceptualized as an odd or aberrant event (or series of events) in Canadian multiculturalism. It is interesting to consider in this context how bodies and cultural practices are translated in multicultural contexts to manage the "crisis" of multiculturalism.[64] Whereas in most conventional practices of translation, the original is prioritized as the criterion against which the translation, which comes subsequently, must try to measure up, in both Mukherjee's and Marjara's narration the original appears to be inferior, or lacking, precisely through the act of translation. Official translation renders the grief of the Sikh couple in " The Management of Grief" and the narrator's mother in *Desperately Seeking Helen* as indicators of backwardness and the inability of immigrants (i.e., the multicultural subject) to integrate. On the other hand, Mukherjee's narrator Shaila and Marjara's narrator Eisha, who appear "well-balanced" on the surface, having effectively suppressed their intense sorrow, can be quickly turned into model mourners and model minorities. Yet, while the dominant gaze positions both the unassimilated minority and the seemingly conforming minority as knowable bodies, the two creative texts discussed here indicate otherwise.

Mukherjee's story points to the irony of Templeton's juxtaposition of Shaila against the other mourners as "one of the few whose grief has not sprung bizzare obsessions"[65]—because Shaila is haunted by the visions and voices of her dead family members and prophetic dreams.[66] In an abandoned temple in a tiny Himalayan village, her husband appears to her and, in Queen's Park, in Toronto, she hears voices of her dead family, who direct her toward the future. On the other hand, unlike Shaila, the Sikh couple, in interpreting the bombing as an instance of God providing and God taking away, appears to have found a way to deal with their loss. Similarly, Marjara does not offer us much insight into Eisha's inner life. Remaining mostly silent about Eisha's struggles with anorexia and the loss of her sister in the Air India bombings, she makes it difficult for us to claim that we "know" Eisha.[67] If, as Cathy Caruth argues, "the traumatized carry an impossible history within them, or they become themselves the symptom of a history they cannot entirely possess,"[68] how can the reader or cinematic viewer "know" the experiences of those who carry only a partial knowledge of these losses in the first place? These incomplete, fragmented accounts underline the very impossibility of "knowing" the other's grief and affirm the enduring attachments to the lost object that no work of mourning can sever. In addition, they challenge us to a new kind of listening and urge us to be attentive to the intricacies and complexities of silence.

Sara Ahmed, in her reading of Gurinder Chadha's *Bend It Like Beckham*, explains that "happiness is imagined as what allows subjects to embrace futurity, to leave the past behind, where pastness is associated with custom and the customary."[69] Yet, in *Desperately Seeking Helen*, happiness is imagined as what would allow the mother to embrace the past, as the past is associated with possibilities that do not exist in her present. It is the mother's forced placement within the home that prompts her to recreate her sense of self through obsessive cleaning, cooking Punjabi food, and mothering her children. In other words, it is racism that results in her attempts to hold on to cultural practices of the lost homeland as reparative. Moreover, while traditional attire and food in " The Management of Grief" and *Desperately Seeking Helen* mark immigrants as "ethnic" or other in the dominant gaze, these remnants of a lost homeland signify diasporic belonging, community, and family to the racialized subjects. As Angela

Failler notes, for Eisha's mother, "keeping one foot in India...served to keep India, or at least an identification with India, alive within herself."[70]

With both creative texts raising questions about how the everyday and the unpredictable are represented and experienced in order to contest more established renditions of the past, the understanding of Canadian multiculturalism as a tool of managing and governing others takes on critical import. Eva Mackey explains, "the story of Canada's tolerant nationhood has often been framed in terms of its policy and mythology of 'multiculturalism,' a policy defined in official government ideology as 'a fundamental characteristic of Canadian heritage and identity.'"[71] Similarly, Vijay Mishra claims that multiculturalism is central to the project of nation building in Canada, as it "actually encourag[es] and mak[es] possible national unity."[72] Yet the premise of "happy" multiculturalism necessitates that immigrants demonstrate that they are worthy to be granted the rights of citizenship and to be treated as citizens. As Ahmed argues, for their own "happiness," migrant subjects "must first get over their suffering; they must become unstuck."[73] In this way multiculturalism becomes a forward motion.

Both multiculturalism and mourning share in common this compulsion toward closure. In Freud's essay, "Mourning and Melancholia," mourning is constructed as a healthy process of grieving for a lost object. Through mourning, one is able to let go of the object of loss. Melancholia, on the other hand, is about holding on to the lost object; a melancholic does not get over loss. So the good mourner or the model mourner of Air India Flight 182 is the migrant who has accepted the loss of loved ones and has moved on to form new attachments. In other words, the model mourner, unlike the melancholic, does not continue to pine over the loss. As Ahmed succinctly observes about affective forms of shared grief: "if an affective community is produced by sharing objects of loss, which means letting objects go in the right way, then the melancholics would be affect aliens in how they love: their love becomes a failure to get over loss, which keeps them facing the wrong way. The melancholics are thus the ones who must be redirected, or turned around."[74] They have to be turned away from looking behind at the racist past, from uncovering histories of racism and discrimination, and redirected toward securing the nation's (and their) multicultural future. The impetus that racial grief be civilly displayed works to not only mask *uncivil* acts like everyday racisms and the government's apathy toward the loss of lives and the grief of those who lost family and friends on Air India Flight 182, but also functions as a mode of managing racialized subjects. Yet the everyday grief of racialized minorities divests multiculturalism of its naturalization, directing attention to how "the social and subjective formations of the so-called racialized or minority subject are intimately tied to the psychical experience of grief."[75]

In Mukherjee's story, the Sikh couple's continued grief keeps them "facing the wrong way,"[76] prompting the social worker Miss Templeton to enlist Shaila to provide them with direction on how to manage grief. Shaila as model mourner can function as proof of the inclusive and caring Canadian nation; her seeming ability to "move on," as well as help other grieving families, can be construed as the nation's own success at multicultural community building. Yet, as Mukherjee and Marjara clarify, for Shaila and Eisha, respectively, moving forward propelled by visions of their families means staying open to sudden flashes of their loved ones, to memories of loss, and to "the difficult knowledge of...[a] traumatic past as they inevitably live on in the present."[77] With the Canadian state and its agencies setting limits on the kinds of losses that can be avowed as such, Mukherjee and Marjara produce artistic representations of the lived experiences of minorities in Canada by narrativizing the everyday of the minority subject. They offer images of bodies and lives that are not represented in government discourse by interweaving the loss of lives in the 1985 Air India bombings with the simultaneous hidden loss of home, of security, of community, of citizenship, of dreams and hopes, among others. They seem to successfully take up Butler's call "to grieve, and to make grief itself into a resource for politics,"[78] so that grief is no more private or privatizing. These creative works reveal that grief can be regenerative of "a sense of political community of a complex order" that illuminates the relational ties between subjects and communities.[79] Mourning lost lives, lost childhoods, lost relations, and failures of the multicultural state that point to unresolved grief becomes a way of testifying to a fundamental commonality of minoritized communities. In addition, the pushback against the model mourner/model minority discourse suggests a space of solidarity with the "bad" migrant, who, refusing to mask her/his pain, acts out in "uncivil" ways.

In 2010, many years after Mukherjee's short story and Marjara's docudrama, the Canadian government issued a statement on the twenty-fifth anniversary of the Air India bombings (on the heels of the Air India commission of inquiry report).[80] Delivering an apology to family members and friends of those onboard Air India Flight 182, Prime Minister Stephen Harper clarified what the "management of grief" and "moving ahead" with one's life signify in a post-9/11 era of heightened anxiety and increased securitization.[81] While regretting the lack of support from the rest of society and the failures of government agencies for so many years after the bombing, Prime Minister Harper reminded the families that the crime was perpetrated by members of their own community (Indo-Canadians). In other words, he suggested they brought the grief upon themselves by not being able to leave their past behind in India. Racial grief is thus conceptualized as "*the affective cost of not following the scripts of normative existence.*"[82] Thus, even while pointing to an apparent crisis in multiculturalism, the prime minister's statement does not put the state's official multiculturalism policy into question. It does not expose the state as having "failed" *its* multicultural ideal in perpetuating forms of racism. On the contrary, it presents the bombing of Air India Flight 182 as *India's* problem with *its* (Sikh) minorities, ignoring Canada's historical contributions to these racial tensions and failure to protect its minorities—as if what explains the crisis is not the failure of the ideal but minorities' failure to adhere to that ideal. Linking the state's conceptualization of brown bodies as potential terrorists to the Air India bombings—for example, naming June 23 as the National Day of Remembrance for Victims of Terrorism (in 2005) in a deliberate allusion to the bombings—the government, through the apology, urges the Air India families to embrace a multicultural future by endorsing its anti-terrorism initiatives "to prevent another Flight 182."[83] The implication is that the Indo-Canadian community's failure to live up to Canada's multicultural ideal in the past makes its commitment to the government's initiatives in the present all the more urgent. For, as Thobani reminds us, "multiculturalism was intended to further the nation's unity, not its transformation."[84]

The model mourner thus merges seamlessly into the figure of the model minority enunciated in the government's apology and the norms for "managing grief" function as a mode of minority governance, one that is generative of different hierarchical arrangements of racialized bodies and identities. Racialized Canadians are reminded to be on their guard in displaying their emotions—their loss, pain, anger, or frustration—in order to successfully demonstrate that they are, indeed, civil subjects standing "on guard" for Canada.[85] The government's stance is clear: "systematically marginalize" and "not...reach out to" alienated and disgruntled Canadians.[86] Aggrieved, racialized citizens are not perceived as legitimate subjects whose grief and grievance require both recognition and accountability from those in power. Instead, they are positioned as threatening outsiders necessitating increased surveillance and policing by the state.

State versions of happy (Canadian) multiculturalism are rooted in anxieties about the potential "abuse" of Canada as a "generous" and "tolerant" host. Consequently, immigrants are asked to leave behind the old world (transnational affiliations) and the past (such as the government's mistreatment of the Air India families) and show willingness to be directed toward the state's version of the future. Yet this call to be model mourners or model minorities—that is, loyal Canadians—is not neutral; as Mukherjee and Marjara demonstrate, how one moves with grief and in what direction are determined by the subject's relation to a broader history of loss and suffering. While the state declares the past as "resolved, finished, and dead," for the melancholic mourner, "the past remains steadfastly alive in the present."[87] Thus, while the Canadian government urges the Air India families to move on with their lives by securing their (terror-free, grief-free) multicultural future through endorsing the government's anti-terrorism initiatives "to prevent another Flight 182" and "make the skies safe for travel,"[88] Mukherjee and Marjara alert us to the conditions on the ground, conditions that—without an engaged reflection on the state's long history of racism against South Asians (and other racialized minorities), who continue to remember and mourn the past—make the government's projection of a happy multicultural future untenable.[89]

Directing the reader's/viewer's gaze to the lived experiences of Indo-Canadians pre- and post-1985, interweaved with the enduring grief of the Air India tragedy and its aftermath, Mukherjee's and Marjara's creative works insist that the multicultural "ideal" never existed and hence was never lost. Effectively historicizing the grief of minority communities, they offer us a glimpse of the texture of the lives of those who continue to live with loss. As they map the conditions that shape minority identities and communities in Canada, melancholia emerges as an integral part of the everyday lives of racialized minorities—but melancholia not as stasis and the inability to get over one's loss but as a prompt to engage with how the past persists and shapes the present. In speaking directly to the generative aspects of grief, these creative works offer an alternative to state redress projects. Their evocative portrayal of melancholic mourners of Air India Flight 182, who continue to live with the contradictions produced by loss, invites us to imagine alternative strategies to live with and after loss, and to create alternative futures.

Notes

1. Multiculturalism emerged as official governmental policy in Canada during the 1970s in response to tensions between British, French, and other "ethnic" groups demanding "recognition of their place within the nation." Sunera Thobani, *Exalted Subjects: Studies in the Making of Race and Nation in Canada* (Toronto: University of Toronto Press, 2007), 144. Scholars argue that the 1971 multiculturalism policy and the 1988 Multiculturalism Act (Bill C-93) that worked to proclaim Canada's openness and tolerance of diverse populations also functioned as a mode of differentiating between Canadians. See, for example, Thobani, *Exalted Subjects*; Eva Mackey, *The House of Difference: Cultural Politics and National Identity in Canada* (London: Routledge, 1999); Vijay Mishra, *The Literature of the Indian Diaspora: Theorizing the Diasporic Imaginary* (New York: Routledge, 2008).
2. Clark Blaise and Bharati Mukherjee, *The Sorrow and the Terror: The Haunting Legacy of the Air India Tragedy* (Toronto: Viking, 1987), 203.

3. John C. Major, "Opening Remarks by the Honourable John C. Major, C.C., Q.C., on the Release of the Report of the Commission of Inquiry into the Investigation of the Bombing of Air India Flight 182," in *Commission of Inquiry into the Investigation of the Bombing of Air India Flight 182*, last modified June 17, 2010, accessed August 10, 2012, http://epe.lac-.gc.ca/100/206/301/pco-bcp/commissions/air_india/2010-07-23/www.majorcomm.ca/en/reports/finalreport/default.htm.

4. On May 23, 1914, a Japanese ship called the *Komagata Maru* arrived in Vancouver with 276 predominantly Sikh Indians on board—all of them British subjects. The passengers were refused permission to leave the ship because of the continuous journey regulation, which required that passengers come via direct passage from India. The ship had departed from Hong Kong, and most passengers did not have the $200 on their person that was required to enter British Columbia. After two months, on July 23, 1914, the *Komagata Maru* was forced to leave Vancouver. Vijay Mishra writes, " The *Komagata Maru* incident is the most powerful symbol of Canadian racism for the South Asian diaspora." See Mishra, *Literature of the Indian Diaspora*, 142. See also Amber Dean's essay in this volume for a detailed discussion of the *Komagata Maru* incident in relation to the Air India bombings.

5. Thobani argues that official multiculturalism enables Canada to renarrate its history and "'reinvent' itself" in a way that facilitates its "self-presentation on the global stage as urbane, cosmopolitan, and at the cutting edge of promoting racial and ethnic tolerance among western nations." Thobani, *Exalted Subjects*, 144–145. Mackey characterizes multiculturalism as "the great national bandage" that allows the state to "manage diversity without endangering the project of nation-building." Mackey, *House of Difference*, 81.

6. Chandrima Chakraborty, "Official Apology, Creative Remembrances, and Management of the Air India Tragedy," *Studies in Canadian Literature* 40.1 (2015): 111–130.

7. Anne Anlin Cheng, *The Melancholy of Race: Psychoanalysis, Assimilation, and Hidden Grief* (Oxford: Oxford University Press, 2000), x.

8. Here I am drawing upon Arlie Russell Hochschild's definition of "emotional labour," which "requires one to induce or suppress feeling in order to sustain the outward countenance that produces the proper state of mind in others." Arlie Russell Hochschild, *The Managed Heart: Commercialization of Human Feeling* (Berkeley: University of California Press, 2003), 7.

9. Sigmund Freud, "Mourning and Melancholia," in *The Standard Edition of the Complete Psychological Works of Sigmund Freud*, ed. and trans. James Strachey, vol. 14 (London: Hogarth, 1957), 243–258.

10. Judith Butler and David Eng and David Kazanjian argue that in the *The Ego and the Id* (1923), Freud explicitly deconstructs his previous binary of mourning and melancholia

by recognizing that the identification with the lost object is also a crucial aspect of mourning. Judith Butler, "Psychic Inceptions: Melancholia, Rage, Ambivalence," in *The Psychic Life of Power: Theories in Subjection* (Palo Alto, CA: Stanford University Press, 2000), 167–198; David L. Eng and David Kazanjian, eds., *Loss: The Politics of Mourning* (Berkeley: University of California Press, 2003), 4.

11. Butler, "Psychic Inceptions," 167.
12. Judith Butler, " Violence, Mourning, Politics," *Studies in Gender and Sexuality* 4.1 (2003): 19.
13. José Muñoz, "Photographies of Mourning: Melancholia and Ambivalence in Van Der Zee, Mapplethorpe, and Looking for Langston," in *Race and the Subject of Masculinities*, ed. Harry Uebel Stecopoulos and Michael Uebel Stecopoulos (Durham, NC: Duke University Press, 1997), 355–356.
14. Cheng, *Melancholy of Race*, xi.
15. Eng and Kazanjian, *Loss*, 4.
16. Ibid., 5.
17. Bharati Mukherjee, " The Management of Grief," in *The Middleman and Other Stories* (New York: Grove Press, 1988), 179–197; Eisha Marjara, *Desperately Seeking Helen* (Montreal: National Film Board of Canada, 1999), DVD. The film was originally produced in 1998 and re-released in 1999 with a new soundtrack.
18. Cheng, *Melancholy of Race*, xi.
19. Hochschild, *Managed Heart*, 56.
20. Daniel Coleman, "From Canadian Trance to Transcanada: White Civility to Wry Civility in The Canlit Project," in *Trans.Can.Lit: Resituating the Study of Canadian Literature*, ed. Roy Miki and Smaro Kamboureli (Waterloo, ON: Wilfrid Laurier University Press, 2007).
21. Ibid., 29.
22. Ibid.
23. Ibid., 31.
24. Blaise and Mukherjee, *Sorrow and the Terror*, 174.
25. Mukherjee, "Management of Grief," 179.
26. Ibid., 180.
27. Ibid.
28. Ibid.
29. Ibid.
30. Ibid., 183.
31. Butler, "Psychic Inceptions," 186.
32. Mukherjee, "Management of Grief," 183. The report of the commission of inquiry, *The Families Remember*, notes, "It was a common comment that *nobody from the government ever called us*...Some pointed out the absence of grief counselling

services by Canada for the families"; additionally, in his testimony on September 25, 2006, Dr. Bal Gupta, founder of the Air India Victims' Families Association, said that "there was no emotional, psychological, physical or administrative help or grief counselling or guidance from any government agency." Government of Canada, *The Families Remember: Commission of Inquiry into the Investigation of the Bombing of Air India Flight 182, Phase I Report* (Ottawa: Minister of Public Works and Government Services, 2007), 99, 101.

33. Mukherjee, "Management of Grief," 183.
34. Ibid.
35. Ibid.
36. Ibid., 193.
37. Ibid.
38. Ibid., 179. As with this elderly Sikh man in the aftermath of the 1985 bombings, the post-9/11 discourse of terror has made Sikh male bodies excessively visible. It is a sign of the ongoing nature of racist practices against Sikh Indians that the history of racism is being covered over by a reinvigorated discourse on terrorism. In this context, it is interesting that Shaila notes, "My parents are progressive people; they do not blame communities for a few individuals. In Canada it is a different story now." Ibid., 189.
39. Ibid., 193.
40. Ibid., 194.
41. Ibid., 183.
42. Cheng, *Melancholy of Race*, x.
43. Mukherjee, "Management of Grief," 195.
44. Ibid., 186.
45. Ibid., 183.
46. Ibid., 192.
47. Ibid.
48. Cheng, *Melancholy of Race*, 175.
49. Mukherjee, "Management of Grief," 195.
50. Butler, "Violence, Mourning, Politics," 18.
51. Mukherjee, "Management of Grief," 193.
52. Ibid.
53. Cheng, *Melancholy of Race*, 20.
54. Ann Cvetkovich, "Legacies of Trauma, Legacies of Activism: ACT UP's Lesbians," in *Loss: The Politics of Mourning*, ed. David L. Eng and David Kazanjian (Berkeley: University of California Press, 2003), 437.
55. The melancholic's speech, as Butler tells us, "is neither verdictive nor declarative (assertoric), but inevitably indirect and circuitous." Butler, "Psychic Inceptions," 186.
56. Marjara, *Desperately Seeking Helen*.

57. Ibid.

58. Ibid.

59. Firdaus Ali, "In Search of a Vamp," *Rediff.com* (US edition), April 24, 2000, accessed August 10, 2012, http://www.rediff.com/us/2000/apr/24us1.htm.

60. Marjara, *Desperately Seeking Helen*.

61. Janice Kennedy, "Desperately Seeking Understanding: Filmmaker Eisha Marjara Returns to Her Indian Roots in Search of Meaning for Her Own Life and the Stolen Lives of Her Mother and Sister," *Ottawa Citizen*, July 7, 1999, C15.

62. Eng and Kazanjian, *Loss*, 4, 5.

63. See Butler, "Psychic Inceptions."

64. Mishra reminds us that the discourse of multiculturalism has been common in various manifestations in Western civil societies and has functioned as "a structure of control that [has] kept minorities where they are in the guise of a 'colonialist' (white) respect of cultural difference without changing the unified selves of the 'managers' themselves." Mishra, *Literature of the Indian Diaspora*, 135.

65. Mukherjee, "Management of Grief," 192.

66. Shaila wonders, "How do I tell Judith Templeton that my family surrounds me, and that like creatures in epics, they've changed shapes? She sees me as calm and accepting...I cannot tell her my days, even my nights, are thrilling." Ibid.

67. I would like to thank Amber Dean for urging me to develop this point further.

68. Cathy Caruth, ed., *Trauma: Explorations in Memory* (Baltimore, MD: Johns Hopkins University Press, 1995), 5.

69. Sara Ahmed, *The Promise of Happiness* (Durham, NC: Duke University Press, 2010), 137.

70. Angela Failler, "Remembering the Air India Disaster: Memorial and Counter-Memorial," *Review of Education, Pedagogy, and Cultural Studies* 31 (2009): 170.

71. Mackey, *House of Difference*, 2.

72. Mishra, *Literature of the Indian Diaspora*, 139.

73. Ahmed, *Promise of Happiness*, 138.

74. Ibid., 141.

75. Cheng, *Melancholy of Race*, x.

76. Ahmed, *Promise of Happiness*, 141.

77. Failler, "Remembering the Air India Disaster," 171.

78. Butler, "Violence, Mourning, Politics," 19.

79. Ibid., 12.

80. The final report of the commission of inquiry came out on June 17, 2010. Six days later, at the memorial site in Toronto, Prime Minister Stephen Harper apologized on behalf of the government for "the institutional failings of 25 years ago and the treatment of the victims' families thereafter." See Prime Minister of Canada, "Statement by the

Prime Minister of Canada at the Commemoration Ceremony for the 25th Anniversary of the Air India Flight 182 Atrocity" in this volume.

81. For a critical analysis of the apology, see Chakraborty, "Official Apology."
82. Sara Ahmed, *The Cultural Politics of Emotion* (New York: Routledge, 2004), 107.
83. See "Statement by the Prime Minister of Canada" in this volume.
84. Thobani, *Exalted Subjects*, 156.
85. The Canadian national anthem, "O Canada," ends with the repetition of the line, "O Canada, we stand on guard for thee."
86. See "Statement by the Prime Minister of Canada" in this volume.
87. Eng and Kazanjian, *Loss*, 3–4.
88. See "Statement by the Prime Minister of Canada" in this volume.
89. The Air India trials, the government's apology, and the findings of the commission of inquiry work to re-establish Canada as a liberal and multicultural nation that is willing to attend to the grievances of its (minority) citizens; they do not prompt reflections on past and ongoing practices of discrimination against racialized minorities in Canada.

Works Cited

Ahmed, Sara. *The Cultural Politics of Emotion*. New York: Routledge, 2004.

———. *The Promise of Happiness*. Durham, NC: Duke University Press, 2010.

Blaise, Clark, and Bharati Mukherjee. *The Sorrow and the Terror: The Haunting Legacy of the Air India Tragedy*. Toronto: Viking, 1987.

Butler, Judith. "Psychic Inceptions: Melancholia, Rage, Ambivalence." In *The Psychic Life of Power: Theories in Subjection*, 167–198. Palo Alto, CA: Stanford University Press, 2000.

———. "Violence, Mourning, Politics." *Studies in Gender and Sexuality* 4.1 (2003): 9–37.

Caruth, Cathy, ed. *Trauma: Explorations in Memory*. Baltimore, MD: Johns Hopkins University Press, 1995.

Chakraborty, Chandrima. "Official Apology, Creative Remembrances, and Management of the Air India Tragedy." *Studies in Canadian Literature* 40.1 (2015): 111–130.

Cheng, Anne Anlin. *The Melancholy of Race: Psychoanalysis, Assimilation, and Hidden Grief*. Oxford: Oxford University Press, 2000.

Coleman, Daniel. "From Canadian Trance to Transcanada: White Civility to Wry Civility in The Canlit Project." In *Trans.Can.Lit: Resituating the Study of Canadian Literature*, edited by Roy Miki and Smaro Kamboureli, 25–43. Waterloo, ON: Wilfrid Laurier University Press, 2007.

Cvetkovich, Ann. "Legacies of Trauma, Legacies of Activism: ACT UP's Lesbians." In *Loss: The Politics of Mourning*, edited by David L. Eng and David Kazanjian, 427–457. Berkeley: University of California Press, 2003.

Eng, David L., and David Kazanjian, eds. *Loss: The Politics of Mourning*. Berkeley: University of California Press, 2003.

Failler, Angela. "Remembering the Air India Disaster: Memorial and Counter-Memorial." *Review of Education, Pedagogy, and Cultural Studies* 31 (2009): 150–176.

Freud, Sigmund. "Mourning and Melancholia." In vol. 14 of *The Standard Edition of the Complete Psychological Works of Sigmund Freud*, edited and translated by James Strachey, 243–258. London: Hogarth, 1957.

Government of Canada. *The Families Remember: Commission of Inquiry into the Investigation of the Bombing of Air India Flight 182, Phase I Report*. Ottawa: Minister of Public Works and Government Services, 2007.

Hochschild, Arlie Russell. *The Managed Heart: Commercialization of Human Feeling*. Berkeley: University of California Press, 2003.

Mackey, Eva. *The House of Difference: Cultural Politics and National Identity in Canada*. London: Routledge, 1999.

Marjara, Eisha. *Desperately Seeking Helen*. Montreal: National Film Board of Canada, 1999. DVD.

Mishra, Vijay. *The Literature of the Indian Diaspora: Theorizing the Diasporic Imaginary*. New York: Routledge, 2008.

Mukherjee, Bharati. " The Management of Grief." In *The Middleman and Other Stories*, 179–197. New York: Grove Press, 1988.

Muñoz, José. "Photographies of Mourning: Melancholia and Ambivalence in Van Der Zee, Mapplethorpe, and Looking for Langston." In *Race and the Subject of Masculinities*, edited by Harry Uebel Stecopoulos and Michael Uebel Stecopoulos, 337–358. Durham, NC: Duke University Press, 1997.

Thobani, Sunera. *Exalted Subjects: Studies in the Making of Race and Nation in Canada*. Toronto: University of Toronto Press, 2007.

The Management of Grief

BHARATI MUKHERJEE

A WOMAN I DON'T KNOW is boiling tea the Indian way in my kitchen. There are a lot of women I don't know in my kitchen, whispering and moving tactfully. They open doors, rummage through the pantry, and try not to ask me where things are kept. They remind me of when my sons were small, on Mother's Day or when Vikram and I were tired, and they would make big, sloppy omelets. I would lie in bed pretending I didn't hear them.

Dr. Sharma, the treasurer of the Indo-Canada Society, pulls me into the hallway. He wants to know if I am worried about money. His wife, who has just come up from the basement with a tray of empty cups and glasses, scolds him. "Don't bother Mrs. Bhave with mundane details." She looks so monstrously pregnant her baby must be days overdue. I tell her she shouldn't be carrying heavy things. "Shaila," she says, smiling, "this is the fifth." Then she grabs a teenager by his shirttails. He slips his Walkman off his head. He has to be one of her four children; they have the same domed and dented foreheads. "What's the official word now?" she demands. The boy slips the headphones back on. "They're acting evasive, Ma. They're saying it could be an accident or a terrorist bomb."

All morning, the boys have been muttering, Sikh bomb, Sikh bomb. The men, not using the word, bow their heads in agreement. Mrs. Sharma touches her forehead at such a word. At least they've stopped talking about space debris and Russian lasers.

Two radios are going in the dining room. They are tuned to different stations. Someone must have brought the radios down from my boys' bedrooms. I haven't gone into their rooms since Kusum came running across the front lawn in her bathrobe. She looked so funny, I was laughing when I opened the door.

The big TV in the den is being whizzed through American networks and cable channels.

"Damn!" some man swears bitterly. "How can these preachers carry on like nothing's happened?" I want to tell him we're not that important. You look at the audience, and at the preacher in his blue robe with his beautiful white hair, the potted palm trees under a blue sky, and you know they care about nothing.

The phone rings and rings. Dr. Sharma's taken charge. "We're with her," he keeps saying. "Yes, yes, the doctor has given calming pills. Yes, yes, pills are having necessary effect." I wonder if pills alone explain this calm. Not peace, just a deadening quiet. I was always controlled, but never repressed. Sound can reach me, but my body is tensed, ready to scream. I hear their voices all around me. I hear my boys and Vikram cry, "Mommy, Shaila!" and their screams insulate me, like headphones.

The woman boiling water tells her story again and again. "I got the news first. My cousin called from Halifax before six a.m., can you imagine? He'd gotten up for prayers and his son was studying for medical exams and heard on a rock channel that something had happened to a plane. They said first it had disappeared from the radar, like a giant eraser just reached out. His father called me, so I said to him, what do you mean, 'something bad'? You mean a hijacking? And he said, *behn*, there is no confirmation of anything yet, but check with your neighbors because a lot of them must be on that plane. So I called poor Kusum straight-away. I knew Kusum's husband and daughter were booked to go yesterday."

Kusum lives across the street from me. She and Satish had moved in less than a month ago. They said they needed a bigger place. All these people, the Sharmas and friends from the Indo-Canada Society, had been there for the housewarming. Satish and Kusum made homemade tandoori on their big gas grill and even the white neighbors piled their plates high with that luridly red, charred, juicy chicken. Their younger daughter had danced, and even our boys had broken away from the Stanley Cup telecast to put in a reluctant appearance. Everyone took pictures for their albums and for the community newspapers—another of our families had made it big in Toronto—and now I wonder how many of those happy faces are gone. "Why does God give us so much if all along He intends to take it away?" Kusum asks me.

I nod. We sit on the carpeted stairs, holding hands like children. "I never once told him that I loved him," I say. I was too much the well-brought-up woman. I was so well brought up I never felt comfortable calling my husband by his first name.

"It's all right," Kusum says. "He knew. My husband knew. They felt it. Modern young girls have to say it because what they feel is fake."

Kusum's daughter Pam runs in with an overnight case. Pam's in her McDonald's uniform. "Mummy! You have to get dressed!" Panic makes her cranky. "A reporter's on his way here."

"Why?"

"You want to talk to him in your bathrobe?" She starts to brush her mother's long hair. She's the daughter who's always in trouble. She dates Canadian boys and hangs out in the mall, shopping for tight sweaters. The younger one, the goody-goody one according to Pam, the one with a voice so sweet that when she sang *bhajans* for Ethiopian relief even a frugal man like my husband wrote out a hundred-dollar check, *she* was on that plane. *She* was going to spend July and August with grandparents because Pam wouldn't go. Pam said she'd rather waitress at McDonald's. "If it's a choice between Bombay and Wonderland, I'm picking Wonderland," she'd said.

"Leave me alone," Kusum yells. "You know what I want to do? If I didn't have to look after you now, I'd hang myself."

Pam's young face goes blotchy with pain. "Thanks," she says, "don't let me stop you."

"Hush," pregnant Mrs. Sharma scolds Pam. "Leave your mother alone. Mr. Sharma will tackle the reporters and fill out the forms. He'll say what has to be said."

Pam stands her ground. "You think I don't know what Mummy's thinking? *Why her?* That's what. That's sick! Mummy wishes my little sister were alive and I were dead."

Kusum's hand in mine is trembly hot. We continue to sit on the stairs.

She calls before she arrives, wondering if there's anything I need. Her name is Judith Templeton and she's an appointee of the provincial government. "Multiculturalism?" I ask, and she says "partially," but that her mandate is bigger. "I've been told you knew many of the people on the flight," she says. "Perhaps if you'd agree to help us reach the others...?"

She gives me time at least to put on tea water and pick up the mess in the front room. I have a few *samosas* from Kusum's housewarming that I could fry up, but then I think, why prolong this visit?

Judith Templeton is much younger than she sounded. She wears a blue suit with a white blouse and a polka-dot tie. Her blond hair is cut short, her only jewelry is pearl-drop earrings. Her briefcase is new and expensive looking, a gleaming cordovan leather. She sits with it across her lap. When she looks out the front windows onto the street, her contact lenses seem to float in front of her light blue eyes.

"What sort of help do you want from me?" I ask. She has refused the tea, out of politeness, but I insist, along with some slightly stale biscuits.

"I have no experience," she admits. "That is, I have an M.S.W. and I've worked in liaison with accident victims, but I mean I have no experience with a tragedy of this scale—"

"Who could?" I ask.

"—and with the complications of culture, language, and customs. Someone mentioned that Mrs. Bhave is a pillar—because you've taken it more calmly."

At this, perhaps, I frown, for she reaches forward, almost to take my hand. "I hope you understand my meaning, Mrs. Bhave. There are hundreds of people in Metro directly affected, like you, and some of them speak no English. There are some widows who've never handled money or gone on a bus, and there are old parents who still haven't eaten or gone outside their bedrooms. Some houses and apartments have been looted. Some wives are still hysterical. Some husbands are in shock and profound depression. We want to help, but our hands are tied in so many ways. We have to distribute money to some people, and there are legal documents—these things can be done. We have interpreters, but we don't always have the human touch, or maybe the right human touch. We don't want to make mistakes, Mrs. Bhave, and that's why we'd like to ask you to help us."

"More mistakes, you mean," I say.

"Police matters are not in my hands," she answers.

"Nothing I can do will make any difference," I say. "We must all grieve in our own way."

"But you are coping very well. All the people said, Mrs. Bhave is the strongest person of all. Perhaps if the others could see you, talk with you, it would help them."

"By the standards of the people you call hysterical, I am behaving very oddly and very badly, Miss Templeton." I want to say to her, *I wish I could scream, starve, walk into Lake Ontario, jump from a bridge.* "They would not see me as a model. I do not see myself as a model."

I am a freak. No one who has ever known me would think of me reacting this way. This terrible calm will not go away.

She asks me if she may call again, after I get back from a long trip that we all must make. "Of course," I say. "Feel free to call, anytime."

Four days later, I find Kusum squatting on a rock overlooking a bay in Ireland. It isn't a big rock, but it juts sharply out over the water. This is as close as we'll ever get to them. June breezes balloon out her sari and unpin her knee-length hair. She has the bewildered look of a sea creature whom the tides have stranded.

It's been one hundred hours since Kusum came stumbling and screaming across my lawn. Waiting around the hospital, we've heard many stories. The police, the diplomats, they tell us things thinking that we're strong, that knowledge is helpful to the grieving, and maybe it is. Some, I know, prefer ignorance, or their own versions. The plane broke into two, they say. Unconsciousness was instantaneous. No one suffered. My boys must have just finished their breakfasts. They loved eating on planes, they loved the smallness of plates, knives, and forks. Last year they saved the airline salt and pepper shakers. Half an hour more and they would have made it to Heathrow.

Kusum says that we can't escape our fate. She says that all those people—our husbands, my boys, her girl with the nightingale voice, all those Hindus, Christians, Sikhs, Muslims, Parsis, and atheists on that plane—were fated to die together off this beautiful bay. She learned this from a swami in Toronto.

I have my Valium.

Six of us "relatives"—two widows and four widowers—choose to spend the day today by the waters instead of sitting in a hospital room and scanning photographs of the dead. That's what they call us now: relatives. I've looked through twenty-seven photos in two days. They're very kind to us, the Irish are very understanding. Sometimes understanding means freeing a tourist bus for this trip to the bay, so we can pretend to spy our loved ones through the glassiness of waves or in the sun-speckled cloud shapes.

I could die here, too, and be content.

"What is that, out there?" She's standing and flapping her hands, and for a moment I see a head shape bobbing in the waves. She's standing in the water, I, on the boulder. The tide is low, and a round, black, head-sized rock has just risen from the waves. She returns, her sari end dripping and ruined and her face is a twisted remnant of hope, the way mine was a hundred hours ago, still laughing but inwardly knowing that nothing but the ultimate tragedy could bring two women together at six o'clock on a Sunday morning. I watch her face sag into blankness.

"That water felt warm, Shaila," she says at length.

"You can't," I say. "We have to wait for our turn to come."

I haven't eaten in four days, haven't brushed my teeth.

"I know," she says. "I tell myself I have no right to grieve. They are in a better place than we are. My swami says I should be thrilled for them. My swami says depression is a sign of our selfishness."

Maybe I'm selfish. Selfishly I break away from Kusum and run, sandals slapping against stones, to the water's edge. What if my boys aren't lying pinned under the debris? What if they aren't stuck a mile below that innocent blue chop? What if, given the strong currents...

Now I've ruined my sari, one of my best. Kusum has joined me, knee-deep in water that feels to me like a swimming pool. I could settle in the water, and my husband would take my hand and the boys would slap water in my face just to see me scream.

"Do you remember what good swimmers my boys were, Kusum?"

"I saw the medals," she says.

One of the widowers, Dr. Ranganathan from Montreal, walks out to us, carrying his shoes in one hand. He's an electrical engineer. Someone at the hotel mentioned his work is famous around the world, something about the place where physics and electricity come together. He has lost a huge family, something indescribable. "With some luck," Dr. Ranganathan suggests to me, "a good swimmer could make it safely to some island. It is quite possible that there may be many, many microscopic islets scattered around."

"You're not just saying that?" I tell Dr. Ranganathan about Vinod, my elder son. Last year he took diving as well.

"It's a parent's duty to hope," he says. "It is foolish to rule out possibilities that have not been tested. I myself have not surrendered hope."

Kusum is sobbing once again. "Dear lady," he says, laying his free hand on her arm, and she calms down.

"Vinod is how old?" he asks me. He's very careful as we all are. *Is*, not was.

"Fourteen. Yesterday he was fourteen. His father and uncle were going to take him down to the Taj and give him a big birthday party. I couldn't go with them because I couldn't get two weeks off from my stupid job in June." I process bills for a travel agent. June is a big travel month.

Dr. Ranganathan whips the pockets of his suit jacket inside out. Squashed roses, in darkening shades of pink, float on the water. He tore the roses off creepers in somebody's garden. He didn't ask anyone if he could pluck the roses, but now there's been an article about it in the local papers. When you see an Indian person, it says, please give him or her flowers.

"A strong youth of fourteen," he says, "can very likely pull to safety a younger one."

My sons, though four years apart, were very close. Vinod wouldn't let Mithun drown. *Electrical engineering*, I think, foolishly perhaps: this man knows important secrets of the universe, things closed to me. Relief spins me lightheaded. No wonder my boys' photographs haven't turned up in the gallery of photos of the recovered dead. "Such pretty roses," I say.

"My wife loved pink roses. Every Friday I had to bring a bunch home. I used to say, Why? After twenty-odd years of marriage you're still needing proof positive of my love?" He has identified his wife and three of his children. Then others from Montreal, the lucky ones, intact families with no survivors. He chuckles as he wades back to shore. Then he swings around to ask me a question. "Mrs. Bhave, you are wanting to throw in some roses for your loved ones? I have two big ones left."

But I have other things to float: Vinod's pocket calculator; a half-painted model B-52 for my Mithun. They'd want them on their island. And for my husband? For him I let fall into the calm, glassy waters a poem I wrote in the hospital yesterday. Finally he'll know my feelings for him.

"Don't tumble, the rocks are slippery," Dr. Ranganathan cautions. He holds out a hand for me to grab.

Then it's time to get back on the bus, time to rush back to our waiting posts on hospital benches.

Kusum is one of the lucky ones. The lucky ones flew here, identified in multiplicate their loved ones, then will fly to India with the bodies for proper ceremonies. Satish is one of the few males who surfaced. The photos of faces we saw on the walls in an office at Heathrow and here in the hospital are mostly of women. Women have more body fat, a nun said to me matter-of-factly. They float better.

Today I was stopped by a young sailor on the street. He had loaded bodies, he'd gone into the water when—he checks my face for signs of strength—when the sharks were first spotted. I don't blush, and he breaks down. "It's all right," I say. "Thank you." I had heard about the sharks from Dr. Ranganathan. In his orderly mind, science brings understanding, it holds no terror. It is the shark's duty. For every deer there is a hunter, for every fish a fisherman.

The Irish are not shy; they rush to me and give me hugs and some are crying. I cannot imagine reactions like that on the streets of Toronto. Just strangers, and I am touched. Some carry flowers with them and give them to any Indian they see.

After lunch, a policeman I have gotten to know quite well catches hold of me. He says he thinks he has a match for Vinod. I explain what a good swimmer Vinod is.

"You want me with you when you look at photos?" Dr. Ranganathan walks ahead of me into the picture gallery. In these matters, he is a scientist, and I am grateful. It is a new perspective. "They have performed miracles," he says. "We are indebted to them."

The first day or two the policemen showed us relatives only one picture at a time; now they're in a hurry, they're eager to lay out the possibles, and even the probables.

The face on the photo is of a boy much like Vinod; the same intelligent eyes, the same thick brows dipping into a V. But this boy's features, even his cheeks, are puffier, wider, mushier.

"No." My gaze is pulled by other pictures. There are five other boys who look like Vinod.

The nun assigned to console me rubs the first picture with a fingertip. "When they've been in the water for a while, love, they look a little heavier." The bones under the skin are broken, they said on the first day—try to adjust your memories. It's important.

"It's not him. I'm his mother. I'd know."

"I know this one!" Dr. Ranganathan cries out suddenly from the back of the gallery. "And this one!" I think he senses that I don't want to find my boys. " They are the Kutty brothers. They were also from Montreal." I don't mean to be crying. On the contrary, I am ecstatic. My suitcase in the hotel is packed heavy with dry clothes for my boys.

The policeman starts to cry. "I am so sorry, I am so sorry, ma'am. I really thought we had a match."

With the nun ahead of us and the policeman behind, we, the unlucky ones without our children's bodies, file out of the makeshift gallery.

From Ireland most of us go on to India. Kusum and I take the same direct flight to Bombay, so I can help her clear customs quickly. But we have to argue with a man in uniform. He has large boils on his face. The boils swell and glow with sweat as we argue with him. He wants Kusum to wait in line and he refuses to take authority because his boss is on a tea break. But Kusum won't let her coffins out of sight, and I shan't desert her though I know that my parents, elderly and diabetic, must be waiting in a stuffy car in a scorching lot.

" You bastard!" I scream at the man with the popping boils. Other passengers press closer. " You think we're smuggling contraband in those coffins!"

Once upon a time we were well-brought-up women; we were dutiful wives who kept our heads veiled, our voices shy and sweet.

In India, I become, once again, an only child of rich, ailing parents. Old friends of the family come to pay their respects. Some are Sikh, and inwardly, involuntarily, I cringe. My parents are progressive people; they do not blame communities for a few individuals.

In Canada it is a different story now.

"Stay longer," my mother pleads. "Canada is a cold place. Why would you want to be all by yourself?" I stay.

Three months pass. Then another.

"Vikram wouldn't have wanted you to give up things!" they protest. They call my husband by the name he was born with. In Toronto he'd changed to Vik so the men he worked with at his office would find his name as easy as Rod or Chris. "You know, the dead aren't cut off from us!"

My grandmother, the spoiled daughter of a rich *zamindar*, shaved her head with rusty razor blades when she was widowed at sixteen. My grandfather died of childhood diabetes when he was nineteen, and she saw herself as the harbinger of bad luck. My mother grew up without parents, raised indifferently by an uncle, while her true mother slept in a hut behind the main estate house and took her food with the servants. She grew up a rationalist. My parents abhor mindless mortification.

The *zamindar*'s daughter kept stubborn faith in Vedic rituals; my parents rebelled. I am trapped between two modes of knowledge. At thirty-six, I am too old to start over and too young to give up. Like my husband's spirit, I flutter between worlds.

Courting aphasia, we travel. We travel with our phalanx of servants and poor relatives. To hill stations and to beach resorts. We play contract bridge in dusty gymkhana clubs. We ride stubby ponies up crumbly mountain trails. At tea dances, we let ourselves be twirled twice round the ballroom. We hit the holy spots we hadn't made time for before. In Varanasi, Kalighat, Rishikesh, Hardwar, astrologers and palmists seek me out and for a fee offer me cosmic consolations.

Already the widowers among us are being shown new bride candidates. They cannot resist the call of custom, the authority of their parents and older brothers. They must marry; it is the duty of a man to look after a wife. The new wives will be young widows with children, destitute but of good family. They will make loving wives, but the men will shun them. I've had calls from the men over crackling Indian telephone lines. "Save me," they say, these substantial, educated, successful men of forty. "My parents are arranging a marriage for me." In a month they will have buried one family and returned to Canada with a new bride and partial family.

I am comparatively lucky. No one here thinks of arranging a husband for an unlucky widow.

Then, on the third day of the sixth month into this odyssey, in an abandoned temple in a tiny Himalayan village, as I make my offering of flowers and sweetmeats to the god of a tribe of animists, my husband descends to me. He is squatting next to a scrawny *sadhu* in moth-eaten robes. Vikram wears the vanilla suit he wore the last time I hugged him. The *sadhu* tosses petals on a butter-fed flame, reciting Sanskrit mantras, and sweeps his face of flies. My husband takes my hands in his.

You're beautiful, he starts. Then, *What are you doing here?*

Shall I stay? I ask. He only smiles, but already the image is fading. *You must finish alone what we started together.* No seaweed wreathes his mouth. He speaks too fast, just as he used to when we were an envied family in our pink split-level. He is gone.

In the windowless altar room, smoky with joss sticks and clarified butter lamps, a sweaty hand gropes for my blouse. I do not shriek. The *sadhu* arranges his robe. The lamps hiss and sputter out.

When we come out of the temple, my mother says, "Did you feel something weird in there?"

My mother has no patience with ghosts, prophetic dreams, holy men, and cults.

"No," I lie. "Nothing."

But she knows that she's lost me. She knows that in days I shall be leaving.

Kusum's put up her house for sale. She wants to live in an ashram in Hardwar. Moving to Hardwar was her swami's idea. Her swami runs two ashrams, the one in Hardwar and another here in Toronto.

"Don't run away," I tell her.

"I'm not running away," she says. "I'm pursuing inner peace. You think you or that Ranganathan fellow are better off?"

Pam's left for California. She wants to do some modelling, she says. She says when she comes into her share of the insurance money she'll open a yoga-cum-aerobics studio in Hollywood. She sends me postcards so naughty I daren't leave them on the coffee table. Her mother has withdrawn from her and the world.

The rest of us don't lose touch, that's the point. Talk is all we have, says Dr. Ranganathan, who has also resisted his relatives and returned to Montreal and to his job, alone. He says, Whom better to talk with than other relatives? We've been melted down and recast as a new tribe.

He calls me twice a week from Montreal. Every Wednesday night and every Saturday afternoon. He is changing jobs, going to Ottawa. But Ottawa is over a hundred miles away, and he is forced to drive two hundred and twenty miles a day. He can't bring himself to sell his house. The house is a temple, he says; the king-sized bed in the master bedroom is a shrine. He sleeps on a folding cot. A devotee.

There are still some hysterical relatives. Judith Templeton's list of those needing help and those who've "accepted" is in nearly perfect balance. Acceptance means you speak of your family in the past tense and you make active plans for moving ahead with your life. There are courses at Seneca and Ryerson we could be taking. Her gleaming leather briefcase is full of college catalogues and lists of cultural societies that need our help. She has done impressive work, I tell her.

"In the textbooks on grief management," she replies—I am her confidante, I realize, one of the few whose grief has not sprung bizarre obsessions—"there are stages to pass through: rejection, depression, acceptance, reconstruction." She has compiled a chart and finds that six months after the tragedy, none of us still reject reality, but only a handful are reconstructing. "Depressed Acceptance" is the plateau we've reached. Remarriage is a major step in reconstruction (though she's a little surprised, even shocked, over *how* quickly some of the men have taken on new families). Selling one's house and changing jobs and cities is healthy.

How do I tell Judith Templeton that my family surrounds me, and that like creatures in epics, they've changed shapes? She sees me as calm and accepting but worries that I have no job, no career. My closest friends are worse off than I. I cannot tell her my days, even my nights, are thrilling.

She asks me to help with families she can't reach at all. An elderly couple in Agincourt whose sons were killed just weeks after they had brought their parents over from a village in Punjab. From their names, I know they are Sikh. Judith Templeton and a translator have visited them twice with offers of money for airfare to Ireland, with bank forms, power-of-attorney forms, but they have refused to sign, or to leave their tiny apartment. Their sons' money is frozen in the bank. Their sons' investment apartments have been trashed by tenants, the furnishings sold off. The parents fear that anything they sign or any money they receive will end the company's or the country's obligations to them. They fear they are selling their sons for two airline tickets to a place they've never seen.

The high-rise apartment is a tower of Indians and West Indians, with a sprinkling of Orientals. The nearest bus-stop kiosk is lined with women in saris. Boys practice cricket in the parking lot. Inside the building, even I wince a bit from the ferocity of onion fumes, the distinctive and immediate Indianness of frying *ghee*, but Judith Templeton maintains a steady flow of information. These poor old people are in imminent danger of losing their place and all their services.

I say to her, "They are Sikh. They will not open up to a Hindu woman." And what I want to add is, as much as I try not to, I stiffen now at the sight of beards and turbans. I remember a time when we all trusted each other in this new country, it was only the new country we worried about.

The two rooms are dark and stuffy. The lights are off, and an oil lamp sputters on the coffee table. The bent old lady has let us in, and her husband is wrapping a white turban over his oiled, hip-length hair. She immediately goes to the kitchen, and I hear the most familiar sound of an Indian home, tap water hitting and filling a teapot.

They have not paid their utility bills, out of fear and the inability to write a check. The telephone is gone; electricity and gas and water are soon to follow. They have told Judith their sons will provide. They are good boys, and they have always earned and looked after their parents.

We converse a bit in Hindi. They do not ask about the crash and I wonder if I should bring it up. If they think I am here merely as a translator, then they may feel insulted. There are thousands of Punjabi-speakers, Sikhs, in Toronto to do a better job. And so I say to the old lady, "I too have lost my sons, and my husband, in the crash."

Her eyes immediately fill with tears. The man mutters a few words which sound like a blessing. "God provides and God takes away," he says.

I want to say, But only men destroy and give back nothing. "My boys and my husband are not coming back," I say. "We have to understand that."

Now the old woman responds. "But who is to say? Man alone does not decide these things." To this her husband adds his agreement.

Judith asks about the bank papers, the release forms. With a stroke of the pen, they will have a provincial trustee to pay their bills, invest their money, send them a monthly pension.

"Do you know this woman?" I ask them.

The man raises his hand from the table, turns it over, and seems to regard each finger separately before he answers. "This young lady is always coming here, we make tea for her and she leaves papers for us to sign." His eyes scan a pile of papers in the corner of the room. "Soon we will be out of tea, then will she go away?"

The old lady adds, "I have asked my neighbors and no one else gets *angrezi* visitors. What have we done?"

"It's her job," I try to explain. "The government is worried. Soon you will have no place to stay, no lights, no gas, no water."

"Government will get its money. Tell her not to worry, we are honorable people."

I try to explain the government wishes to give money, not take. He raises his hand. "Let them take," he says. "We are accustomed to that. That is no problem."

"We are strong people," says the wife. "Tell her that."

"Who needs all this machinery?" demands the husband. "It is unhealthy, the bright lights, the cold air on a hot day, the cold food, the four gas rings. God will provide, not government."

" When our boys return," the mother says. Her husband sucks his teeth. "Enough talk," he says.

Judith breaks in. "Have you convinced them?" The snaps on her cordovan briefcase go off like firecrackers in that quiet apartment. She lays the sheaf of legal papers on the coffee table. "If they can't write their names, an X will do—I've told them that."

Now the old lady has shuffled to the kitchen and soon emerges with a pot of tea and two cups. "I think my bladder will go first on a job like this," Judith says to me, smiling. "If only there was some way of reaching them. Please thank her for the tea. Tell her she's very kind."

I nod in Judith's direction and tell them in Hindi, "She thanks you for the tea. She thinks you are being very hospitable but she doesn't have the slightest idea what it means."

I want to say, Humor her. I want to say, My boys and my husband are with me too, more than ever. I look in the old man's eyes and I can read his stubborn, peasant's message: *I have protected this woman as best I can. She is the only person I have left. Give to me or take from me what you will, but I will not sign for it. I will not pretend that I accept.*

In the car, Judith says, " You see what I'm up against? I'm sure they're lovely people, but their stubbornness and ignorance are driving me crazy. They think signing a paper is signing their sons' death warrants, don't they?"

I am looking out the window. I want to say, *In our culture, it is a parent's duty to hope.*

"Now Shaila, this next woman is a real mess. She cries day and night, and she refuses all medical help. We may have to—"

"—Let me out at the subway," I say.

"I beg your pardon?" I can feel those blue eyes staring at me.

It would not be like her to disobey. She merely disapproves, and slows at a corner to let me out. Her voice is plaintive. "Is there anything I said? Anything I did?"

I could answer her suddenly in a dozen ways, but I choose not to. "Shaila? Let's talk about it," I hear, then slam the door.

A wife and mother begins her new life in a new country, and that life is cut short. Yet her husband tells her: Complete what we have started. We, who stayed out of politics and came halfway around the world to avoid religious and political feuding, have been the first in the New World to die from it. I no longer know what we started, nor how to complete it. I write letters to the editors of local papers and to members of Parliament. Now at least they admit it was a bomb. One MP answers back, with sympathy, but with a challenge. You want to make a difference? Work on a campaign. Work on mine. Politicize the Indian voter.

My husband's old lawyer helps me set up a trust. Vikram was a saver and a careful investor. He had saved the boys' boarding school and college fees. I sell the pink house at four times what we paid for it and take a small apartment downtown. I am looking for a charity to support.

We are deep in the Toronto winter, gray skies, icy pavements. I stay indoors, watching television. I have tried to assess my situation, how best to live my life, to complete what we began so many years ago. Kusum has written me from Hardwar that her life is now serene. She has seen Satish and has heard her daughter sing again. Kusum was on a pilgrimage, passing through a village, when she heard a young girl's voice singing one of her daughter's favorite *bhajans*. She followed the music through the squalor of a Himalayan village, to a hut where a young girl, an exact replica of her daughter, was fanning coals under the kitchen fire. When she appeared, the girl cried out, "Ma!" and ran away. What did I think of that?

I think I can only envy her.

Pam didn't make it to California, but writes me from Vancouver. She works in a department store, giving makeup hints to Indian and Oriental girls. Dr. Ranganathan has given up his commute, given up his house and job, and accepted an academic position in Texas where no one knows his story and he has vowed not to tell it. He calls me now once a week.

I wait, I listen, and I pray, but Vikram has not returned to me. The voices and the shapes and the nights filled with visions ended abruptly several weeks ago.

I take it as a sign.

One rare, beautiful, sunny day last week, returning from a small errand on Yonge Street, I was walking through the park from the subway to my apartment. I live equidistant from the Ontario Houses of Parliament and the University of Toronto. The day was not cold, but something in the bare trees caught my attention. I looked up from the gravel, into the branches and the clear blue sky beyond. I thought I heard the rustling of larger forms, and I waited a moment for voices. Nothing.

"What?" I asked.

Then as I stood in the path looking north to Queen's Park and west to the university, I heard the voices of my family one last time. *Your time has come*, they said. *Go, be brave.*

I do not know where this voyage I have begun will end. I do not know which direction I will take. I dropped the package on a park bench and started walking.

Source

■

Desperately Seeking Helen

Film Synopsis

EISHA MARJARA

DIRECTOR Eisha Marjara's story takes us first to her childhood in snowbound small-town Quebec and then to Bombay, India, where she desperately tries to track down Helen, a famous movie star in the world's largest dream factory. Helen becomes a passage into Marjara's real world—her unsettling youth, life-threatening anorexia, and the devastating 1985 Air India bombing, which took the lives of her mother and sister. This video revisits the '70s pop culture of Marjara's youth and enters the fascinating world of the Bombay movie industry—"Bollywood."

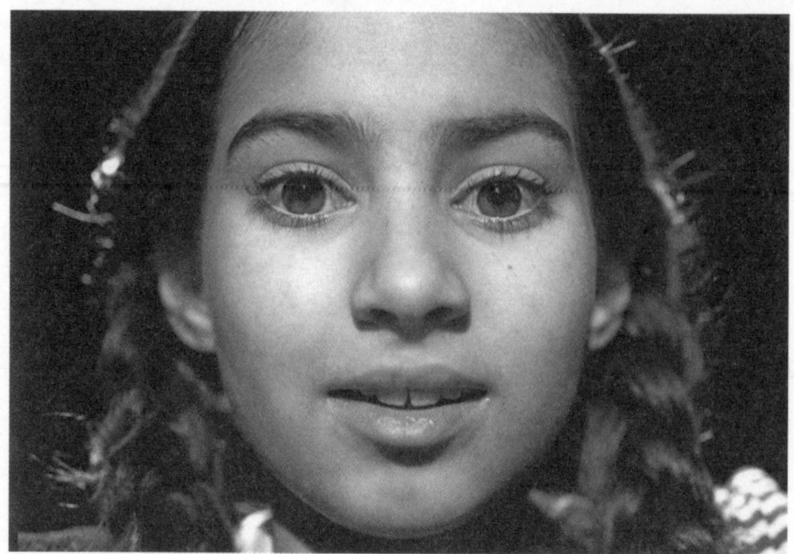

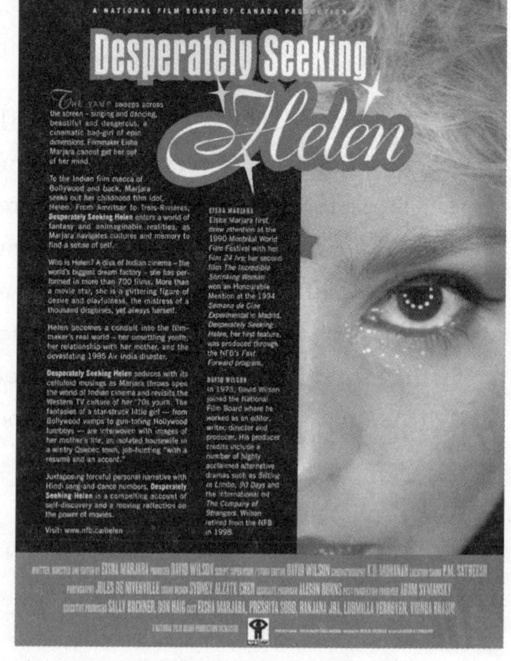

Film still and poster from Eisha Marjara's Desperately Seeking Helen. *Copyright © 1998 by National Film Board of Canada. All rights reserved, reprinted by permission of the National Film Board of Canada and by permission of the artist.*

Source

National Film Board of Canada, *Desperately Seeking Helen*: Description, last modifed April 8, 2013, accessed Feburary 28, 2015, http://onf-nfb.gc.ca/en/our-collection/?idfilm=33640.

air india, unsent / letters from the archive

RENÉE SAROJINI SAKLIKAR

Dear Cousin, this letter unsent,

flying Canada to Ireland
on winds, Atlantic,
the names of the Air India dead
held, released—
documents numbering thousand-hundred-thousand
the unimaginable turned fragment,
littering a coastline: Ireland a jigsaw,
waves puzzle over bodies
long dispersed
in the deep Atlantic
surface tremour, hunted,
hunting June 23, 1985
blasted into being
these mathematical devices
51°3.6'N 12°49'W
these words settled,
settling 6,700 feet
Pacific to Atlantic
25 years, a generation calling
add the new years
forgetting, remembering
Air India
over and across, Ireland
to Canada
time and its dimensions
water and numbers
words and families, their children,
82 under the age of 13
floating and forgetting
1985-2010-2011-2012-2013-2014-2015-2016—

from the archive, this morning as mourning,

Why did all this so affect you?
bodies exist, whole and fractal
    these letters, unsent, reside—
    sequence to space: a ratio in search of meaning.

Where does one go from here?
to seek the page as shelter,
    as with the names of the dead.

Do you claim you are the author of these terms?
Of course and off
    course as coordinates, ocean a site of recovery,
re-membering
    a condition not of agency. Subaltern status.
    And of forgiveness? Who dares to name it, let her bow, forehead to documents.

Answering to what, exactly?
Love, which is its own test
also, the means to—alternate response: Citation. A number of volumes.

When did this happen?
The date is documented and well known, effaced and forgotten.
One continuing gesture, happened, never happened.

Is this your actual level of despair?
I am upright, writing, Dear Cousin—
The longing is for sutra. It will be refused. The way of grief,
if pronounced long, will slow time
    the way the past, brute, will bring tears,
        tearing a fabric of living

unexpected, unwanted in this, our North America—

as if outside history, unaccountable. Air India: happened to someone else.

—procedures for unaccompanied sorrow:

mourners must present an object, valid enough
        for experience, there is a body
reaction as serialized itemization: groin, gut. The tear ducts.
        As for the mind, unlawful seepage
                accruing inside the passenger—
memory
        and underneath,
the everlasting—

June 23, 1985: morning over the Atlantic—

Dear Cousin, these moments of inscription

accept as memorial, shards stranded and
        numbering on the line of days,
10226.8, 1985–2013
always reoccurring, this month
ritual
        all around us digital: age of staccato,
        already the epistolary is cliché:
everyone addresses
someone, these letters
remain un-
sent

testimony
that space between
tear   and
terror

about the body
they will tell us,
        move on—

Dear Cousin, I lose count of the years,

each letter about to be sent
    instead, hidden inside a packet:
Your loss everything, and I, mother of no one
    have made other children,
my own: is it monstrous,
to conjure ghosts when they, free to float elsewhere
    must travel long distances—

Today I am inventory
limbs as notebooks
written upon
with visitation
~~strike sentiment.~~
Begin again, the lists,
endless saga, marking time—
    Bring us the bodies?
    No, not even three hundred and thirty-one:
out of catastrophe, away from monuments
    cousin to cousin: between us, ocean, language (Gujarati), fractured family,
between us a coroner's report, decades old.

They will make our story
about good and evil, about laws and nations, about systems: their analysis of what went wrong
between us the bodies, flesh of our flesh,
    and the long-wailing that is song.

Dear Cousin, into this space seen by no one,

except that most intimate stranger,

the reader:

Add your longings,

Add your dreams

to banish June 23, 1985: this:

morning in the garden up at the home-house, in the town of towns—

cigar smoke rises—there is your father, in the far corner, past the roses,

down by the peonies, lush magenta.

I cannot name for you

the fragrance—

Dear Cousin, without warning, yes

visitations occur.
Voices: children and others.
Impossible to explain.
Have given up trying.
Instead, welcome.
Communion with the dead.
And some of them, also offended,
to find me as receptacle,
still open
after all these years, insistent on chronicle.
It is transgression. It is witness, to record the extreme.
And we who remember are a kind of sect,
archive as cloister, where the contemplative might gather
amid the grand narratives, a few outcast moments, "—a child's battered shoe."

Portrait of Two Children: pre-pubescent
Photographs found in yellowed newspaper,
acrid smell of the last century
Location: summer holidays, south Vancouver.
Name: [redacted]
Name: [redacted]
Surviving relatives: " Tell me, again, G——, how they played, so happy to be going—"

*

Note: error is common: when redacting information, remember not to use the wrong method. Review is necessary. Below is a partial list of methods NOT to use

[redacted]
[redacted]
[redacted]

Dear Cousin, there you are in the before-time,

pampered, beloved of two
        was there lightness in you,
                do you remember the weeks before?
the past, carved sandalwood,
        a chest made devoid of scent.
Open the lid of this box, behind its cover, runs a small boy.
My calls do not reach him.

*

Today we are again in that before-time, the past
        June 23, 1985. The days before—
                See the young woman walking, swinging her hips down a hill.
                It is the town of towns.
She is eager
        a shining twenty-three-year-old.
She lives in Empire's outpost, pacific coastal,
shelf of the Americas. We must address her.
She is forever in that moment just before:
        O woman, do not shine so!
        They will mistake your luminescence.

un/authorized interjection archival transmission

from the line of Volume 2, Part I

Heightened threat
Had requested
Were events
Were as
So it was
Chronologies and gaps
Repercussions or stigma
A number of discrepancies
Stated that—

*

dear archive,

No photographs of the dead.
          Still, the dust.
No tokens withdrawn,
          a jeweled box, held, rubbed.
          Still, the dust, entering even, your electronic files—

These letters, a song for you,
holder of—

*

Moment: June, 1985
Depiction: a family says goodbye
Photographer: he who is absent
Architecture: Airport divider. A kind of glass.
Status: YVR
Relations: Aunt who is mother,
                    Uncle who is father,
                    two daughter-nieces
                              mothers of no one
Location of original photograph: lost
Appearance: infrequent
Source: photograph published in a newspaper
Owner: news corporation

*

It is Vancouver. June. 1985.
A family separated by farewell.
        our glass good-byes.
Only a literalist
        would dream of shattering
this memory.

June 23, 1985

Always, you are—
Always, I am—

And they, who are lost, with us
            the forever.

Dear Cousin,

This space   hollow
    hallowed,

for you to enter
    your own story:

Your date of birth
Your toddler days—

Childhood, an absence:

perhaps an empty playroom: unseen birthday parties, photographers, day-trips, posters, heroes, pets, bicycles, watches, tee-shirts, soccer games, cricket glove, talismans, small objects,

your pockets,
emptied.

Your earliest memories
Your cherished—
    echo

Dear Cousin, it is the end of June.

I am twenty-three. Every day I write to you on my way to work, my walking,
writing,
            rhythm inside my head—up and down the hills in this town of towns.
messages sent telepathically, stored only
in absence and—until—

(interception from the future,
that dark box
where this pen, as if laser,
will engrave the past, tiny and miniature
a Mughal painting
            textured)

Dear Cousin,

Our house has gone quite still, after all the crying,
the days ahead, vast,
without buoys—

Dear Cousin, now we are in the after-time.

A friend is here. He is helping with math. We are in the dining room.
There is so much friendliness here. Our friend is rugby.
Our friend is United Church.
We are all United Church and there is belonging.
There is friendship. There is the
not looking   writing   there is the not looking

Friend: *I don't see why our tax dollars should have to pay for that over there in Ireland, I don't agree with it.*

Dear Cousin,

I am getting ready
for my trip to India.

March 31, 1987, Gujarat.

I walk narrow dusty streets, cow-dung-patties fat disks,
        where goats and hens wander.
Crows cry out.
Far off, in the paddocks owned by our family, the bullocks moan.
Around our grandfather's long deserted home,
coconut, eucalyptus—

There you are, outside the hospital
        built by your surgeon mother—

Un/authorized memory: your mother: "you know, many women would
come to me.
        I would help them."

Photograph-Memory

We are outside your home-clinic.
up against its blue washed stucco,
          your name in large steel letters, bougainvillea blossoms
                    magenta profusion
bottom left hand corner, a dog.
          Black hind-quarters—

Memory inside the photograph

We sit in the home built by your dead parents.
Inside: blue tile. Cool concrete. The sun's glare shuttered.
Outside, crows scream against the wind.
Inside: we sit side by side, our shoulders do not touch
in the blue room,
          your father's people stare—

Photograph prohibited

I am at the graveyard on the hill, in the village J . . . .
Dry earth, burnt red, stone mounds
barbed wire narrow paths to my aunt, your mother
          who lies beside her mother
Our grandmother who lies beside grandfather
          our dead sunk into
          the ground, rose petals—
Did I scatter these upon arrival?
          They blow with the wind and away—
what is the Gujarati word for sirocco?

*

(Mother to Daughter: *you went all that way. Your letters told us nothing.*)

*

from the Atlantic they brought her
          Ireland to India
Is it true, that thousands came to say good-bye—
          our laughing one,
                    diamond in the groove of her nose—
I have never asked you for your memories,
          seeing as in relief: shadow,
                    a small boy:
          behind him a long line—

from the archive, your parents

The photograph exists.

Scalloped edges.

Wedding day portrait.

Husband and wife, seated, hands linked. They are smiling into each other's eyes.

*

Artifact: plastic folder, cover emblazoned, Expo '86.

*

Dear Cousin,

I never look at it.

*

Coroner's report: [notes redacted]

Dear Cousin, accept within today's letter, this story.

Dedication: for our dead.

*

1988. It is the after-time. I am still a believer.

First year criminal law class: a guest speaker arrives. He is a crown prosecutor, in the Attorney General's department. This man: fine boned, dapper, his words come out fast in a clipped rhythm, he speaks about wiretapping and uses as his case study, Air India.

He asks us to consider *opening the packet:*

Authority is an explanation, is the RCMP-CSIS. Desire is spying. Desire is wanting: Canadian citizens originally from the Punjab and their religion, Sikh. There will be a requirement: by law. There will be the need to get permission. A judge. There will be the making of a case. There will be the why's and wherefore's established: this phone, this device, this home, watched. It is the way of *Surveillance.*

And the arguments accumulate: to spy on resident-citizens, there must be justification, which itself is often gathered through more spying. Action and theory collated in a series of documents: *the Packet.* And sealed. At the request of the authorities, information. And secreted away from those who might have questions.

Sealing the Packet and Opening the Packet. This is what the prosecutor wants us to learn.

At the end of his lecture, the prosecutor asks us to consider the instance of Air India and the accused bomb makers. Should *the accused be given the right to open the packet?* The stakes: full disclosure, in order to know, to assess what they are up against—And on the other side, the public interest, to keep society safe from *terrorists* although in 1988 that word doesn't get much play.

The prosecutor asks for a show of hands: *Yes:* to open the packet, favour the accused. *No:* to keep the packet sealed, society's secrets kept safe. When he asks, *No?* Most of the class will raise their hands. When he asks, *Yes? Yes. Open the packet—*

Let the accused breathe in the dust of his accusers. The prosecutor counts the hands raised, *No* v. *Yes* and out of one hundred students: ninety-seven *No's*, ninety-seven law students raise their hands against the rights of the men accused of Canada's worst mass murder. Three *Yes's.*

Three hands up for the rights of the accused. *The case for the defense.*

And my hand, one of them. It is 1988, the long years of the after-time—I am still a believer. And now—

Dear Cousin: inside Courtroom #20

from the home-house in the town of towns, we take you,
from the reach of evening, to inside a suburban movie theatre,
we take you to the word, *Coquitlam*, linked to the words, *Port Coquitlam*
    (let history summon as under-over layer:
        those murdered, missing, the future
    not spoken, not acknowledged.
    still present.)

It is March, 2005.
We take you to a big-box cinema-complex
silver in its raucous X-Box yearning, your eyes
tell me nothing.
We eat French fries and hamburgers.
We see *The Matrix*.
    Inside the dark,
I turn, and watch
        the whites of your eyes.

We never speak of it.
—your day inside the body of the court.

Dear Cousin, during these days, questions surface, un-asked:

There you are, upstairs in the home-house, bedroom where once they slept
Your parents—do you dream of them, waking—
    to step onto floorboards,
    the wood, Douglas Fir, varnished, yellow-brown
    milled from early in the last century,
    where forests—

un/authorized interjection archival transmission

Inquiry on the line of Vol 2, Part One, Chapter v

descent entered
busy morning
was served
sought to
one suitcase
was not
was able
had paid

Time
drags fate,
          an unknown
was too much

a long flight—

Dear Cousin, the time of the trial is like a demarcation zone:

Bomb-makers.

Ticket-takers.

Their stories.

And ours?

[redacted], her shaking hands.

Dear Cousin, embedded in these letters, my witness for you:

Memory-Artifact

Location: June 23, 1985 and the after-time

Dimension: perjury trial, jury verdict.

Mother: *Deekrah*, it's been so long: I just fade with it.

Cousin: How are you? We are thinking of you today.

Reporter: (off camera). I lost my father. I lost my father.

N: (street side). Was it sudden?

Reporter: Yes.

N: : am sorry

: am sorry—

un/authorized interjection archival transmission

Found on the line of twenty-seven: transcript

[reporter name redacted] with regards to [redacted] NO SLUG Modif. WTR Media. Host.
Source. Transcript. SCRIPTS.[redacted] TOTAL subjects Comment [redacted]
[redacted] modified subject comment regards [redacted] Air India CBC [redacted]
Regards NO SLUG Modif. WRT [redacted]Air India [redacted] 3/8/2010 SOURCE COPY
Aud/vid Air India [redacted] accused. Lying. NO SLUG. Modif. WTR Media. Host.
[redacted] Aud/vid Air India outdoors[redacted] Air India outdoors aunt and uncle bomb
[redacted] perjury [redacted] soaks up the sun [redacted] NO SLUG ALL OF US Air India
[redacted] regards to [redacted] Air India [redacted] Soaks up the sun HOW CAN YOU
COME TO TERMS Modif. WRT Media. Host. IF HE WAS LYING. 27 TIMES. [redacted]
Host SOURCE COPY Aud/vid TOTAL [redacted] Modif. WTR [redacted] Supreme Court
unmitigated liar NO SLUG Type Host SOURCE COPY Aud/vid What it feels like
Air India [redacted] seven years CAPTIVE TO A PROCESS tape in: for the CBC lying
Runs:1:16 out: news, Vancouver [redacted] 3/8/2010 [redacted] 27 times
Perjury CAPTIVE [ERN]People.SCRIPTS.[redacted] 27 times soaks up the sun TIME Air
India false CBC WTR Media ERN Host Source TIME Air India 2005 Supreme Court
[redacted] SUPREME COURT JUSTICE [redacted] Judge, TIME. Air India NO S LUG.
Modif. 3/8/2010. SCRIPTS. [redacted] soaks up the sun TIME COPY Lying 27 times
CAPTIVE trial [redacted] 1985 2005 2007 3/8/2010 NO SLUG [redacted] with regard to
[redacted] CBC soaks up the sun time Families Air India murder Canadian history takes
in the sounds Modif. WTR Media APP TIME soaks up the sun CAPTIVE lying 27 times
lying times
lying times
lying times
lying times
lying times
lying times
[redacted] Court. Supreme Sun TIME Air India families murder NO SLUG Modif.

Dear Cousin,

What orphan means:
the measure of the world.

*

Object:
on a TV set, *Breakfast Television:*
            woman adjusting her legs
sheen of commerce, ready smile
preparation to interview
about Air India,
    this Subject.

from the archive: method

Find: a document.

Result: found.

Insert caption: "August 20, 2009, 12:01pm, Reporter [name redacted],

Newspaper [name redacted].

Insert Title: [redacted].

Invent Title: Once there was a man who built a bomb

Method:

1. Print out document from internet
2. Cut out photo of a man
3. Insert photo into shredding machine
4. Gather shreds onto page and create a shape
5. Paste shape into place
6. Re-insert into news story
7. Repeat
8. Videotape steps 1–7
9. Post on You Tube
10. Repeat

un/authorized interjection archival transmission

from the line of 1. 9. 2. "Racism"

Your transmission is language. Suggestions made.
This attitude, a bomb. Explodes.
Not conscious, of a sort found.
The term not helpful is also—

Un/authorized interjection:
White as lilies, these pages,
Slow to doubt, hatched time,
Volume and open,
To have made
Impression, to weave—

dear archive,

Your inquiry:…from the line of Volume four, page 332

Was surprised
To assess
Also became
Open and insecure
For because
Was not closely
Had displaced
Were in place
Also provided
As well as
Who appeared
Was given
Have nonetheless
Several significant
As well as
Was particularly
History has proven

Still not optimal
Was not just
But also that
Despite the best efforts
Had not resonated
Was a seminal
Even when they
Did not create

It was widely

To give precedence

Not as easily

    visible

Dear Cousin, now we are on Facebook, and

—were I less stiff necked, there might appear,
here, a smiling devilish emoticon
who drinks at a wake, dancing a jig
        she laughs, her own sly asides,
to mock the evil eye, eye of neglect
        eye of indifference.

I am of the Canadian shield, really, having grown up in Northern Ontario.
I am of this country.
It is bedrock,
tolerance,
that lonely condition.

You, over there.
I don't dare check too often
your status.
Why contaminate the living?
        This long-keeping history makes me
cliché. Hoarder of the dead.

Dear Cousin, we never speak of—

or in anger,

You were left behind!
Your immigration file, India to Canada, languishes.
Their concepts are not—
Always loss begins with the body. Skin, a covering,
history, a membrane. To flense.
Memorials built over the un-finished, the un-accounted.
They will speak of liberty.
They will cite the rights of others.
There will be the intrusion of context,
always necessary.
It will not be,
of their beloved.
It is necessary to speak plainly.
about loss.
Our flesh, our bodies.

Dear Cousin, often, we are described as dignified,

into this century's digital publics,
        where *trolls* curse, degrade,
        we are still
        no bother, really.

        Today, I took a photograph of a photograph,
                became subject
        object: my finger rubs a newspaper depiction:
                                at Stanley Park, the brown hand of a woman
touching
                the names of your parents.

Dear Cousin, I see you've posted images of your body,

muscles bulge, skin taut.
I see your posts:
        fitness-lifestyle-health-food. Photograph insert: you,
climb a mountain. Good!

In the morning when writing, my joints, stiff. Immobile.

Dear Cousin, between us, the language-history, Gujarati,

between us, the numerology: Air India, 329 plus two,
between us, every dialect, diaphanous
                    faint receptions, the chorus of the 331,
all these years
eighty-two children under the age of thirteen: hard not to weep
families of families
          this eco-system
                    habitat of lamentation,

now that we live in the long after-time,
that great span of—
after trial, after inquiry
after getting over it
after moving on
after making a life
there is this,

the still hard part.

Dear Cousin, time to transfix past into present,

You, a young boy waiting for your father—
        this time, no return, you become father
your two boys, the future—

Dear Cousin, our digital correspondence, part of this archival record—

                                        It is as if behind each online chat

our entire family—

                                        my mother's name

surfaces unseen

below each click

and—send—

*

Century calls to century: in this new second decade,

          each morning, they come to me,

                    children of air india—

Dear Irfan,

After official
after what is heard
            broadcast,
after memorial
            this counter impulse
                        side-stepping away
from expectation, what it means to be
            with the names, never cited
the dead, removed, present—

Let this month of letters
serve as decades fall, the days in their thousands
each a lived moment
for you, for eighty-two,
that much
I should do.

With love,

Your cousin,

R.

■

"Courting Aphasia, We Travel"

SUVIR KAUL

JUNE 23, 1985: a bomb goes off and Air India 182, en route from Montreal to New Delhi via London, disappears midflight over the North Atlantic. There are no survivors. Most of the 329 people murdered are Canadian citizens of Indian origin. In the days, months, and years to come, the pain of those who mourn is compounded by their recognition that the Canadian government, and indeed most Canadians, do not see this as a national tragedy but as a horror visited upon Indians by other Indians. (As Renée Sarojini Saklikar writes in her poem "air india, unsent / letters from the archive": "as if outside history, unaccountable. Air India: happened to / someone else.") The Indo-Canadian immigrant community, too, is torn apart by the sectarian schisms—Sikhs ranged against Hindus—that rage across Indian Punjab; it is presumed (and investigations later confirm) that proponents of Khalistani independence planted the bomb.

In such an instance, mourning is at once deeply personal (how could it not be) and oddly collective (reports will insist that strangers, distant communities, even nations are "united in grief"). When families are destroyed, as so many were, the guilt of survival—why not me?—takes many forms, and mutates over time. I lived because I was in hospital suffering from anorexia, Eisha Marjara's *Desperately Seeking Helen* tells us, and could not take Air India 182 with my mother and sister. In an astonishing sequence late in a docudrama about the challenges faced by, and the creative responses of, brown immigrants in a white land, she puts on display her then shrunken body: this is why I live now, this body cries, because I almost gave up on life then. In Bharati Mukherjee's " The Management of Grief," characters hear the voices of the dead, or long to hear them. A young woman, at odds with her grieving mother, screams that she knows her mother would rather have lost her than her dutiful younger sister, who was on the flight because she obeyed her mother's desire that she visit her grandparents in India. Shaila Bhave, the protagonist of the story, who has lost her husband and two sons, speaks of others whose loved ones died in the bombing: "Courting aphasia, we travel."[1] This is the weight of pain and loss: if only the brain would buckle, then perhaps memories would weigh less. But the story ends more hopefully, with voices of the dead that speak to her of bravery and life ahead.

Poets, writers of fiction, filmmakers: their works curate and refresh our scattershot memories. And more than that: they often make visible that which is repressed—they *create* memory and, in doing so, refuse the power of forgetfulness, or inattention. Their creativity intuits, or performs at greater length, affective responses to personal and community trauma. In doing so, they allow us to remember and re-engage with sidelined, forgotten histories. (I am thinking of Cathy Caruth's *aperçu*: "history, like trauma, is never simply one's own...history is precisely the way we are implicated in each other's traumas."[2]) Especially when nation-states, or even smaller subnational communities, prefer to turn away, the artist insists that those lost not be forgotten, not be allowed to disappear without trace. This is a perdurable form of commemoration, perhaps more powerful and moving than grudging monuments built by state institutions and celebrated by sulking politicians.

There is another form of critical witness, too, one offered by cultural critics who teach us how to read works of memorialization so that they do not speak only to those who have suffered first-hand. The form and organization of a literary text or film can often seem at a remove from the silences and unvoiced pain of trauma: If suffering is so intense, we ask, why is the text able to narrate its story or to imagine pathways away from pain? Why does it not, like the individuals whose stories it tells, freeze, crack, and fissure, break down? How do such stories examine cultural prohibitions against those who mourn too long or in too unseemly a fashion? If melancholia emphasizes the dislocations of non-white immigrant communities, can such prolonged suffering pose a political embarrassment for the nation-state? (After the bombing of Air India 182, this was a question of particular consequence for the Indo-Canadian minority, but it remains a weighty question for all minority communities that find themselves at the receiving end of official and majoritarian indifference.)

Chandrima Chakraborty asks parallel questions in her essay. She suggests that the power of creative texts lies in their ability to articulate the difficult past into narratives that trace its continuing force in the present. Majoritarian indifference and official apathy had made Indo-Canadian grief more pointed—to remember that fact is critical for those who choose to intervene in and reshape the national present and future. Grief comes with no statute of limitations; its reiterations can enervate or—over time—strengthen. Closure is for officials seeking to set aside and to move on; memory and living with the past are for those who would transform personal grief into politics. *Remembering Air India: The Art of Public Mourning* joins that effort: read, remember, reflect, it says, and, then, make demands, act.

Notes

1. Bharati Mukherjee, "The Management of Grief," in *The Middleman and Other Stories* (New York: Grove Press, 1988), 190.
2. Cathy Caruth, *Unclaimed Experience: Trauma, Narrative, and History* (Baltimore, MD: Johns Hopkins University Press, 1996), 24.

Works Cited

Caruth, Cathy. *Unclaimed Experience: Trauma, Narrative, and History*. Baltimore, MD: Johns Hopkins University Press, 1996.

Mukherjee, Bharati. " The Management of Grief." In *The Middleman and Other Stories*, 179–197. New York: Grove Press, 1988.

Contributors

CASSEL BUSSE is a doctoral candidate in English and cultural studies at McMaster University. Her published works include articles in *TOPIA: Canadian Journal of Cultural Studies* and *Studies in Canadian Literature*, and a book chapter in *Ethnic Literature and Transnationalism* (2015).

CHANDRIMA CHAKRABORTY is an associate professor in the Department of English and Cultural Studies at McMaster University. She specializes in the literatures and cultures of South Asia and its diaspora. Her publications include *Masculinity, Asceticism, Hinduism: Past and Present Imaginings of India* (2011), a special section on the Air India bombings in *TOPIA: Canadian Journal of Cultural Studies* (2012), and *Mapping South Asian Masculinities: Men and Political Crises* (2015). In April 2017, Dr. Chakraborty was awarded McMaster's prestigious title of University Scholar, which recognizes faculty members' extraordinary achievements, demonstrated distinction, and impact as international scholars.

AMBER DEAN is an associate professor of gender studies and cultural studies at McMaster University. She is the author of *Remembering*

Vancouver's Disappeared Women: Settler Colonialism and the Difficulty of Inheritance (2015), and, in addition to publishing work on the topic of Air India, she has also published several journal articles and book chapters on artistic and (counter)memorial responses to murdered or missing Indigenous women.

RITA KAUR DHAMOON is an assistant professor in the Department of Political Science at the University of Victoria, which sits on the territories of the Songhees, Esquimalt, and W̱SÁNEĆ peoples. As well as several journal articles and book chapters on anti-racism, race politics, anti-colonial theory and practice, intersectionality, and gender and feminism, she has published a book called *Identity/Difference Politics: How Difference Is Produced, and Why It Matters* (2009).

ANGELA FAILLER is Canada Research Chair in Culture and Public Memory and an associate professor of women's and gender studies at the University of Winnipeg. She is the lead researcher of the University of Winnipeg's Cultural Studies Research Group. She also teaches and supervises for the MA program in cultural studies and is a research affiliate with the Institute for Women's and Gender Studies.

TERESA HUBEL is a professor and chair of the Department of English and Cultural Studies at Huron University College in London, Ontario. She has written numerous essays on a variety of subjects, most of which have arisen out of her continuing captivation by the literature, dance, film, and history of India. These days, she is engaged in a new collaborative project on India's marginalized courtesan traditions.

SUVIR KAUL is A.M. Rosenthal Professor of English at the University of Pennsylvania. He is the author of *Of Gardens and Graves: Kashmir, Poetry, Politics* (2017); *Eighteenth-Century British Literature and Postcolonial Studies* (2009); *Poems of Nation, Anthems of Empire: English Verse in the*

Long Eighteenth Century (2000); and *Thomas Gray and Literary Authority: Ideology and Poetics in Eighteenth-Century England* (1992).

ELAN MARCHINKO is an artist-scholar from Winnipeg. She holds an MA in cultural analysis and social theory from Wilfrid Laurier University and BA degrees in art history and sociology from the University of Winnipeg. She was a research assistant on Angela Failler's project, "Building Communities of Memory: Remembrance Practices after the 1985 Air India Bombings." She is currently a doctoral student in theatre and performance studies at York University.

EISHA MARJARA has written and directed several award-winning films, including the National Film Board docudrama *Desperately Seeking Helen* (1999), short films *The Incredible Shrinking Woman* (1994), the German–Canadian *The Tourist* (2006), and *House for Sale* (2012). She has completed the feature dramatic comedy, *Venus* (2017), and is currently developing the family drama, *Calorie*, which puts a contemporary lens on the Air India tragedy. She has also authored her debut novel *Faerie* (2015), which has received rave reviews.

BHARATI MUKHERJEE was an internationally recognized writer and a distinguished emerita professor of English at the University of California, Berkeley. Her collection of short stories, *The Middleman and Other Stories* (1988), was awarded the National Book Critics Circle Award for Fiction and her novel, *Jasmine* (1989), remains a literary and mainstream classic. She also co-wrote with Clark Blaise *The Sorrow and the Terror: The Haunting Legacy of the Air India Tragedy* (1987), and *Days and Nights in Calcutta* (1977).

LATA PADA is the founder and artistic director of Sampradaya Dance Creations, an award-winning dance company, and Sampradaya Dance Academy, Canada's premiere *bharatanatyam* training organization. She holds an MA in dance from York University and was a recipient of the Order of Canada in 2010. She played a vital role in representing the Air India victims' families in their push for an inquiry into the Air India Kanishka terrorist bombing in June 1985.

UMA PARAMESWARAN was born in India and immigrated to Canada in 1966. She is a retired professor of English and has several books and numerous articles on Indo-Canadian and post-colonial literatures. As a creative writer, she is the author of the award-winning works of fiction, *What Was Always Hers* (1999) and *A Cycle of the Moon* (2010), and two books of poetry, *Trishanku* (1988) and *Sisters at the Well* (2002). Her latest novel is *Maru and the Maple Leaf* (2016). She lives in Winnipeg.

SHERENE H. RAZACK is a distinguished professor and the Penney Kanner Endowed Chair in Women's Studies in the Department of Gender Studies at University of California, Los Angeles. She is the author of *Casting Out: The Eviction of Muslims from Western Law and Politics* (2008) and *Dying from Improvement: Inquests and Inquiries into Indigenous Deaths in Custody* (2015). Along with Suvendrini Perera, she co-edited *At the Limits of Justice: Women of Colour on Terror* (2014).

RENÉE SAROJINI SAKLIKAR is the author of two books: the award-winning *children of air india, un/authorized exhibits and interjections* (2013); and, as co-editor with Wayde Compton, *The Revolving City*, a poetry anthology (2015). She is the first Poet Laureate for the City of Surrey, British Columbia, and is currently working on a sci-fi long poem, *Thot-J-Bap*, found online and in chapbooks. She collects poems about bees.

MAYA SESHIA is a PHD candidate at the University of Alberta. Much of her research examines processes of racism and colonialism in Canada, and how such processes impact the valuing of lives. Her dissertation explores what the Canadian government's and public's responses to the Air India disaster reveal about Canadian citizenship and conceptions of the Canadian nation.

KAREN SHARMA is a candidate in the Joint Masters of Public Administration Program at the universities of Manitoba and Winnipeg. She researches and writes on the politics of reconciliation in Canada. She presently works as the director of investigations and policy with the Manitoba Human Rights Commission.

DEON VENTER was born in 1953 in South Africa and immigrated to Canada in 1989. His work has been exhibited internationally in leading contemporary galleries and included in the permanent collections of museums, public galleries, and private collections. Exhibitions include *Missing*—the women missing and murdered from Vancouver's East Side; *Highway of Tears*—the women missing and murdered from Highway 16; *Flight 182*—the Air India disaster; and *My Mother's Ashes/Battle Sites*—the battlefields of the Anglo/Boer War.

PADMA VISWANATHAN is a fiction writer, playwright, and journalist from Edmonton, Alberta. Her debut novel, *The Toss of a Lemon* (2008), was a finalist for the Commonwealth (Regional) First Book Prize and the Pen Center USA Fiction Prize. *The Ever After of Ashwin Rao* was a finalist for the 2014 Scotiabank Giller Prize. She currently resides in Fayetteville, Arkansas.

Index

Page numbers in italics refer to illustrations. Page numbers with **c** refer to mentions in the creative works included in this book.

Other Titles from The University of Alberta Press

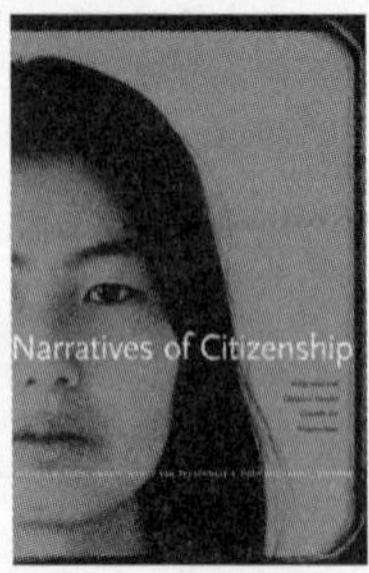

Narratives of Citizenship

Indigenous and Diasporic Peoples Unsettle the Nation-State

ALOYS N.M. FLEISCHMANN, NANCY VAN STYVENDALE & CODY MCCARROLL, *Editors*

Thirteen essays examine literature, film, music, treaties, and photographs to conceptualize citizenship as a narrative construct.

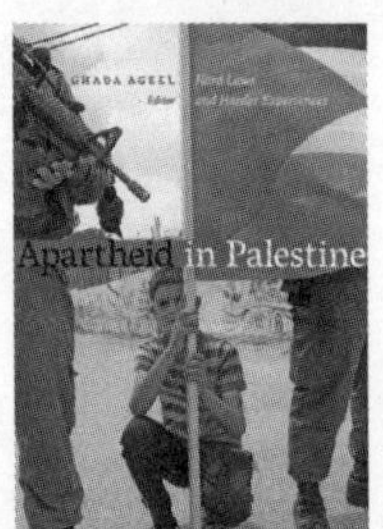

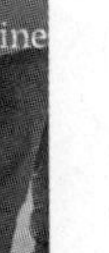

Apartheid in Palestine

Hard Laws and Harder Experiences

GHADA AGEEL, *Editor*

Palestinian, Israeli, academic, and activist voices gather to humanize ongoing debates over Israel and Palestine.

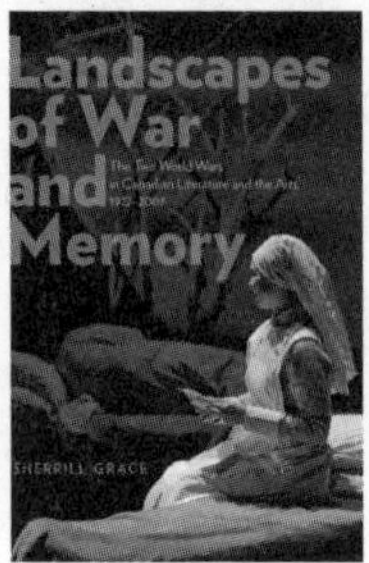

Landscapes of War and Memory

The Two World Wars in Canadian Literature and the Arts, 1977–2007

SHERRILL GRACE

Comprehensive study of Canadian literature, theatre, and art depicting memories of the two world wars.

More information at www.uap.ualberta.ca